FRIENDS
OF ACPL

D1506656

AUG 25'65

Strange Clamor

. . . Suprême Clairon plein de strideurs étranges,
Silences traversés des Mondes et des Anges . . .

(Arthur Rimbaud, "Voyelles")

Strange Clamor

A Guide to the Critical Reading of French Poetry

by Frederic O. Musser

Wayne State University Press   *Detroit, 1965*

Copyright © 1965
Wayne State University Press
Detroit, Michigan 48202

All rights reserved

Published simultaneously in Canada
by Ambassador Books, Limited, Toronto, Ontario, Canada

Library of Congress Catalog Card Number 65-10729

1309907

Matri meae

Contents

Foreword

A foreword to a book is like the esoteric text of an insurance policy: it spells out in detail what is suggested by the title, indicates the nature and extent of the coverage, and implies for what kind of person the document is intended. And since these candid disclosures sometimes turn out to be useful, they tend to go unread. All the same, the spirit of fair play demands that the reader be forewarned before he plunges into the text, so let it be understood at the outset that this book has been written for the speaker of English with some ability to read French who would like to tackle French poetry in the original with more than superficial understanding.

The phrases "some ability to read French" and "more than superficial understanding" require a little amplification. In a sense, anyone who has ever studied French beyond the first-year level is in a position to begin reading French poetry, though he may need to review his grammar and pronunciation and be willing to look up the meanings of a distressingly large number of unfamiliar words. He will find a great source of comfort and strength, however, in the rapidly expanding list of bilingual translations of French poetry which are now available, since these will eliminate much of the need for dictionary-thumbing. Naturally, the more French he knows to begin with, the easier the reading will be; but the more one reads, the more one learns, so it is almost never too early to start. This book, then, is intended to be of help to the general reader as well as to the student, the only requirement being "some ability to read French" and a willingness to work at increasing that ability.

By "more than superficial understanding" is meant a degree of comprehension that represents more than what can be readily inferred from a knowledge of French syntax and the dictionary definitions of words. This volume is intended not to replace but rather to follow the grammars and lexicons that furnish the basic information which makes it possible to read in a foreign language. The first step is to know what the words and phrases literally say. That knowledge will be taken for granted here, and the English version in bilingual translations will normally provide it adequately. But full enjoyment of the poem requires much more than comprehension of the purely denotative meaning of the words, and the development of this deeper understanding will be our principal concern in these pages.

French verse differs from English verse chiefly in the way in which it handles various manifestations of sound, such as meter, rhythm, and rime. On the other hand, the extent of resemblance between French and English poetry is far greater than the amount of difference, so that much that can be said of English poetry is equally applicable to French. For this reason, the expert in English poetry has only to absorb those particular principles that govern the treatment of sound phenomena in French verse to be fully prepared to deal with a French poem, at least from the analytical point of view. Some knowledge of the history of French verse may also be useful to him, but otherwise he will require no further help, assuming, of course, that he has "some ability to read French." But the non-expert in English poetry, by definition, may profit from suggestions about techniques for reading poetry in general. Since this book is intended for him primarily, whether he be a student of French literature or a "layman," Part I has been devoted to the question of the general approach to poetry. Because this is a broad and fundamental subject, its treatment is necessarily somewhat abstract. Nevertheless, every attempt has been made to confine the discussion to matters that lead directly to conclusions of immediate practical importance to the reader of French or English poetry.

Part II, which is concerned with the French poem in particular, concentrates on the close critical reading of the text itself. Here are discussed not only those elements of French versification which distinguish the French poem from its English counterpart, but also many other significant poetic devices that tend to occur in poems written in either language. Whenever possible, the technical points considered are illustrated by quotations from, or complete texts of, poems in both English and French. As a glance at Part II will indicate, a certain amount of critical jargon is unavoidable in any discussion of literary technicalities. This jargon is a shorthand system intended to make it possible to refer to recurring literary devices without having to describe them in detail every time they are mentioned. The various terms that make up the standard vocabulary of poetry criticism need not much concern the general reader whose primary aim is simply to recognize the phenomenon referred to when it occurs in a poem he is reading. The student, on the other hand, is likely to want to formulate his insights for purposes of class discussions, papers, and examinations. He may also wish to read books and articles of literary criticism in which these technical words tend to crop up. For this reason, a Glossary of critical terms (in both French and English) which may be of some help even to the non-academic reader has been placed at the back of the book. Preceding the Glossary will be found an Appendix consisting of "questions to ask of a poem" that it is hoped will stimulate thought and insight.

Finally, Part III raises the question of the historical aspect of French poetry. A brief account of the history of the major trends in French poetry is presented as an introduction to the Bibliography in which are suggested sources of information on specific movements, schools, and poets, as well as on other subjects taken up earlier in the text.

It is hoped that being exposed to a treatment of the three sides of literary study—theory, criticism, and history—will be profitable, though perhaps in different ways, to both the "layman" and the "professional" student of French literature.

Before we engage in a general discussion of poetry we should consider one more point, which is the difference in treatment between the longer poetic forms (represented by the epic, the narrative poem, and the drama in verse). While it is possible to analyze brief passages from large works with great attention to detail, the treatment of a full-length epic, a versified romance, or a drama will naturally bring up special considerations of characterization and plot-structure. On the other hand, the analysis of plot and characterization in a drama composed in verse would, from the point of view of technique, be little different from the analysis of the corresponding elements of a drama in prose; and the same point could be made with regard to prose and versified narratives, including the epic. In that sense these techniques are not involved specifically in the analysis of poetry but rather in the analysis of dramatic and narrative structures of any kind. What makes the analysis of dramatic and narrative poetry different from that of dramatic and narrative prose is therefore the special contribution of the very elements of sound, rhythm, pace, diction, rhetoric, and imagery that are of such vital importance to the structure of a lyric poem, together with the need to possess some knowledge of various historical conventions that have been applied in different periods to narrative and dramatic poetry. Whenever possible we shall consider the particular applications to plays and extended narratives of the techniques and historical facts under consideration in this book, but without attempting to deal with

those matters of plot and characterization which are not limited to poetry but are equally applicable to prose. Thus the
assumption will be made that the reader will bring to bear
on extended narrative and dramatic works whatever experience he may have gained from the study of plot and characterization in English or French literary prose. Any alternative
to making this assumption would involve us in a study of
poetic *drama* and poetic *narrative* (as opposed to dramatic
and narrative *poetry*) and would carry us far beyond the
range of what is usually thought to be the province of poetry,
as distinguished from that of literature in general.

I should like to express my gratitude to the Reverend
Rowan A. Greer, Frederick Hammond, V. Frederic Koenig,
Fred B. Millett, Norman R. Shapiro, Susan Stavropoulos, and
Carl A. Viggiani, for their painstaking detailed reading of
the complete text and their invaluable criticisms of it from
all possible perspectives. I am also most grateful to Wesleyan
University for a Sabbatical leave which greatly facilitated
preparation of the book. The footnotes and Bibliography will
provide a clue to the extent of my obligation to many predecessors in the field; in this respect I hope not to be completely
unworthy of Denham's line on Cowley which is quoted and
commented upon by John Ciardi in *How Does a Poem Mean?*
"He did not steal but emulate."

F. O. M.

Towson, Maryland
July 1, 1964

PART I
THEORY

1
The Approach to the Poem

Once upon a time, a primeval ancestor of ours probably invited his wife to admire the handsome bison he had just painted on the wall of their cave. What her reaction may have been we can only guess, but in the light of modern art criticism it seems likely that if she did not say: "It has the right number of legs, but isn't the body too long?" then she undoubtedly sighed deeply and announced that although she had no idea why, the painting gave her a lovely warm feeling inside. Certainly if we judge by the writings of some of our more recent critical forebears we can only conclude that these are the two possible responses to art: the intellectual and the emotional, that of the mind and that of the "heart." In fact the artist himself often appears to be inviting one of these reactions. He seems either to be hoping to melt, depress, or elate his public, or else to be trying to provoke a thoughtful meditation or even a change in moral conduct.

The history of poetry and of literary criticism reveals on the part of writers in both fields a persistent tendency to vacillate between these same two poles. We have the impression that certain poems, such as most of those of Verlaine and Poe, are calculated to enchant rather than to alert the mind, while those of Boileau and Pope, at least on the surface, seem to appeal primarily to the intellect. Correspondingly, Romantic critics like Matthew Arnold or Sainte-Beuve were more inclined to favor the literary gasp of approval or disapproval than the kind of cerebral probing and dissection practiced by such later critics as Jean-Pierre Richard or Cleanth Brooks.

This distinction between the intellectual and emotional approaches to the reading of a poem has sometimes been corrupted into a simple rule-of-thumb used to differentiate between the general reader of poetry and the student of poetry. The rule is often expressed in the form of a polite social question, such as: "Do you study poetry, young man, or do you read it for pleasure?" the suggestion being that since enjoyment is emotional and study is intellectual, they must be mutually exclusive. There may in fact be still another implication hidden in this infuriating question; namely, that the two possible approaches to the poem consist of what we might call the active and passive responses. By "passive response" is meant "letting the poem (or its sounds, or its images) wash over you" with a consequent pleasurable emotional sensation. "Active response," on the other hand, is "studying the poem"; that is, thinking about it, criticizing it, analyzing it—in short, working at it, as opposed to enjoying it.

Clearly, there is a solid historical reason for supposing that the primary reaction to a given poem should be emotional or intellectual, but not both in equal degree. A number of well-known poems seem designed to invite such a unilateral approach, and many respectable critics have accepted the invitation and responded in just that way. But the source of the "active-passive" polarity, with its implied opposition between enjoyment and study, may be a shade less objective. The idea that the student of literature reads a poem exclusively in order to pass the course and therefore cannot possibly take pleasure in it is based at least partly on some people's recorded experience. That fact gives the notion a certain aura of plausibility that makes it difficult to refute.

We are really dealing here, of course, with two essentially unrelated "either-or" approaches to poetry. The critic who treats Pope primarily intellectually and Poe primarily impressionistically may simply be reacting to the fact that Pope seems to *express* more ideas than Poe does. The disillusioned former student, on the other hand, is thinking of the way he was expected by his teachers to *experience* either Pope or Poe; *viz.*, purely intellectually, and therefore disagreeably. Needless to say, this is merely the impression he is left with as he recalls papers to be ground out laboriously and examinations that had to be passed. But the result is that he proclaims his lifelong hatred of Pope and Poe (or Boileau and Verlaine), the poets he was forced to "dissect" in the classroom, though he has perhaps learned to enjoy some other poets who were fortunate enough to escape the contamination of the university. He might even confess to devoting a little thought to these unpolluted writers, but in a casual way having nothing to do with the pedantic textual analysis of the literature course.

The ex-student's antipathetic response to, let us say, Pope and Poe, and the contradictory reactions of critics to poems of various kinds, raise two obvious questions: first, "Is the intellectual response to poetry a sure way to kill the poem?" and second, "Do some poets really demand an intellectual reaction, while others simply arouse strong feelings?" Both questions hinge on the differentiation between the intellectual and the emotional responses, except that in the first question the terms are changed so that the implied distinction is between study and enjoyment. In order to answer both questions negatively we have only to see clearly that intellect, emotion, study, and enjoyment are all part of the normal full response to a poem; and that fact is easy to demonstrate. Obviously, if Poe called for a purely emotional response he could not be studied—and yet he is. If Pope required an exclusively intellectual approach he could not be enjoyed—and yet he is. It is clear that Pope has "something to say," i.e., one could write out a series of propositions in prose that would bear a strong resemblance to the *Essay on Man*. If one did the same thing for "The Raven" the results would be comparatively meager, even supposing that due allowance were made for the respective lengths of the two poems. Pope provides more food for thought than Poe does. And Poe may give us more of a pleasant, shuddering sensation than Pope affords. But if we ask *why* we experience this sensation we are calling for a reply that requires thought, and perhaps even "dissection." By the same token, if we compare the *Essay on Man* with our prose paraphrase of its ideas we may notice that the paraphrase leave us cold, while the poem evokes a response that is quite clearly more than intellectual and therefore must be emotional as well. In short, poetry is more than the organized expression of pure propositional statements; and since only such statements can be completely divested of overtones of feeling, poetry necessarily requires emotional involvement. Furthermore, unless the poem consists entirely of nonsense syllables, it must mean something and thereby call for the use of the mind to determine what the meaning is. Even if the poem were in fact made up of pure nonsense syllables any emotional response it could evoke would tend to raise the question: "Why does it have this effect?" and only analysis—an activity demanding thought—could provide an answer. So any poem is bound to require both thought and emotion if it is to receive a full response from its reader, even though his critical reaction to it may favor one tendency over the other. And if enjoyment is in any way bound up with the fullness of the reader's involvement, the ability to enjoy the poem cannot depend on the non-use of the intellect. Of course a pedantic worrying of the text that makes the term "dissection" leap to mind can damage, perhaps permanently, a reader's ability to enjoy a poem. But dissection implies death—if not before, at least after. Proper analysis of a text is more accurately imagined as the equivalent of an X-ray picture: it tells a good deal about the inner structure of the patient, but it does not kill him.

Since a full participation in the pleasure that can be derived from a poem requires that it receive both the active and passive responses, the intellectual as well as the emotional, a willingness on the part of the reader to think actively about poetry in general and individual poems in particular will be taken for granted here, with the understanding that we are concerned with using our minds as X-ray machines, not as scalpels. By approaching our subject in this way we should find it possible to transform the strange clamor that the unfamiliar sounds of French poetry sometimes seem to resemble to the foreign ear into an agreeable and comprehensible harmony. Then too, the more we know about a poem, the more we can say about it; and there is a certain delight to be had in responding to poetry with words as opposed to grunts.

Of course, the sort of grunt that seems appropriate on a first reading may provide the initial clue to what sort of analytical approach the poem calls for. The first step in dealing with any poem, needless to say, is to read it; and this is the first (though not the last) time to let it "roll over you." The important point is to acquiesce in what the poet is doing while bearing in mind that the shift from reading prose to reading poetry is inevitably accompanied by a certain mental dislocation, a shock that has to be anticipated. Poetry, even when read somewhat passively, requires much closer attention than prose does, especially if the poem happens to be obscure. Reading it alone and undistracted by noise is a virtual necessity if the right degree of attention is to be paid to what the poet is saying, partly because one should be "hearing" the sounds of the words and phrases even if one is not actually reading aloud.

There is, of course, another reason for focusing one's mind on a poem apart from the sheer ecstasy of thinking, namely, the need for making a correct interpretation. It is undoubtedly possible to derive great pleasure from a wrong reading of a poem; some of the best and most experienced readers find this happening to them quite frequently. But there is a certain satisfaction to be gained from reading rightly, and doing so requires more than simply absorbing impression- istically the flavor of the text.

If we agree, then, that learning how to see beneath the surface of a poem is a worthwhile undertaking, our next ap- propriate step would seem to be to place a sonnet behind our X-ray screen and learn which buttons to push. Readers who are constitutionally opposed to theoretical principles as against direct action will accordingly be well advised to turn imme- diately to Part II of the book which concerns itself with essen- tially practical questions. However, for the sake of those who would like to know how the machine works and who its in- ventors were before knowing which levers to pull, the rest of Part I will be taken up with basic principles, the rationale behind the cogs and wheels of the mechanism.

2

First Principles

We noted in the last chapter the tendency on the part of the professional critics to favor at one time an inspirational and at another time a rational approach to poetry. There often seems to have been a functional relationship between the direction in which the critics have leaned and the period in which they were writing. Thus some of the nineteenth-century Romantic critics may have placed a heavy emphasis on feeling partly because of their antipathy toward scientific materialism. There can be little doubt, in any case, that the spectacular influence and prestige of science has in recent decades contributed significantly to a critical enthusiasm for the controlled, intellectual approach to poetry. Criticism is now generally thought to be the *study* of literature, not merely its appreciation. This rational orientation explains why teachers of "literature" so often join Northrop Frye[1] in pointing out that they do not in fact teach literature at all, any more than an economist teaches money or a chemist teaches sulphuric acid. What they teach is literary criticism, a body of knowledge *about* literature. And not unnaturally, they

[1] See *Anatomy of Criticism* (Princeton: Princeton University Press, 1957), pp. 11 ff., where many implications of this point are developed.

9

would prefer that criticism be a rationally organized body of knowledge.

This situation resulted several decades ago in a verbal clash between two groups of critics: those who would like to think of a poem as a detached, purely literary object, susceptible of being studied dispassionately as an entity existing in its own right; and those who feel that a poem is so conditioned by its historical origins that it cannot be adequately analyzed, and certainly cannot be evaluated, except in terms of its relative historical context. Although our principal concern is with the best way to read poetry, not with abstract literary theory, this critical debate requires our attention if only briefly, since it involves two very different approaches to the study of a poem. The question is: Do we treat the text as a chemist deals with a molecule, caring only about its structure and properties and not a bit about its date of origin, or do we concentrate on the poet's life and times and judge the poem by the standards of its own day? Or can we do both without being hopelessly inconsistent?

The answer to these questions clearly depends on what we consider the essential nature of a poem to be. Admittedly, this is a highly theoretical problem, but it also leads directly to very practical conclusions. If we are going to read a poem with greater understanding it behooves us to reach some agreement about the *general* nature of the object we are trying to comprehend *specifically*. If we can arrive at a clear conception of the internal mechanism of poetry, we should then be in a better position to X-ray the anatomy of a given particular poem.

But here we find ourselves involved in a vicious circle; for the only way to understand the constitution of a poem in particular is to have some notion of the nature of poetry in general, and the only way to learn about the nature of poetry in general is, precisely, to generalize from the comparison of poems in particular. When a doctor diagnoses a back ailment as a curvature of the spine he is in a position to make the judgment because he knows what a straight spine looks like. But he acquired that information only because he and the predecessors who taught him had examined a great many individual spines. Happily for us we are not the first investigators to inspect the backbone of poetry. Other readers have been doing so for several millennia, and they have arrived at a number of general principles. Unfortunately, however, the general principles evolved have not at all times been identical; like medicine and time-tables, poetic theory is subject to change. And as is the case with time-tables, though perhaps not with medicine, it is possible to doubt whether these changes always represent progress. We must remember, indeed, that among the great variety of feelings, views, and even theories about the nature of poetry that are constantly being expressed and passionately defended, a number can be justified at least as convincingly as the notions about to be set forth here. Our approach is therefore not to be thought of as an incontrovertible statement of eternal truths; it is merely one of many possible ways of looking at the problem of poetry. Nonetheless, since we live in the scientifically oriented twentieth century, let us for the time being adopt a view in general conformity with the position of those who prefer to concentrate primarily on the aspects of a poem that are to some extent independent of the poem's historical context. It need not be a theory to be accepted permanently and absolutely; it will simply serve us as a temporary vantage-point from which to examine particular poems, and once we have done that we can draw our own conclusions.

Let us postulate then, along with most modern critics and a good many older ones, that a poem is a *structure*. This fits nicely with our X-ray analogy; the function of X-rays is to reveal hidden structures. But the question that leaps immediately to mind is, of course, "A structure of what?" and it is in the way in which they reply to this question that the critics just alluded to tend to differ with one another. Before we proceed to leap into the fray by attempting to answer the question ourselves, we had better stand back and see what we have accomplished merely by saying, "A poem is a structure."

René Wellek and Austin Warren, in *Theory of Literature*,[2] demonstrate conclusively that calling a poem a "structure" is the only way to avoid a number of unpleasant ontological dilemmas that crop up if one tries to locate its essence in some other way. For example, if we think of a poem as a physical object (paper and ink) we overlook the fact that it can exist in memory. If we regard it as an experience, or as a system of sounds, we run into the objection that no two experiences of the poem and no two recitations of its sounds are ever identical. This predicament has led the authors of *Theory of Literature* to conclude that a poem is a "structure of stratified norms." Restraining ourselves from answering prematurely the question of what the components of the poetic structure are, let us first consider what practical reasons there may be for supporting the use of the term "structure" itself.

The most obvious advantage of the structural approach is that it agrees with what we have said and implied about the analysis of a text. Structures can be analyzed. An intelligent study of a poem should tell us what components make up its structure and how the structure is organized. And if we know that we must be very close to understanding the poem.

Furthermore, if a poem has an independent structure it can be studied in terms of its own coherence and need not be approached as a mere element in some larger structure of which it is a part. This means that we can study a poem as a poem, as an independent phenomenon existing in its own right, as an end-product, and not merely as a psychological experience, or a fact of history, or an economic symptom.

Perhaps the most important reason for endorsing the idea that a poem is a structure is the fact that this notion does not violate our experience of individual poems. It is clear that almost everything that occurs in a poem has some bearing on

[2] (2nd edition; New York: Harcourt, Brace and Company, 1956), pp. 129–139.

other elements of the text. The sounds of the words often re-inforce the emotion evoked by the meanings of the words; the images are linked not only to the ideas but to each other as well, so that they form a pattern in their own right; sounds and rhythm are tied to one another; and the meanings, con-notations, feelings, and attitudes that emerge from the inter-action of all of these elements seem to exist in a balanced harmony of their own. The poem, in short, is significantly coherent, and the coherence seems to involve more aspects of communication than the mere ideas expressed by the text. This coherence of many levels of events in the poem is surely one of the most obvious characteristics that distinguish it from a piece of pure scientific prose.

There is a certain kind of rhythm in an ordinary prose propositional sentence, such as the one you are now reading, but in terms of what makes this sentence significant the rhythm is inconsequential. All that really matters is the idea that the sentence expresses. Scientific prose, in short, has a logical structure; but that seems to be the extent of its internal co-herence, apart from matters of pure syntax. But in poetry all of the elements—such as rhythm, sound, imagery, idea, and implied attitude—are important, and indeed are part of the meaning of the text. Therefore none of these elements can be neglected; they are all vital to our understanding. By the same token, no single element can by itself establish the structure of the poem. Our definition implies the categorical rejection of any tendency to elevate one aspect of a poem to a status of pre-eminent importance, since this procedure would amount to reducing the poem to a part of the totality of its significant components. It is in the over-all interrelation of these parts that the essence of the poem is to be found.

Thus, our definition forces us to reject the idea that the poem is a nosegay, a collection of pretty—but separate—flow-ers. If it were merely a package of attractive sounds, or words, or images all one would have to do to evaluate the poem would be to "extract" these glittering trinkets from the text and judge it by how many of them it contained. According to our definition this is impossible; it is the manner in which these elements interact with one another that makes the beauty of the poem. The poem can be judged only in terms of its wholeness, its structure, not in terms of its simple "ingredients." The total pattern may incorporate into itself many items which are intrinsically beautiful or ugly, but the beauty of the poem as *poem* depends on the way in which these separate elements become part of a unity.

Furthermore, our definition repudiates the notion that the poem is a *container* for anything. It rejects as invalid the term "content" which has often been used to refer to the ideas expressed in poetry. If the poem is a structure it is an ordering of materials. The manner or means by which items are related to one another cannot be thought of as a container for the items, since a manner or a means cannot contain. A relationship does not contain the related items. Therefore, the ideas of the poem, which have been frequently termed its "content" as opposed to its "form" (the manner in which they are expressed), are not in fact contained by the poem. The ideas may well be logically related to each other, but this logical structure is not the structure of the poem itself, any more than the rhythmic, sound, and image structures form in themselves the structure of the poem. They cannot do so, because by themselves they fail to encompass each other.

Since the poetic structure is clearly not the logical structure of the raw concepts expressed or implied by the poem, the theory that the poem is simply an ornament clothing an idea has been dubbed the "heresy of communication" by Cleanth Brooks, while Allen Tate has branded as the "fallacy of communication" the attempt on the part of a writer to use a poem as a vehicle for communicating ideas or feelings that should properly be conveyed by prose. Northrop Frye, in the same spirit, has gone so far as to say[3] that literature as such is "a hypothetical verbal structure" in the sense that

[3] *Op. cit.*, p. 71 and *passim*.

nothing in literature is properly speaking true or false. By this he seems to mean that literature involves primarily attitudes, and attitudes are subjective in nature; as such they may be appropriate or inappropriate, or morally right or wrong, but unlike objective facts they cannot accurately be called "true" or "false." In this sense, statements and ideas in literature are hypothetical; rather than having a truly independent existence (like an event referred to in a history book), within the poem they exist only in terms of the structure of which they are a part. It is this fact that permits a reader to disagree with a statement in a poem while holding to the belief that the poem is a great work of art. From this point of view the work of art is formally *unreal*, which is to say that it is not *simply* a piece of objective reality to be experienced like any other manifestation of objective reality. The detachment of the reader who makes this distinction between art and reality is what is sometimes called psychic distance or, by the New Critics, "esthetic distance."

The difficulty with the critical position just outlined is that it suggests that poetry is cut off from reality entirely, which is manifestly untrue. It is the way in which a poem orders a perception of reality that determines its very nature. If it had no connection with reality we would hardly be interested in it. The problem is largely verbal, in fact. The point is that the truth of poetry is primarily moral or psychological truth. Poetry is involved with emotions and attitudes that are not verifiable in the sense that cold, scientific facts are verifiable. The experience of reading poetry is not identical in nature with the direct experience of other kinds of reality. In that sense only, poetry is "unreal." And this "unreality" is part of its virtue since it permits the expression of a kind of truth not easily perceived in ordinary experience of reality. The point of the term "hypothetical," therefore, is to underscore the fact that while some elements of the poetic structure, such as ideas, may resemble similar elements of non-poetic experience, they are not necessarily to be treated in the usual way.

On the practical level, then, let us make it our first general principle to consider the poem as a structure of supralogical meanings, recognizing that every element or event in the poem that influences or affects any other element is a significant part, but not the whole, of this structure of meanings.

We can see now that the question "A structure of what?" is not an easy one to answer. Recent attempts to reply in a word or two have ranged from "a structure of stratified norms" by Wellek and Warren to Cleanth Brooks' "a structure of attitudes." If we felt obliged to play this game we might propose "a structure of connotations" for reasons that will become apparent later. In any case, our practical concern in studying a poem will be to determine the nature of its structure, and that will require us to discover first of all what significant elements are operating in the poem and how they are related to one another: how they balance, sustain, reinforce, or otherwise affect one another so that charged meanings emerge. The structure of the poem will then be revealed by the way in which these meanings support or oppose each other in what we might envisage architecturally as a harmony of stresses. The structure will be a unity of controlled tensions, a coherence of meanings which we may call "connotations" or, with Mr. Brooks, "attitudes" (to avoid confusing "meanings" with ideas, propositions, true or false statements).

But in looking at the poem in this way, have we not forgotten that it also stands in relation to objects outside itself, including the poet and ourselves? After all, the poet wrote the poem for a reader or readers, even if the reader is only the poet himself. The poet intended the poem to be something and to do something; and we, as readers, are affected by the poem: it does something to us. Is it not the case that the poet is trying to communicate with us, so that the poem is really a vehicle, a conveyor between the poet and the reader? And do we not have to judge the poem by the way in which it affects us, by the results of its success in communicating, or at least by the quality of whatever the poet was trying to convey?

Certainly if the poet stated somewhere what his intention was in writing the poem and this statement reached us it would help us to understand and ultimately to evaluate his work—if we were sure that he was entirely aware of his intention and that he had fully carried it out in the poem. Unfortunately, neither of the latter conditions is ever completely fulfilled. The poem probably represents a number of "intentions" that were only intuitively felt by the poet when he wrote it. Furthermore, he may not in fact have succeeded in doing even what he consciously wanted to do, or he may quite accidentally have done a good deal more than that, or even something quite different. The only way to be sure is to investigate the poem itself. It is, after all, a public document; it exists as an independent entity, and we are free to read it, to inspect it, and to try to determine what it is. The stated intention of the poet may provide us with a clue about where to look first, but we must never fall into the trap of assuming that what he claims is in the poem is in fact there, or that nothing else is there. The way to be sure is to examine the text. Any preoccupation with the poet's intention that distracts our mind and averts our gaze from the actual text has done us more harm than good. The value of the poem, in short, is the value of the *poem,* not the value of the author's intention. The failure to realize this is what the "New Critics," with justifiable annoyance, call the "intentional fallacy." If, on the other hand, we use the word "intention" to refer to the conclusions we reach after our examination of the poem, then we are simply assuming that the nature of the poem is fully commensurate with what the poet had in mind when he wrote it. We are free to make that assumption, but in doing so we are no longer criticizing the poem; we are psychoanalyzing the poet, which is a very different thing.

It should be noted, in this connection, that we ought never to confuse the speaker in the poem with the real author of the poem unless there is unquestionable justification for doing so. Just as ideas are hypothetical in literature, so normally are persons. The pronouns *I* or *je* are elements in the structure of the poem, but an external referent such as the real poet is not usually a factor in the poem at all. What the *I* or *je* means is determined primarily by the interaction of all the other elements in the text, and only exceptionally by historico-biographical data that lie outside of it. When Victor Hugo wrote elegies on the death of his daughter Léopoldine he referred in these poems to real people and events, including himself. But that fact has no bearing on the value of the poems, which would be the same if all the people and events were totally imaginary. Hugo was not always entirely accurate in his portrayal of details if we judge by actual history. But that in itself has no effect on the quality of the poem as a work of *fiction*.

Our second general principle, then, will be to avoid thinking of poems as works to be judged in terms of the poet's intention, or in terms of whether or not the poem has adequately communicated his ideas, or in terms of the truth of those ideas.

The next point brings us to the edge of a philosophical precipice which, since our primary purpose is practical, we may prudently attempt to skirt. In the course of doing so, however, we shall permit ourselves a fleeting glance into the abyss. There we find a group of theorists who would like to draw us into a philosophical position the acceptance of which, though it may tempt us at first, would make it impossible for us to deal pragmatically with a poem. We cannot undertake to refute the position of these theorists here, but we can at least make clear the relationship between our practical stand and their theoretical one. The idea that they put to us is that it is absurd to talk about "the" existence of a poem, because "a poem" has as many existences as there are potential psychological reactions to it. Our only way of knowing that a poem exists at all is our individual perception of it; what we perceive is "the poem"; but since, taken individually, we each have a modified experience of the poem every time we encounter it (not to speak of the infinite number of highly varied reactions to the poem that occur when different people come into contact with it), "it" must in fact be an infinite number of *poems*. When you and I think we are talking to each other about "The Raven" we are in reality each referring to entirely different "Ravens": the "Raven" in *my* mind and the "Raven" in *yours*. It is consequently impossible to speak meaningfully of "the poem itself"—there is no such thing.

Now we need not fall off the cliff of practicality and lose ourselves in a theoretical debate that will probably still be underway when the Last Trump sounds. We cannot, however, ignore this theoretical position altogether, since its implications have evident bearing on our treatment of a poem. So our first step should be to try to determine what the advocates of this view of the nature of poetry are driving at, that is, what they are afraid of. They are obviously concerned about the impossibility of defining theoretically or locating physically the "real nature" of a poem. They are afraid we will fall back on the "text" (a short term we may use in this context to refer to symbols expressed either in writing or in sound) as being the "poem itself." Naturally, we cannot do that. If we defined the essence of the poem in terms of physical sounds or of paper and ink we would raise the question of which printed copy or which recitation was the "real" poem, and we would also have to deal with the fact that the poem can survive in the memory of a single individual. So no definition of the poem in physical terms is possible.

The second cause for alarm on the part of our theorists is that we may attempt to divorce what we call the "objectively real" poem from the psyches of the individuals that experience it. Indeed, when we say "objectively real" we seem to be trying to do just that. But how can we possibly imagine an *unexperienced* poem? And even if we could, how could we possibly define, limit, or in any other way come to grips with it? What clue to its nature would we have? After all, what we have to work with is an infinite number of *different* experiences, none of which could possibly constitute a direct contact with a single, objective reality.

We must now remind ourselves that our principal concern

is pragmatic, not theoretical. We need not feel obliged to deal here with problems of ontology or epistemology. Indeed, we need not feel obliged to *define* the "real nature of the poem," though we may for certain purposes characterize it as a kind of "structure." Beyond that, we need not try to specify its mode of existence. It will be sufficient for our purposes to establish that it *does* exist, whether or not we can locate it precisely in time, or space, or the human psyche. But it is essential that we do convince ourselves that there is such a thing as the "real poem." We need not conceive of it as something totally separated from each human experience of it, but rather as something distinguishable from (i.e., not identical with) those experiences. Unless we can do this we can no longer speak to each other about poetry at all. If all our experiences of "The Raven" were not only different but entirely unique (having nothing to do with each other), we could not discuss "The Raven," we could not criticize or judge it even according to the most relative standards; we could only rejoice in our personal, incommunicable state of mind. So we must either stop talking about poetry altogether or else be prepared to grant that, whether or not we can define it, "The Raven" itself exists. This assertion simply implies that every experience of "The Raven" has something in common with every other experience of it. This shared element cannot be divorced from the other elements of each experience, but it must be at least theoretically distinguishable as an element common to all experiences of "The Raven," and it must correspond to the common source of these experiences. It is often impossible to conceive of a cause apart from its effect, but we can still distinguish theoretically between the two. Indeed, whenever our theorists use the words "experience," "perception," "reaction," or "effect," they imply that something exists which is perceived or experienced, which we react toward or are affected by. This "something," the common source of a series of experiences, is the poem. To say that the experience *is* the poem is to say that the effect is its own cause, which is logically impossible. The theorists may of course grant that every effect produced by what we call "The Raven" has a cause, but they might still insist that in each individual case the cause is different. My "Raven" is not your "Raven"; what caused my experience is not what caused yours. "The Raven" is a separate cause with a separate existence every time it provokes a separate effect. We may accept this theoretical possibility if we like, while denying its practical importance. The same point can be made, after all, of the color green, or of our own personalities, or of anything else that can be experienced. Probably no two of us ever perceive in the same way what a scientist would insist was the same shade of green. We may never, at two different moments, experience ourselves identically. But these facts need not and do not prevent us from postulating the real existence of the given shade of green and of ourselves; we assume these existences and act accordingly. There is really only one reason for not doing the same with "The Raven," and that is the fact that, unlike ourselves, the real entity which is "The Raven" is not directly perceivable. Nonetheless, this difficulty can be circumvented by admitting, not that the text of "The Raven" is the poem itself, but rather that the text is the symbolic expression of the poem. The text, i.e., the system of audible, visible, or memorable symbols that we associate with "The Raven," is perceivable. And we know empirically that while the text is not the real poem, the real poem must operate *through* the text (in its printed, heard, or remembered form) for us to have any experience of it at all. Furthermore, we can, for practical purposes, agree to a canonical text of "The Raven." Since this is as good as agreeing to the existence of a given shade of green, we may pragmatically assume the existence of a single, real "Raven" which, though it is not itself the text, is approachable through (and only through) the text.

To summarize briefly our conclusions on this point, we may say that no matter how different our reactions to "The

Raven" may be, they can be assumed to have a common source which, though we cannot place or define it precisely, can at least be recognized as operating through a vehicle of symbolic expression which we call the text. The text is identifiable by means of its sounds and/or written symbols, in physical or mental (memorized) form. It is usually possible to agree to a given set of symbols as the accepted version of the text of a given poem. And that is really all that is necessary for our purposes, even though we have left many theoretical dilemmas untouched. Pragmatically we will treat the text as a surrogate of the real poem. If we are to criticize the poem we can do so only through the text. This is not meant to imply that we can treat the text as totally independent of our reactions to it. It is, however, meant to suggest that we can place a limitation on those reactions as proper grounds for criticism. We may reasonably postulate, for example, that any effect of the poem which is based on an error with regard to its text is invalid as evidence on which to found a judgment of the poem. Similarly, any apparent "effect" which is not in fact related to the text at all (having been caused, let us say, by an attack of indigestion at the time the poem was read) is of course not a real effect of the poem and therefore would not constitute a proper basis for discussion, criticism, or judgment of the poem. Thus, even though we cannot define the poem, i.e., we cannot categorically say what it is, we can often for practical purposes say what it is *not*. It is possible to err sensorially with regard to the text (by misreading or mishearing a word), and it is possible to err intellectually (for example, by naïvely misconstruing irony that is generally recognized to be such). Sensory errors we may probably take to be absolute; intellectual ones, unless they are very naïve, must no doubt be regarded as relative, i.e., theoretically unprovable. Emotional errors, if they exist, would be even harder to condemn in any absolute sense, though we might feel that emotional reactions stemming from sensory errors were at least tainted, since they really do not in any way correspond to the accepted text of the poem. The same would be true of aspects of any reaction dependent upon personal idiosyncrasies or other irrelevancies. Judgment of poems must always be made in relative terms, of course. But even the limitations imposed by the mere existence of a perceivable text may be useful in clearing the critical underbrush, as can be seen from a glance at the evidence adduced by I. A. Richards[4] with regard to the way in which even very well educated people literally misread.

As our third general principle, then, we may make it a point to be wary of assuming that all of the possible psychological effects that the poem may seem to have upon us are equally valid as bases for criticizing, judging, or even simply discussing it. We may at the same time try to disarm some defenders of the total validity of all poetic experiences by calling attention to the fact that we have in no sense denied the pleasure and even profit that we may derive *individually* from whatever purely personal, idiosyncratic contributions we may bring to our own experiences of the poem. If these contributions please us or help us in any other way, so much the better. But it is only *we* who will be helped. And since criticism, judgment, and discussion imply a communication of ideas involving *more* than one person, they cannot be usefully predicated on matters that do not pertain to the shared part of our common experience of the poem. If I call attention to the fact that I like "The Raven" because it reminds me of my pet crow, you will probably not be very much helped in your own experience of "The Raven." If on the other hand I call your attention for the first time to the fact that sound phenomena are important to the poem, you may find your own experience enriched as a result. This distinction is one we should bear in mind in all cases in which we are criticizing a poem for the benefit of someone other than ourselves.

[4] In *Practical Criticism: A Study of Literary Judgment* (London, 1929).

Now the question is: Have we in fact divorced the poem from everything outside itself, including us? We can safely reply in the negative. We have insisted, admittedly, that the poem is real, that it corresponds to (but is not identical with) a theoretically distinguishable part of each psychological re-action to it, and that this correspondence is achieved through the agency of the perceived text. The poem is not, therefore, something in its author's mind (an intention) or in ours (an effect), nor is it a window-pane between two souls. But all that this means practically is that we must not identify the poem with its effects even though it is ultimately significant only in terms of them. W. K. Wimsatt and M. C. Beardsley have observed that to judge a poem exclusively in terms of its effect upon the reader would represent "a confusion be-tween the poem and its *results* (what it *is* and what it *does*) . . .,"[5] and they stigmatize this misapprehension with the term "affective fallacy." We may agree with them that a poem is not its own effects, and that we would risk arriving at in-valid conclusions if we tried to judge a poem in terms of the total complex of emotions and ideas that we experience in any given reading of it, since some elements of that complex might be purely personal contributions of our own, not true effects of the poem. They would be our fault (or our good fortune), not the poem's. We are of course affected by poetry, and that is precisely what makes it so valuable to us. But if we try to establish the degree of that value by completely subjective means, by assessing the poem's worth exclusively in terms of its apparent effect upon us, we automatically limit the poem to precisely the extent that we are limited ourselves. The poem, after all, may be a potential source of effects we were not aware of when we first read it. If we learn more about its structure by examining the text itself, we may thereby greatly increase the extent of the enjoyment we can derive from it. And of course the effect the poem has upon

[5] *The Verbal Icon: Studies in the Meaning of Poetry* (2nd paperbound edition; New York: The Noonday Press, 1960), p. 21.

us is bound to furnish the first clue to the nature of its structure, which is why the initial reading is so important. The only risk we run lies in equating the poem with its apparent effects. If we carefully consider the nature of the text, thereby learning more about the poem, we will be in a better position to respond to it in a way that is more nearly commensurate with its real nature. We see then that far from cutting the poem off from us, we have in fact greatly increased our chances of gaining more benefit from it by the very act of treating it as something exterior to the total psychic response it may seem to evoke.

The same point may be made concerning the poet's intention. We need not divorce the poem from the poet; on the contrary, the more we know about him the better, since biographical and psychological knowledge may give us a hint of what to look for in the text. But again the poem must corroborate what this information may suggest. We should never trust the implications of extraliterary facts without verifying them in the text, for the only really relevant source of information about the poet's intention is finally the poem itself. Any kind of knowledge—historical, biographical, political, or psychological—is potentially useful, so long as it leads to further discoveries in the poem (and does not turn into a mere source of unverified assumptions about what may or may not be there), and so long as the poem does not become simply a piece of evidence intended to prove something about the poet, or the psychology of creation, or a historical period. If we permitted that to happen we would have ceased being concerned about the poem as a poem.

The fear has been expressed on the part of some critics that limiting the possible range of absolute errors in the reading of a poem to sensory mistakes would make it impossible to reject readings based on anachronisms. Any reading that fitted the structure in a coherent way would be automatically acceptable, whether or not it represented a meaning that was possible at the time the poem was written. If in reading

Racine's *Bérénice* I encounter the line: "Dans l'Orient désert quel devint mon ennui," and if the word *l'Orient* makes me think of the Far East and *ennui* suggests to me a vague state of melancholy, have I not in fact misread the line? Racine certainly intended *l'Orient* to refer to the Near East, and *ennui* in the seventeenth century meant a very precise and not necessarily melancholy perturbation of the mind. It is possible that my reading makes perfect sense in the context; it may be entirely coherent; but surely it will be a wrong reading all the same.

This objection has become all the more acute since certain modern critics, such as William Empson in *Seven Types of Ambiguity,* have suggested that any word that means more than what it literally says is, by definition, ambiguous. After all, in poetry every significant word "means" more than what it literally says (in the sense that its meaning is enriched by other elements in the poetic structure), so on this basis the analysis of poetry ought really to consist of the proper placing of every ambiguity. All connotations of words are ambiguous, of course, since they mean more than the denotations of the words. Analysis, then, should consist of the disclosing of all the connotations of a poem. But what about the connotation "China" that I derived from Racine's word *l'Orient?* Is it not erroneous? The answer is that this wrong meaning is not in the *poem,* it was simply in *my mind* as I read the poem. It was part of the effect that the poem had on me, and in this case it was an improper effect. The reader's experience of the poem is not the poem itself, as we have seen. The erroneous connotation of the word *l'Orient* was a potential effect of the poem, and when I was affected by that connotation it became an actual effect of the poem. But neither potential nor actual effects are part of the poem itself; they are not part of its structure. They are merely uses, proper or improper, to which the structure can be put. To confuse an effect with the poem itself is to be subject to the "affective fallacy." So we can properly declare an anachronistic reading to be a wrong reading, meaning that the effect upon the reader was not commensurate with the true nature of the text. And since we can avoid such errors only by having adequate historical knowledge, we have said nothing that reduces in any way the importance of historical or biographical information in dealing intelligently with a poem. No one will ever read a poem perfectly in the sense of being affected by it in a way which is in total conformity with its true nature. To do so, in fact, we would have to avoid, among hosts of other possible errors, all anachronisms of sound. For example, in the days of Racine the diphthong *oi,* as in the words *roi, loi,* and *bois,* was pronounced not "wah" but "weh." Consequently, a line such as "Oui, c'est Agamemnon, c'est ton roi qui t'appelle," should be pronounced ". . . c'est ton rouè . . ." if we are to recapture the original sound of the words. Inevitably, anachronisms will occur in any reading of a poem written before our own time. But with the aid of historical knowledge we can at least come closer to a state of perfection than would be possible if we overlooked history completely.

If we hope, then, to reach the fullest and most accurate possible understanding of a poem we shall need to respond to it actively by analyzing its structure, but we shall also have to bring to bear on our analysis whatever extraliterary data may be appropriate to the comprehension of the text in question.

PART II
CRITICISM

3
The Analysis of the Poem

Having emerged safely from the jungle of theory with a handful of basic principles as trophies, we are now ready to get down to the practical business of criticism. Our first concern is with analysis, the inspection of the poem's structure. As can be readily imagined, a great many elements of the structure of a French poem have direct counterparts in English poetry, but because of certain fundamental differences between the two languages most of the aspects of sound and rhythm that must be dealt with in the analysis of a French poem have no direct English parallels. With this major exception, however, much of what can be said about French verse should not seem too strange to the reader accustomed to Anglo-American literature.

It would be highly convenient if a series of rigid rules could be set down making it possible for us to analyze a poem automatically, as though we were following the directions for disassembling a model engine. Unfortunately, the analysis of poetry is not a simple mechanical process. The key to criticism has always been, and perhaps will always be, personal insight. Here again the importance of even the first reading as a source of information about where to begin cannot be overemphasized. There is no substitute for reading with heightened sensitivity and sharpened perceptions; their absence is likely to lead to what I. A. Richards called the "stock response," an unthinking reaction to a text based on purely conventional grounds. Madison Avenue advertisers thrive on eliciting stock responses, but if they happen in poetry reading all is lost. Even if we were able to draft a perfect set of rules for inspecting a poem, insight would still have a role to play since knowing where to look is one thing while seeing is another.

We have already noted that poetry analysis is something one does with a fluoroscope, not with a scalpel. It is true that as we focus our attention on one element of the poetic structure at a time we may momentarily lose sight of the over-all structure. But we have not destroyed the poem in the process. We have only to reread it, with a consequent improvement in our knowledge of what its constituents are, in order to restore it; and it should then seem more alive than ever before. The rereading, however, is vital. Analysis is only a step leading to it, not an end in itself. As John Ciardi has said, "The only reason for taking a poem apart is that it may then be put back together again more richly."[1]

It is also important to avoid confusing analysis with the French *explication de texte*. An *explication* is a formal presentation of the results of analysis and of other, extraliterary, approaches to the poem; it is essentially a prescribed method of exposition. Since most teachers have their own favorite formula for the structure of an *explication,* none will be outlined here. With the aid of the Glossary at the end of this book a student should find it possible to present an *explication* in whatever external form of development the teacher may prefer.

One of the basic principles we arrived at laboriously in Part I was the rejection of the notion that the poem is a sort

[1]*How Does a Poem Mean?* (Boston: Houghton Mifflin Company, 1960), p. 664.

of disposable container for an idea, a formal embellishment which, if we threw it away, would leave us with the "content," the only really valuable part of the poem. This fallacy, which Cleanth Brooks calls the "heresy of paraphrase"[2] because it often leads readers to restate the ideas of a poem in order to express the "meaning" of the text, is more commonly referred to as "message-hunting." It is one of the most readily understandable, though thoroughly misguided, approaches to the meaning of a poem. Essentially it represents the way in which we are accustomed to reading and elucidating prose; and since it is far easier to think of poetry as embellished prose than it is to look upon it as an entirely different order of language, we naturally tend to adopt the simpler approach. But if we agree to be steadfast and to follow the rougher but straighter path, we must then abandon the old "form versus content" method of analysis. It will do no good merely to change the names of the same categories to "vehicle" and "tenor," or "expression" and "thought." A fallacy by any other name is just as false. The point is that a successful poem expresses what cannot be expressed by prose, since prose does not have at its disposition all the connotation-evoking factors that are a part of poetry; and the meaning of the poem cannot be rendered without the aid of these significant elements.

René Wellek and Austin Warren[3] have made a sound suggestion for avoiding the form-content dilemma. They distinguish between "materials" and "structure," the materials being the "aesthetically indifferent" elements of a poem, i.e., the denotations of the words themselves, and the "structure" being the manner in which the materials "acquire aesthetic efficacy." We shall have occasion to adopt this useful distinction at least in part, though a change in the key terms may

[2] *The Well Wrought Urn* (New York: Harcourt, Brace and Company, 1947), chap. 11.

[3] *Theory of Literature* (2nd edition; New York: Harcourt, Brace and Company, 1956), p. 129.

prove advisable. But now it is time to stop talking about poetry in general and turn to the poem in particular.

As we pick up a French poem with the intention of trying to analyze it, it becomes painfully evident that there are some preliminary and elementary facts that must be dealt with at the outset; namely, the denotations of the words, syntactical arrangements, and references to external objects and events. These are the items that give the native Frenchman a slight advantage in dealing with the poem, yet they will probably prove to be the least important factors in the final analysis. Unfortunately, if we do not clarify these questions first we shall never reach a final analysis. The denotations are no doubt what Wellek and Warren mean by their term "materials," the esthetically indifferent elements of the poem, as opposed to "structure," the manner in which these elements become esthetically effective. We had better avoid using the term "structure" in this sense in order not to confuse it with the way in which the various significant elements of the poem are related to one another; so let us instead distinguish between *denotations* and *connotations* in their customary sense. The denotations of the poem, then, are the meanings that are to be found in dictionaries, grammars, and reference works.

The foreigner who encounters the phrase "writhing fingers" and recognizes "writhing" as a present participle can look up the verb "writhe" in the dictionary and discover that it means "to twist or contort"; and "fingers" will turn out to be the "five terminal members of the hand." He will then know that the denotation of "writhing fingers" is "the five terminal members of the hand in a process of contortion." With the exercise of a little imagination he will probably also recognize the general flavor of the connotations that are implied by the phrase. The same procedure applies to aggregates of words with a fixed meaning, such as idioms and proverbial expressions. Our only essential advantage over the foreigner lies in the fact that we should not have to look up the words or idioms in a dictionary, since their denotations are perfectly familiar to us; and when we read in French it is in just this one respect that we lag behnd the native Frenchman. With a little time and effort we can overcome his initial advantage quite sufficiently to carry us far into the poem.

Without straining the meaning of the word absurdly it is even possible to apply the term "denotation" to standard grammar and syntax. In scientific prose, to cite the extreme case, syntax and grammar are so used as to arouse no feelings and reflect no attitudes. They are in effect neutral, merely associating one denotation with another so as to express a proposition. In rhetoric certain syntactical constructions are so arranged that they do suggest the attitude of the speaker, and here they may be said to take on connotative overtones. But our first concern must be to recognize the denotations of grammar, the normal patterns of prose syntax and word inflections, which can be learned (or relearned if they have been forgotten) with the help of a standard review grammar of French. And here again the use of bilingual translations will often be of assistance so long as we remember that a poem when translated ceases to be the same poem; its sounds, rhythms, and connotations have changed. What we need is a literal translation to save us the trouble of untying syntactical knots and leafing constantly through dictionary pages, but that is the only proper use to which we can put an English version of the poem. It will not in any way replace the French original.

Finally, we must learn the denotations of the references the poet may make to ideas, facts, events, persons, or things, in the world of reality or the world of art. Typical examples of such references are proper names that designate real or imaginary beings or objects that exist outside the poem, such as the names of the Muses or other mythological creatures. These references have a denotative meaning. When the Faun in Mallarmé's "Après-midi d'un faune" speaks of Etna, the denotative meaning of his reference is a specific mountain in Sicily, though the connotative meaning involves the notion of Vulcan's forge. This sort of denotation can usually be clarified by consulting appropriate reference works such as dictionaries of mythology, atlases, or encyclopedias. In cases where the poet refers to events in his own life or in world history, or to other works of literature, we shall need to know the facts of the poet's biography or of the relevant historical period or literary work. Thus it is important to know, when reading Valéry's poem "Au Bois dormant," that "La Belle au bois dormant" is the French translation of "Sleeping Beauty." Usually in annotated editions the textual footnotes will solve this kind of problem for us.

Now the point of this extended laboring of the obvious is to indicate that because denotative words, syntactical constructions, or references are merely signs pointing to specific concepts, word relations, and concrete facts, it is usually perfectly possible to "decipher" semi-mechanically the denotative meaning of a poem either with the help of annotated translations of the text or, failing that, with the aid of standard reference works. Once we have performed this operation of decoding the poem, we could "extract the ideas it contains" (to use a phrase every word of which implies a fallacy), and we could write "a prose paraphrase of the propositions stated in the poem"—provided that we had no interest in the poem itself. But having just spent a chapter establishing the fact that the poem does not contain anything, that it does not really express propositions, and that a paraphrase is not a statement of the meaning of the poem, we may justifiably feel that such a "deciphering" would not advance us very far. Actually, of course, a correct understanding of all the denotations of a poem is a *sine qua non* if our analysis is to proceed. The essential point is not to stop when we have merely comprehended the raw signs of the poem. These signs are also symbols with rich implications, and any explanation of them that overlooks their connotative possibilities is totally inadequate.

Connotations, which are the implied meanings of words, grammatical constructions, and references are deeply involved

in attitudes and feelings. They partake of the nature of ambiguity in William Empson's sense of the word; namely, any
significance that extends beyond purely denotative meaning.
Since connotations are plays on, or distortions of, or enrich-
ments of denotations, we must learn the denotations first; but
this is only the initial attack in what will develop into a fairly
elaborate campaign of interpretation.

We all know that words have connotations. We saw earlier how easily we could misjudge the connotations of the
word *ennui* if we thought of it in a post-Romantic sense,
rather than in terms of the seventeenth-century classical meaning which Racine intended when he wrote: "Dans l'Orient
désert quel devint mon ennui." What is less obvious is that
even syntactical constructions sometimes have the ability to
confer connotative value on the denotations of words. The
phrase "Va, je ne te hais pas," as used by Chimène in *Le Cid*
means, denotatively, "Je t'aime." But connotatively, the mere
use of "litotes" (the negating of the opposite of what is really
meant) has made the statement imply a modest reluctance on
Chimène's part to confess that she really loves Rodrigue. The
effect here is one of understatement, just as in the corresponding English phrase: "I am not altogether displeased," meaning, denotatively, "I am very glad indeed." So if we simply
use the word "not" with a term that means the opposite of
what we really intend to convey it is not entirely unlikely
that we will produce an effect not utterly dissimilar to that
of understatement. And understatement has an ironic connotative significance; it underscores an attitude which can be
suggested by the mere use of litotes. Here the new meaning,
the implied attitude, results from the interaction of the syntactical construction (litotes) and the denotations of the
words used in the construction. If we introduced more factors, such as certain kinds of rhythm, still further meaning
would emerge. Any change that we made in the participating
elements would alter the connotative meaning of the phrase.
And this is why pure denotative meaning is not equivalent to

poetic meaning, which involves the interplay of many more elements than these three.

The function of analysis is first to determine precisely what factors are engaged in the creation of a poem's meaning and then to allow us to see how the resulting connotations are interconnected so as to form the poetic structure. We must examine various aspects of the poem one at a time in order to learn how to recognize these basic elements. This will permit us to discover the special forms they may take and the sort of significant relationships they are likely to enter into with one another. It is important to remember that these relationships are brand new entities, not simply aggregates of their components. Sodium can burn us, and chlorine can poison us, but the compound of sodium and chlorine is a new substance whose absence from our bodies would kill us: sodium chloride, or common table salt.

The seven chapters that follow might have been divided into two groups. Chapters Four, Five, and Six are concerned with the physical aspect of a poem: its sounds, its shape (which is determined by the lengths of its lines, the number of lines in a stanza, and the pattern of rimes that binds the stanza together), and its rhythm. These properties of the poem are not in themselves either denotations or connotations, but they help to cause connotations to emerge from denotations. The shape of a poem, for example, may involve a rhythm which will bring certain sounds into prominence, and these sounds may evoke a feeling about the words which they express that produces a level of connotative meaning. It is the interaction of these "physical" properties of the poem with the power of the words to express meanings that makes possible the poem's structure.

Chapters Seven, Eight, Nine, and Ten address themselves to the problem of meaning itself. They concentrate on the kinds of words, the type of language, that the poet uses; the ways in which, by stimulating the reader's senses and imagination, he implies more than he actually says; the possible extraliterary approaches to the poem that may lead to the discovery of further levels of meaning; and the manner in which the resulting connotations become associated with one another in such a way as to create the structure that we call a poem.

Chapters Four, Five, and Six are necessarily somewhat technical, like the scoring of a game of contract bridge or the statistics involved in the evaluation of racehorses and football teams. As these similes demonstrate, however, even technicalities need not rule out enjoyment, and there is always the consoling thought that, compared with football, the mathematics of poetry is pure child's play.

4
Sound

Poetry is sometimes referred to as "verbal music"—very misleadingly, since the two arts have almost nothing in common except what is rather vaguely implied by the word "euphony." Nevertheless, the importance of pure sound to the meaning of a poem is inestimable. It is through the sound system of the poem that its structure reaches us. Even when we are reading poetry silently we should be listening to the sounds with our "inner ear," as we saw earlier. We have also previously noted the fact that no two recitations of a poem are ever identical, so that even apart from anachronisms the perfect reading of a poem will never be heard by human ears. But some readings are better than others. Even though the recitation of a French poem by a foreigner is likely to differ significantly from that of a native Frenchman no matter how good the foreigner's pronunciation is, at least the grosser errors can be avoided. Anyone who feels it necessary to polish his pronunciation should ask his teacher or tutor to drill him on speech rhythms as well. Rhythm is as important in poetry reading as the pure sounds themselves, and sometimes more so. Some rhythmic patterns that occur in poetry are rarely if ever heard in prose speech, and we shall discuss these when we come to the topic of rhythm.

Significant manifestations of sound in poetry range from the effects that can be caused by the sounds of a single word, through the considerable variety of phenomena involving repetitions of similar or identical sounds, to the over-all verse texture of the poem. We may begin with the smallest unit, the sound of the individual word.

There are two ways in which the very sound of a word can reinforce the word's denotation so that a heightened connotative effect is produced. The first of these is the familiar "onomatopoeia," the resemblance between a word's sound and the sound of what the word denotes, as in the French *roucoulement* for the cooing of a dove, or the English word *coo* itself. The French word is a more elaborate—and possibly, therefore, a more accurate—imitation of the dove's sound than is the English *coo*. It is, in short, a more effective onomatopoeia. The slight roll of the initial *r* makes possible an imitative effect in the French which cannot be reproduced in English. On the other hand, the diphthongization that is characteristic of English makes *miaow* a better representation of the sound made by a cat than the French *miaulement*. Onomatopoeias occur in poetry whenever a sound is imitated and are usually rather easy to recognize. Their connotative power lies in the fact that there is a real connection between the actual form of the onomatopoeic word itself and what the word signifies. Ordinarily, words are quite arbitrary symbols, as can be seen by the fact that while *Blatt, feuille,* and *hoja* all mean "leaf," there is no clear reason why any of these groups of sounds should necessarily have to do with foliage. As far as the meaning of the words is concerned, the actual sounds are purely arbitrary.

The second way in which a word's sound can reinforce its denotation is far more common and basic than onomatopoeia; and for that reason, no doubt, it has no generally accepted name in English. Sometimes it is called "pseudo-onomatopoeia"; John Ciardi, in *How Does a Poem Mean?*,[1] avoids

---

[1] (Boston: Houghton Mifflin Company, 1960), p. 764.

this jaw-breaker by using the term "mimesis" (adjective "mimetic"), the Greek word for "imitation," and we shall follow his example. Mimesis is a rather more subtle effect than onomatopoeia. It occurs when the sound of a word "imitates" its denotation in cases where the denotation is not itself a sound. This imitation may be what Ciardi calls a "muscular enactment" of the denotation, or the relationship between sound and meaning may be of an even more delicate, though no less perceptible, kind. A notable example of "muscular enactment" occurs in the closing lines of Joachim Du Bellay's villanelle, "D'un Vanneur de blé, aux vents," in connection with the word *j'ahanne,* "I toil":

> De votre douce haleine
> Eventez cette plaine,
> Eventez ce séjour,
> Cependant que j'ahanne
> A mon blé, que je vanne
> A la chaleur du jour.[2]

The silent *h* of *j'ahanne* requires the reader to pronounce the two *a*'s separately but in one breath, and the result is a gasp of the kind the wheat-sifter might himself exhale as he labors at his task. The lungs of the speaker seem to enact in sound the effort of the peasant.

A similar effect, also caused by a silent *h,* is produced by the French noun *la haine,* "hatred," one of the most dramatic words in the language and a sheer delight to tragedians. Here again, the so-called aspirate *h* creates a hiatus, the immediate juxtaposition of two vowel sounds one of which succeeds the other in the same breath with no consonant sound to intervene between them. The result is an unusual prolongation of vocalized breath, a phenomenon often avoided in French poetry and therefore a very noticeable one to the ear when

[2] The spelling has been modernized. A literal translation would be: "With your gentle breath / fan this plain, / fan this place, / while I toil / at my wheat, which I sift / in the heat of the day."

it does occur. The *l* of *la* and the *n* of *haine* both permit the voice to be heard before and after the hiatus, and the speaker may extend the sound of the *n* beyond its normal limit of duration: "la-è-è-nnn." This tends to produce an effect analogous to that of a protracted wail which, combined with the muscular tension and shift at the change of the vowel sounds, seems extremely appropriate for expressing the emotion denoted by the word "hatred." The same principle applies to the corresponding verb, *haïr,* "to hate," which also begins with an aspirate *h.* In Act I of Racine's first tragedy, *La Thébaïde,* we find the following examples of the two words:

> Prendrait-elle pour roi l'esclave de Mycène,
> Qui pour tous les Thébains n'a plus que de *la haine.* . . ?

> *Je hais* ses ennemis, et c'est là tout mon crime. . . .

> De lâches courtisans peuvent bien *le haïr,*
> Mais une mère enfin ne peut pas se trahir.

> Je le dois, en effet, distinguer du commun,
> Mais c'est pour *le haïr* encor plus que pas un;
> Et je souhaiterais, dans ma juste colère,
> Que chacun *le haït* comme *le hait* son père.

> Mais un père à ce point doit-il être emporté?
> Vous avez trop *de haine.*

Mimetic effects can be created in many ways. The French word *l'huile* might be thought by some to be more expressive of the tactile quality of oil than the word "oil" in English, though they operate on the same diphthongal principle. *Suinter* in French and "ooze" in English, on the other hand, though they mean the same thing and are both clearly imitative of their common denotation, share not a single sound between them, nor do they even involve a similar muscular play. This may serve to remind us that sounds as such convey no meaning whatever (except in the case of the purest onomatopoeias, where they really denote themselves). If you say "ooze" or "oil" to a Frenchman who speaks no English, he will be very unlikely to guess even approximately what you mean. It is the combination of sound and denotation that produces the new, more effective meaning.[3]

Onomatopoeic effects are usually very brief, though by no means insignificant. The effect can sometimes be prolonged, however, by repeating the key sounds of the imitative word in later words of the same sentence. This process has been called "extended onomatopoeia."[4] The classic illustration of the device in English is Tennyson's line from *The Princess:* "The *moan* [onomatopoeia] of doves in *immemor*ial *elms* [extended onomatopoeia]." An example in French would be Racine's celebrated line from *Andromaque*, "Pour qu*i* sont *c*es serpents qu*i* *s*ifflent *s*ur vos têtes?" where the extension is backwards, so that the alliterative *s* sounds and the assonanced *i* sounds suddenly take on fuller significance as a result of the onomatopoeic word *sifflent*, "hiss." To realize that this extended onomatopoeia has contributed to the meaning of the line one has only to rephrase it in some such way as: "For whom are intended the reptiles which are emitting their characteristic utterance upon your heads?" The denotative significance of the question has scarcely changed, if at all, but the connotative meaning has been markedly altered. If we translated the line as "For whom are those snakes who are hissing on your heads?" some of the original connotative power would remain, since an extended onomatopoeia would again be operating.

[3] For a very elaborate treatment of muscular play between jaw, tongue, and lips and its effect on the reader of poetry, see André Spire, *Plaisir poétique et plaisir musculaire; essai sur l'évolution des techniques poétiques* (New York: S. F. Vanni, 1949).

[4] Edward A. Bloom, Charles H. Philbrick, and Elmer M. Blistein, *The Order of Poetry: An Introduction* (New York: The Odyssey Press, 1961), p. 123.

The total effect of pure sound in a poem is usually called "verse texture" or "harmony," and the quality of this texture at any point in the verse is often described as euphonious or cacophonous. Euphony is the effect produced by a series of easily pronounced, "musical" sounds, as opposed to cacophony, which results from a succession of harsh, grating, or not easily pronounced sounds. In English we can create a cacophonous effect by a heavy use of consonant clusters, as in the line from "The Outlaw of Loch Lene" by Jeremiah Joseph Callanan, "O would that a freezing sleet-wing'd tempest did sweep . . ." (*dth-fr-ngsl-tw-ngdt-mp-std-dsw*). In French, by the nature of the language, this is more difficult to do, though there are other ways of achieving a similar result.

Euphony and cacophony in both English and French tend to accompany the repetition of a particular characteristic of sound; for example, the quality of explosiveness (such as is produced by the heavy use of *p, k, t, b,* hard *g,* and *d*), or of smoothness (as represented by *l, r, m, n, sh,* and *z*). The element of repetition is necessary to prolong the effect to the point at which it will be perceived at least unconsciously by the listener. The result will normally be a reinforcing of the denotations of the passages that are affected, in much the same way that mimesis operates in a single word. Thus Ronsard plays on the sounds of the last syllable of *hélas,* "alas," to augment the feeling of shocked sadness he wishes to evoke in the second stanza of his ode, "A sa maîtresse." He also uses related but not quite identical sounds, a technique called "dissonance" which we shall discuss shortly. The significant sounds are italicized:

> Mignonne, allons voir si la rose
> Qui ce matin avait déclose
> Sa robe de pourpre au Soleil
> A point perdu cette vêprée
> Les plis de sa robe pourprée,
> Et son teint au vôtre pareil.

> *Las!* voyez comme en peu d'esp*ace,*
> Mignonne, elle a dessus la p*lace*
> *Las! las!* ses beautés *laissé c*hoir!
> O vraiment marâtre Nature,
> Puisqu'une telle fleur ne dure
> Que du matin jusques au soir!
>
> Donc, si vous me croyez, mignonne,
> Tandis que votre âge fleuronne
> En sa plus verte nouveauté,
> Cueillez, cueillez votre jeunesse:
> Comme à cette fleur la vieillesse
> Fera ternir votre beauté.[5]

The following poem by Baudelaire contains some notable examples of cacophony, caused by the coincidence of the gloomy, claustrophobic denotations of the lines with explosive consonants and somber vowels:

SPLEEN

> Quand le ciel bas et lourd pèse comme un couvercle
> Sur l'esprit gémissant en proie aux longs ennuis,
> Et que de l'horizon embrassant tout le cercle
> Il nous verse un jour noir plus triste que les nuits;
>
> Quand la terre est changée en un cachot humide,
> Où l'Espérance, comme une chauve-souris,
> S'en va battant les murs de son aile timide
> Et se cognant la tête à des plafonds pourris;
>
> Quand la pluie étalant ses immenses traînées
> D'une vaste prison imite les barreaux,
> Et qu'un peuple muet d'infâmes araignées
> Vient tendre ses filets au fond de nos cerveaux,

---

[5] The spelling has been modernized.

Des cloches tout à coup sautent avec furie
Et lancent vers le ciel un affreux hurlement,
Ainsi que des esprits errants et sans patrie
Qui se mettent à geindre opiniâtrement.

—Et de longs corbillards, sans tambours ni musique
Défilent lentement dans mon âme; l'Espoir,
Vaincu, pleure, et l'Angoisse atroce, despotique,
Sur mon crâne incliné plante son drapeau noir.

Contrast with this oppressive atmosphere the ethereal quality of another Baudelairian poem, in which the airy freedom of the poet's imaginary voyage is emphasized by the prominence of liquid consonants and unchecked vowels:

Elévation

Au-dessus des étangs, au-dessus des vallées,
Des montagnes, des bois, des nuages, des mers,
Par delà le soleil, par delà les éthers,
Par delà les confins des sphères étoilées,

Mon esprit, tu te meus avec agilité,
Et, comme un bon nageur qui se pâme dans l'onde,
Tu sillonnes gaiement l'immensité profonde
Avec une indicible et mâle volupté.

Envole-toi bien loin de ces miasmes morbides;
Va te purifier dans l'air supérieur,
Et bois, comme une pure et divine liqueur,
Le feu clair qui remplit les espaces limpides.

Derrière les ennuis et les vastes chagrins
Qui chargent de leurs poids l'existence brumeuse,
Heureux celui qui peut d'une aile vigoureuse
S'élancer vers les champs lumineux et sereins!

Celui dont les pensers, comme des alouettes,
Vers les cieux le matin prennent un libre essor,
—Qui plane sur la vie, et comprend sans effort
Le langage des fleurs et des choses muettes!

There is in French an interesting exception to the English rule that a predominance of vowel sounds tends to be euphonious. The phenomenon of hiatus, the immediate succession of two fully pronounced vowel sounds with no intervening consonant sound, is cacophonous to the French ear. We foreigners may find it melodious, but the French miss the supporting consonant. We have already felt the cacophonous effect of the hiatus in the French word for "hatred," *la haine.* To illustrate the point further, here is a gloriously jarring line, one meant to be spat out in the theater in such a way that the harshness of its three hiatuses will fully support the peremptory quality of the question asked: "D'*où* es-*tu, où* vas-tu, d'où viens-t*u à* cette heure?"

Sometimes, as we have seen, the phenomena of sound recurrence that are deliberately built into a poem involve the use of consonants or vowels of a similar general quality, such as explosive sounds, or liquids, or open vowels. Between this rather vague category of sound associations and the specific use of repetitive identical vowels or consonants falls the class of closely related but not quite identical sounds. Here the technique is to emphasize different shades of the same vowel, such as open and closed *o*'s, *a*'s, or *e*'s, or the voiced and unvoiced forms of the same basic consonant sound, such as *p* and *b*, *t* and *d*, *k* and hard *g*, *s* and *z*. The only difference between, for example, a *p* and a *b* is that when you pronounce a *b* your vocal cords vibrate, whereas they do not do so when you utter a *p* sound. This matter of the use or non-use of the voice is all that differentiates the two consonants; the lips operate identically in the production of each. Similarly, a *t* is the unvoiced equivalent of a voiced *d*, and the same is

true of *s* and *z*, *k* and hard *g*, *f* and *v*, etc. The close proximity of words beginning with *k* and *g*, *d* and *t*, and *v* and *f*
sounds in the following lines from Mallarmé's "Après-midi
d'un faune" produces a muted alliteration, not so obvious as
if the words all began with exactly the same consonant, but
nonetheless detectable.

. . . CONTEZ
"Que je *c*ou*p*ais ici les *c*reux roseaux *d*omptés
"Par le *t*alent; *q*uand, sur l'or *g*lauque *de* lointaines
"Verdures *d*édiant leur *v*igne à *d*es *f*ontaines,
"Ondoie une blancheur animale au repos. . . ."

Needless to say, the general effect is enhanced by the echoes
of significant consonants in the interior of the words, especially when the consonants begin stressed syllables. The initial *b* of *blancheur*, for example, is reinforced by the stressed
p of *repos;* the first four riming syllables all begin with *t*, and
we have additional *d*'s in *verdure, dédiant,* and *ondoie;* and
the *g* of *glauque* is accentuated by the *q* that follows it in
the same word.

The result of this sort of sound association is sometimes
onomatopoeic, sometimes mimetic, and sometimes simply euphonious or cacophonous; but whatever the effect may be, it
normally influences the denotations of the lines involved so
as to enrich their meaning. This repetition of not quite identical sounds is occasionally called "dissonance," though unfortunately the term "dissonance" is also substituted at times
for the word "cacophony." Such, alas, is the ambiguous nature
of critical terminology.

The repetition of absolutely identical sounds has a variety
of names depending on whether consonants or vowels or both
are being repeated, and depending on their relative position
in the word or line of verse. To some extent these distinctions
are academic; what really counts is the fact of sound repetition, whatever form it may take. Sometimes, however, the
particular type or category may be quite important. The four

basic terms covering the repetition of identical sounds are "consonance," "alliteration," "assonance," and "rime."

Consonance occurs whenever the same consonant sound is repeated, regardless of the positions occupied by the consonant in any of the given words; for example: "The *m*oan of doves in i*mmem*orial el*m*s." Consonance is the genus of which alliteration is a particular species. The term consonance is also used to describe the placing at the ends of lines of words whose last syllables contain identical consonant sounds but dissimilar vowel sounds, such as "black-block," "share-shore." This substitute for rime is very rare in French, but consonance often occurs in the interior of a line with great effect, as in Tristan Corbière's "La Fin," where he contrasts the pale Death of the landlubber with the sailor's violent but glorious end in the sea:

> Vieux fantôme éventé, la Mort, change de face:
> 　La Mer! . . .

Or we may cite Charles Cros' "Hiéroglyphe" in which the same consonance is extended to include *l'amour:*

> J'ai trois fenêtres à ma chambre:
> 　L'amour, la mer, la mort,
> Sang vif, vert calme, violet.
>
> O femme, doux et lourd trésor!
>
> Froids vitraux, cloches, odeurs d'ambre,
> 　La mer, la mort, l'amour,
> Ne sentir que ce qui me plaît . . .
>
> Femme, plus claire que le jour!
>
> Par ce soir doré de septembre,
> 　La mort, l'amour, la mer,
> Me noyer dans l'oubli complet.
>
> Femme! femme! cercueil de chair!

"Alliteration," sometimes called "head rime," is the repetition of the same consonant sound at the beginning of words. We have already seen an example: "Pour qui *s*ont *c*es *s*erpents qui *s*ifflent *s*ur vos têtes? Another occurs in the third line of the poem just quoted: "Sang *v*if, *v*ert calme, *v*iolet."

"Assonance," also called "ablaut," is the inverse of consonance, being the repetition of identical vowel sounds without regard to preceding or following consonant sounds. At the end of lines, where the repeated vowel is in the last accented syllable, assonance can replace rime. This was standard in the medieval *chansons de geste,* such as *La Chanson de Roland* (of which a sample passage will be found on pages 78–9), and it has been used by a few twentieth-century poets.

"Rime," the most standard technique involving sound in both English and French verse, consists of the repetition of a combination of identical consonant and vowel sounds. Depending on the number and position of such sounds, various qualifying adjectives such as "rich," "adequate," or "weak" are used to modify the word "rime" in order to distinguish its possible forms.

Recognizing the presence in a given poem of an assonance, a consonance, an alliteration, or a rime is of course only the first step in assessing its significance, and the same is true of locating examples of euphony or cacophony, dissonances, onomatopoeias, or mimetic effects. It is not enough to announce triumphantly: "Eureka! An alliteration!" The real problem is to discover how the alliteration is functioning in relation to other elements of the poem. The possible services that may be performed by these sound phenomena are legion, but there are several typical ones that can be mentioned here.

A repeated sound may focus attention on a particular word, thereby increasing its effectiveness. The voltage of the word *la mer* as it occurs in Corbière's "La Fin," having been prepared for by *la mort,* is very considerable. Not only does the consonance associate the two words particularly tightly, it also causes them to stand out from the text far more vividly than would normally be the case.

Repetitions of identical sounds may in turn produce euphony, cacophony, or extended onomatopoeias, as we have
seen; and these secondary effects may harmonize with the tone
of what is otherwise being expressed by the text. The cacophony of the line, "O would that a freezing sleet-wing'd tempest
did sweep . . . ," caused by the consonantal clusters involving four *t*'s and four *d*'s among other explosive sounds, not
to mention the threefold assonance in *ee,* is in perfect keeping
with the harshness of the weather being described.

Assonance, consonance, or rime, when used at the ends of
lines of verse, serve to mark the very fact that the line has
ended. In French, where, as we shall see, no regular system
of frequent stresses indicates the meter as it does in English,
the rime is of the utmost importance in enabling a listener to
detect the ends of the lines. Furthermore, a regular pattern
of rimes makes it possible to perceive aurally how the stanza
is constructed. Thus the rime scheme communicates the
shape of the poem to a listener. For this reason unrimed verse
was a great rarity in French until the advent of free verse not
much more than a century ago.

Before turning our attention to the kinds of rime that
occur in French poetry, we may pause to note, for the sake of
those intrepid readers who like to push ideas to their ultimate
conclusions, that it is possible to detect in poetry sound phenomena of a far greater degree of refinement than those we
have already considered. Kenneth Burke, in his article "On
Musicality in Verse,"[6] has called attention to a number of
such subtleties in English, all of which can be found equally
frequently in French. One of these is what he terms "tonal
chiasmus." Chiasmus, which means "crossing," normally refers to a verbal sequence in which, for rhetorical effect, a series
of words or grammatical functions is repeated in reverse order, thus: "One should *eat* to *live,* not *live* to *eat.*" Applying
this notion to sounds, as Burke does, one discovers that some
very interesting poetic effects can be explained as examples

[6] First published in *Poetry,* reprinted in *The Philosophy of Literary Form*
(New York: Vintage Books, 1957), pp. 296–304.

of tonal chiasmus. The simplest form of the device is exemplified in such lines as these, from Keats' "Ode to a Nightingale":

> Fast-fading violets cover'd up in leaves;
>   And mid-May's eldest child,
> The coming musk-rose, full of dewy wine,
>   The murmurous haunt of flies on summer eves.

In line one, the *v* and *l* of "violets" recur in reverse order in the *l* and *v* of "leaves"; in the third line, the *com* of "coming" returns as the *mu-k* of "musk"; and in line four, three elements of the last two syllables of "murmurous" (*mûr-ŭ-s*) are reversed in the word "summer" (*s-ŭ-mûr*). Often a related sound will be repeated instead of the identical sound, as in "drop of blood," *d—p, b—d,* where the dissonance softens the effect. Variety in the use of consonance, as Burke notes, can also be achieved by repeating consonant clusters with the component consonants spaced out, as in "*gl*eaming *g*o*l*d." This he calls "augmentation," as opposed to the reverse order of presentation ("*g*o*r*y and *gr*im") which he labels "diminution."

In a volume dedicated largely to questions of poetic technique, a French critic surrendered unconditionally some fifteen years ago when faced with the problem of trying to explain the musical magic of Malherbe's great line from the "Prière pour le roi Henri le Grand, allant en Limousin": "Et les fruits passeront la promesse des fleurs." His conclusion was that the line is a miracle of sound because its harmony is sweet to the French ear. Armed with Kenneth Burke's "tonal chiasmus," "augmentation," and "diminution," we can avoid this kind of tautology by pointing first to the initial consonants of the four stressed words in the line: "fruits," "passeront," "promesse," and "fleurs." These initial consonants form a perfect tonal chiasmus: *f, p, p, f.* Furthermore, we have in the two words beginning with *f* a nice case of "augmentation": "*fr*uits—*fl*eurs": "*fr*—*f*-*r*; and in the two words beginning with *p* we find an instance of diminution: "*p*asse*r*ont—*pr*omesse," *p-r—pr*. Perhaps the euphony of the line is not so hopelessly mysterious after all.

Rime, for the reason we have noted, is usually felt to be almost essential to French poetry. The degree of attention we normally pay to the kind of foot that sets up the meter of a line of English verse is accorded in French versifying circles to the rime. French rimes have been classified in three categories: rich rime, sufficient (or adequate) rime, and insufficient (or weak) rime, according to the number of identical sounds involved. The more, the richer, and the better, since the listener is surer to catch the repetition. Also, those poets who feel that difficulties are to be sought after for their own sake naturally favor rich rime. The nineteenth-century Parnassians called it the "clou d'or," the golden nail that tacks the line in place. The easiest way to distinguish categories is to count the identical sounds. The rime is rich if there are three, sufficient if there are two, and insufficient if there is only one. There must always be an identical vowel sound in any rime, and the tonal identity must include the very last sounds in the riming words; thus, "*mère-amère*," "*port-sport*," "*serve-verve*," "*tordu-perdu*" are all rich, since the last three (audible) sounds are identical. Silent written letters do not count, of course; all for the ear, nothing for the eye. The end of Leconte de Lisle's "La Tête du comte," which is cited on pages 81–2 as an example of terza rima, illustrates the typical Parnassian insistence on rich rime. "Splend*eur*-hâbl*eur*," and aig*u*-ambig*u*" are sufficient rimes, having two identical final sounds. The fact that it takes two written letters to express the *eu* sound makes no difference; the sound itself is a single pure vowel. Examples of sufficient rime can be found in almost every poem quoted in this book. Weak or insufficient rimes have just one identical final vowel, and are therefore really a form of assonance: "armée-épée." The "mute" *e* at the end, being silent, is not counted. Though they are technically inadequate, insufficient rimes have often been used by French poets, as in these lines by Voltaire:

Quand l'âme fuit avec la vie
A-t-on des yeux pour voir Délie?

All told, it has been calculated, there are 571 possible rimes in French, some of them with very limited uses, at least until the advent of a French Ogden Nash.

A further peculiarity of French rimes is the rule of alternation. This depends on another way of classifying rimes: as masculine or feminine. These categories have nothing to do with grammatical gender; they depend solely on the absence or presence of a final unaccented *e*, the so-called "mute" *e*, at the ends of the riming words. If the words end in an *e* unadorned with a written accent, they are feminine; otherwise they are masculine. "Donné-fâné" constitutes a masculine rime; "donnée-fânée" is a feminine rime. The two categories cannot be mixed, that is "donné-fânée" is an illegal rime, because although the "mute" *e* is allegedly silent, it is actually felt to prolong ever so slightly the sound preceding it, so that the final syllable of *fânée* would not be strictly identical with the last syllable of *donné*. The rule of alternation is that masculine and feminine rimes must alternate with each other to avoid monotony. This was regarded for centuries as an inviolable law, and the French ear is so accustomed to hearing it obeyed that even modern poets have been loath to try other arrangements of sound except when striving for a special effect. Almost any poem in French verse apart from certain relatively recent ones will illustrate the phenomenon, so no examples need be quoted here. Verlaine was one of the first to defy the edict, as in the following poem in which all the rimes have been kept feminine, presumably to enhance the fluidity of the verse:

MANDOLINE

Les donneurs de sérénades
Et les belles écouteuses
Échangent des propos fades
Sous les ramures chanteuses.

C'est Tircis et c'est Aminte,
Et c'est l'éternel Clitandre,
Et c'est Damis qui pour mainte
Cruelle fait maint vers tendre.

Leurs courtes vestes de soie,
Leurs longues robes à queues,
Leur élégance, leur joie
Et leurs molles ombres bleues

Tourbillonnent dans l'extase
D'une lune rose et grise,
Et la mandoline jase
Parmi les frissons de brise.

Rimes do not always occur at the ends of lines, to be sure. For purposes of amusement, a few virtuoso technicians have even worked out what the French call *olorimes*, lines that rime with each other throughout, from beginning to end, as in the following example (which I plead guilty to having contrived):

Riche et rare, à belle âme, et douce—on t'aima. Leurre!
Ris, chère Arabella. Mais d'où sont tes malheurs?

This sort of game does not produce great poetry, though it can be as much fun to work out as any other puzzle. Internal rime, however, is a very potent device when kept under control. A word in the interior of a line that rimes with another such word, or with the end of the line, or even with a word in the next line, can strike the ear like the ringing of a distant bell. The point is to keep it distant. Older French autocrats of versification objected to internal rime on the grounds that it confused the listener who counted on sound identities to fix the end of the lines in his mind. Modern poets, as might be expected, have stopped worrying about this, and one hears in Verlaine, for example, a great many such rimes:

CLAIR DE LUNE

Votre âme est un paysage choisi
Que vont charmant masques et bergamasques,
Jouant du luth et dansant et quasi
Tristes sous leurs déguisements fantasques.

Tout en chantant sur le mode mineur
L'amour vainqueur et la vie opportune,
Ils n'ont pas l'air de croire à leur bonheur,
Et leur chanson se mêle au clair de lune,

Au calme clair de lune triste et beau,
Qui fait rêver les oiseaux dans les arbres
Et sangloter d'extase les jets d'eau,
Les grands jets d'eau sveltes parmi les marbres.

There are many striking repetitions of sounds in this poem. If we limit the number by agreeing (arbitrarily) to regard as internal rimes only those repeated sounds which (1) occur at least once *before* the end of the line, and (2) either contain both consonant and vowel elements or else are single vowel sounds falling at the end of a word, we are able to point to the following instances of internal rime in "Clair de Lune":

charm*ant*, déguise*ment*; dan*sant*, *sant*gloter; *dans*ant, *dans*;
chan*tant*, tou*t en*; *chan*tant, *chan*son; jou*ant*, *fant*asque, *grands*;

les, les, les, les, les; lu*th et*, dansant *et*, triste *et*, sanglo*ter*;
et, et, et, et, rêver;
l'air de, clair de, clair de; *est*, *fait*, *jets*, *jets*;
leurs, leur, leur; min*eur*, vainqu*eur*, bonh*eur*;
*mi*neur, par*mi*; *choisi*, *quasi*, *vie*, *qui*;
*char*mant, *ar*bres, *par*mi, *mar*bres;
masques, berga*masques*, fant*asques*;
vont, n'*ont*, chan*son*;

opport*une, lune, lune;*
ch*oisi, oi*seaux;
*l'a*mour, *la;*
tristes, triste;
s*ous,* t*out.*

Thus, of eighty-five words in the poem, sixty-five are involved in internal rimes, and a dozen of them enter into more than one such rime.

The effect of internal rime, beyond the matter of pure euphony, may be to focus attention on the words involved in the sound identity, or even to create a whole unifying texture for the poem. Thus the following poem of Rimbaud might be described as a musical eclogue in *euil* major; the numerous repetitions of the sounds *eu, i,* and *euil* can hardly go unnoticed:

Tête de Faune

Dans la f*euil*lée, écrin vert taché d'or,
Dans la f*euil*lée incertaine et fl*eurie*
De fl*eur*s splendi*d*es où le baiser dort,
V*if* et crevant l'exqu*i*se broder*ie,*

Un faune effaré montre ses d*eux yeux*
Et mord les fl*eur*s rouges de ses dents blanches:
Brun*ie* et sanglante ains*i* qu'un vin v*ieux,*
Sa lèvre éclate en r*ir*es sous les branches.

Et quand *i*l a fu*i*—tel qu'un écur*euil*—
Son r*ir*e tremble encore à chaque f*euil*le,
Et l'on voit ép*eur*é par un bouvr*euil*
Le Baiser d'or du Bois, qu*i* se rec*ueil*le.

Here we have gone beyond simple internal rime, though it is one of the many contributing factors to the total harmony of the poem, just as the emphasis on the single sound *i* is a major element in the effect of this famous but very difficult sonnet of Mallarmé:

Le vierge, le vivace et le bel aujourd'hui
Va-t-il nous déchirer avec un coup d'aile ivre
Ce lac dur oublié que hante sous le givre
Le transparent glacier des vols qui n'ont pas fui!

Un cygne d'autrefois se souvient que c'est lui
Magnifique mais qui sans espoir se délivre
Pour n'avoir pas chanté la région où vivre
Quand du stérile hiver a resplendi l'ennui.

Tout son col secouera cette blanche agonie
Par l'espace infligée à l'oiseau qui le nie,
Mais non l'horreur du sol où le plumage est pris.

Fantôme qu'à ce lieu son pur éclat assigne,
Il s'immobilise au songe froid de mépris
Que vêt parmi l'exil inutile le Cygne.

Rime, like all of the sound phenomena we have discussed, is only one of many important elements in the structure of the poem. For this reason, one should avoid any tendency to hammer the rimes when reading aloud. Riming words should receive no more stress than the sense of the line naturally grants them. The identity of the riming sounds will be apparent to the ear even if not to the conscious mind, and that is all that is necessary for the proper effect to occur.

It cannot be emphasized enough that the problem is always to determine not merely what sound effects can be found in a poem but why they are there. It is interesting to know that the crackling of a fire can be imitated on the radio by kneading pieces of cellophane, but in judging a broadcast it is much more important to consider why the sound of a fire was appropriate or necessary in the first place and what function it performed in terms of the drama being portrayed. In verse, sounds may help us to "hear the shape" of a poem, in the sense that they communicate to the ear the length and pattern of lines; or they may emphasize the rhythm and pace of a given passage. As we take up the question of shape, rhythm, and pace in the next two chapters, we shall have occasion to refer back to sounds quite often as they reappear significantly in new contexts.

So many kinds of sound phenomena have been discussed in this chapter that a schematic summary of the types may now prove helpful. We first mentioned the two cases in which the sounds of words seem to be associated with the meanings of the words. If the sound of the word *is* its meaning we are dealing with onomatopoeia. If the sound merely seems unusually *appropriate* to the meaning we may speak of mimesis. All other effects of sound involve repetition. The case which is the least obvious to the listener is the repetition of a special characteristic of sound, of the kind that occurs when a number of harsh consonant clusters are used in a short space. There is no special term for this device, though possible consequences of its use may be called euphony or cacophony. The next step towards unmistakable repetition is the use of a profusion of very closely related but not altogether identical sounds. This is sometimes called dissonance. It involves a closer connection between the effective sounds than the preceding technique did, but not a total identity. The repetition of identical sounds is called consonance if they are consonants only, assonance if they are all vowels, and rime if both consonants and vowels are involved. All three of these categories may be used systematically at the ends of lines, but they may also occur in the interior. A special term is used for consonance when all of the repeated consonants are at the beginning of words: we then speak of alliteration. Similarly, tonal chiasmus, augmentation, and diminution are species of consonance in which two or more consonants are repeated according to a specific pattern. Though it was not mentioned earlier, it is also perfectly possible to produce any of these three arrangements with vowels (e.g., "l'amour mourra," "le tuer serait une cruauté," "il a plongé dans l'océan"), in which case they become types of assonance instead of types of consonance. All of these devices may produce a variety of effects, the two most general ones being euphony and cacophony.

Finally, the over-all sound quality of an extended passage or of the entire poem is variously named verse texture or harmony. Thus we might say that the texture of Rimbaud's "Tête de Faune," which was quoted above, is essentially euphonious as a result of the unusual amount of assonance combined with a prolonged consonance in *f* supported by a dissonance in *v*.

5
Shape

In an earlier chapter we defined a poem as a structure. We did not, however, attempt to compose our definition in a way that would permit some texts to enter the poetic kingdom while others would be rigorously excluded. This vagueness about literary standards was not a sign of lax permissiveness on our part; it was purely pragmatic. The establishment of a frontier, a clear line of demarcation between prose and poetry, is difficult if not impossible, and would not in any case have been useful to us at that time. It is generally easy when dealing with extreme cases to reach a consensus on whether or not a specific piece of writing is poetry or prose. We would not arouse much of a protest by placing the *Æneid* in the first category and the Penal Code in the second. It is only when we approach the area of overlap that we pass from a state of hesitation to one of hopeless indecision. And the same situation arises when we try to distinguish poetry from verse, or verse from prose.

Few people will doubt, of course, that the little jingle Auntie Lou made up in order to enter a contest sponsored by a soap company was not "poetry," yet it was perfectly scannable verse involving a simple but unmistakable rime scheme and a regular rhythm.[1] It may have been prosaic, but it was not prose. By the same token, most of us will acknowledge that *Paradise Lost* or *Phèdre* are poetry in verse, and many will claim that such "prose-poems" as Rimbaud's *Illuminations* are indeed poetry, though written in prose, meaning "non-verse." We agree therefore that there is poetry in verse and poetry in prose, as well as verse that is neither poetry nor prose. And presumably no one considers his income tax form to be anything but prose at its purest, no matter how unattractive it may be.

What do we glean from these distinctions? First, we perceive that the difference between *verse* and *prose* is usually thought of as being a difference in external form. If rime recurs regularly in a text and the rhythm is clearly marked we are dealing with verse, otherwise with prose. Therefore a poem may be written in verse or in prose, but not in both at once. The mere fact that a printed text is either in verse or in prose does not make it *poetry,* however. The *Illuminations* are not versified, yet they are poetry; the income tax form is not. *Phèdre,* which is written in verse, is poetry; Auntie Lou's jingle is not.

All of this shows that the common inclination to assume that a text which is not "poetry" must be "prose" is inconsistent; Auntie Lou's jingle is neither poetry nor prose by usual standards: it is pedestrian verse. But we tend rather frequently to use both words, "prose" and "poetry," very loosely. The term "poetry" is all too often substituted for the word "verse," meaning a composition that is capable of being scanned. When this is what we really have in mind, we shall

---

[1] The reader accustomed to the usual "poetry-prose" distinction may hesitate here. Often the word "poetry" is used to refer to anything that is written in verse. In this chapter the term "poetry" will be reserved for those works of literature which, *whether or not they are in verse,* are artistically serious and capable of inspiring in the reader complex associations of ideas and strong feelings with the greatest possible economy of literary means. Thus the adjective "poetic" may be opposed in this sense to "prosaic," "prosy," etc.

be much less ambiguous if we use the word "verse" exclusively. The line running from the purest prose to the most obvious verse will then be marked off in terms of the relative constancy of recurrence within the text of such technical phenomena as rime and rhythm. There will be, in fact, a large area on the scale within which we shall have great difficulty proving that a given work is unquestionably verse, not prose, or vice versa; but at least we shall not have further complicated matters by introducing into our discussion the notion of *poetry*, as distinguished from *verse*. Into the twilit region in the center of our scale would fall, for example, texts endowed with some of the qualities of verse, such as a marked, fairly regular rhythm, and some of the properties of prose: no rime, no stanzaic structure, but rather a series of paragraphs of variable length. The kind of text that fits this very loose description is often called "free verse"—*verse*, be it noted; not "free poetry."

The word "poetry," as distinguished from "verse," usually suggests, rather vaguely, the emotionally charged, condensed, and sublime text, as opposed to the pedestrian and prosaic. Here technical matters are not at stake at all. We even use the word "poetic" to describe paintings, situations, landscapes, and certain kinds of justice, where there is no implication whatever that verbal expression is involved. Thus, on the one hand, we determine whether a literary piece is verse or non-verse by looking for rime-words, measuring rhythmic pulses, and the like. We can literally *see* the difference between verse and non-verse; they do not have the same shape. But we can *feel* the difference between poetry and non-poetry. Finally, we compound the felony by assigning to the term "prose" the double function of serving as the antonym of both "verse" and "poetry." To use the same word, "prose," for both "non-verse" and "non-poetry" is to create a hopelessly ambiguous situation; and perhaps that is why both French and English permit this dual usage: ambiguity is, even more than variety, the spice of life.

Most poetry in French has been written in regular verse, and since this chapter is principally concerned with the "shape" of a text in verse, we will have occasion to mention, among other things, the so-called fixed forms, such as the sonnet, the rondeau, and the sestina. These forms are purely technical patterns that have become "fixed" by convention. Their physical structure is governed by such details as the lengths of the lines, the number of lines in a stanza, and the rime scheme of the stanza. While the mere fact that a text is written in accordance with one of these fixed forms does not make it poetry, it definitely makes it verse of a classifiable kind. The simple identification of a sonnet tells us very little, of course. But when we remember that any fixed form represents a difficulty that the poet has deliberately set for himself and which he has presumably overcome, we may find it easier to determine where to look for certain consciously devised effects that enter significantly into the structure of the poem. We shall also know what not to expect, since all fixed forms involve limitations of one sort or another. It would not be easy in a sonnet, for example, to portray the fall of Rome in detail.

Unfortunately, fixed forms like the triolet or the chant royal are sometimes referred to as *genres*, thereby confusing them with such other categories as the elegy, the ode, or the mock-epic. To avoid this ambiguity, let us retain the term "fixed forms" for all the conventional technical patterns of the type we have described, and use the word "genre" when we are classifying those poems of variable shape which have in common nothing more than a particular manner of presentation, a relatively identifiable tone, or a tendency to develop certain types of motifs. Elegies are now usually limited to the subject of death, for example, and satires represent a certain distinguishable attitude, while dramatic monologues at least pretend to call for theater presentation.

As can be readily seen, the fixed form is a matter of *verse*, but genre is more a matter of *poetry*. Generic distinctions are made in accordance with such criteria as tone, theme, and sometimes atmosphere or attitude, and this is precisely the sort of norm that helps us to distinguish poetry from non-poetry. Admittedly, we cannot always make a perfectly clean separation between fixed forms and genre, or between verse and poetry in general. Some overlapping is bound to occur; but despite this difficulty it is possible to discuss verse and poetry separately, and to do so will perhaps help to clarify the distinction between them.

Fixed forms are characteristic shapes of verse, and shape is a function of the combination of lengths of lines, lengths of stanzas, and rime scheme. These elements may of course be organized so as to create entirely new shapes, as opposed to conventional forms. A new shape, one invented by the poet for the sake of the particular poem, may later be imitated by other poets and thus gradually become a conventional form in its own right. In any case, the basic principles remain the same. But before we can speak meaningfully of specific forms we must first consider the elements that operate together to establish the shape of a poem.

The first factor to be considered is the single line of verse. The rhythm of a line in English is determined by the number and kind of "feet" the line contains. The usual English foot consists of a single accented syllable preceded or followed by one or two unstressed syllables. Thus the four commonest types of foot are the *iamb* ($\smile$/), the *trochee* (/$\smile$), the *anapest* ($\smile\smile$/), and the *dactyl* (/$\smile\smile$). The English words "a*lert*," "*pur*pose," "indis*creet*," and "*hes*itate," in that order, represent the rhythms of these four respective feet. The English line is named according to the number and kind of feet that predominate in it, so that a line consisting of three anapests is called an "anapestic trimeter" (from the Greek prefix *tri-*, "three," and *meter*, "measure"):

$$\text{/} \qquad \text{/} \qquad \text{/}$$
"When the *trav*eller's *jour*ney is *done*."

A line of five iambs is an "iambic pentameter" (from the Greek prefix *penta*, "five"):

/   /   /   /   /

"For *who* would *bear* the *whips* and *scorns* of *time*. . . ."

This system is admirably suited to a language characterized by the recurrence of heavy accents which appear in all words of more than one syllable; but it would be clearly inappropriate to French, in which stresses are weak and often widely separated. The only words in French that contain a stress are those that come at the end of a so-called sense group. All other words are pronounced quite evenly. Furthermore, the accent falls on the last syllable of the last word in the sense group, with almost no exceptions. Thus, in such a phrase as "Donnez-moi du *pain*, s'il vous *plaît*," only the italicized syllables are stressed. A sentence such as "Je ne lui téléphonerai *pas*" contains one accented syllable (*pas*), preceded by eight (or in colloquial speech six) unstressed syllables. And unless a speaker is being unusually emphatic, his "stresses" will in fact be little more than changes in musical pitch. For this reason it would be virtually impossible to produce an iambic pentameter in French. The accented syllables would not fall close enough to one another unless each successive group of two syllables were a separate sense unit, as in this hexameter by Victor Hugo: "Il pense, il règle, il mène, il pèse, il juge, il aime." A poet may permit himself this sort of line once in a lifetime, but only if he turns out many thousands of less monotonous ones in which to bury it.

Since in French it is almost impossible to feel any distinct recurring rhythm if one has only the accents to serve as a guide, the nature of a French line is determined not by the number of stresses it contains but by its total number of *syllables*. The number of syllables in English lines of the same basic meter is nearly constant, but not quite. A perfect iambic pentameter in English will contain ten syllables, for example; but if an anapest is substituted for one of the iambs the line will have eleven syllables, thus: "The conquering force

of unresisted steel." This line contains the five accents of a
perfect iambic pentameter, but it has an extra syllable in the
second foot. In French, on the contrary, the number of syllables remains constant, while the number of stresses may
vary. For example, Victor Hugo's frightful hexameter, "Il
pense, il règle, il mène, il pèse, il juge, il aime," has six accents,
whereas the first of the following two lines has three and the
second two or four (depending on whether or not *prince* and
tour are stressed):

/   /   /

Je suis le téné*breux*, —le *veuf*, —l'inconso*lé*,

/   /   /   /

Le *prince* d'Aqui*taine* à la *tour* abo*lie*. . . .

All three lines, however, contain exactly twelve syllables.
The identification of a French line by the number of syllables
that compose it remained the rule for all French verse until the
mid-nineteenth century when Aloysius Bertrand and Maurice
de Guérin (followed shortly by Jules Laforgue) wrote what
was perhaps the first French poetry in free verse. Since that
time a tendency to disregard the number of syllables in a
line has increased enormously, but many contemporary poets
continue to write largely or exclusively in regular verse.

Lines ranging in length from one to more than fourteen
syllables have been known to occur in French, and both odd
and even numbers of syllables may be used. Since the number of syllables is the only criterion for distinguishing types
of French lines, the problem of nomenclature is quite simple.
Whereas in English we need two words to name a line (e.g.,
iambic pentameter), in French a single term is sufficient. A
décasyllabe is a line of ten syllables; a *pentasyllabe* contains
five; a *monosyllabe* is a one-syllable line. Naturally, such
extreme cases as the *monosyllabe* are rarities and are almost
never used alone except in fun. As a game, however, it is
even possible to write sonnets in them, like this one dedicated
to a dead rose:

Fort
Belle
Elle
Dort:

Sort
Frêle!
Quelle
Mort!

Rose
Close,
La

Brise
L'a
Prise. . . .

Note the typical rime scheme of the Italian sonnet (*abba, abba, ccd, ede*) and the alternation of masculine and feminine rimes, the last of which is actually rich.

The longest line regularly found in French verse is the twelve syllable line called an *alexandrin* (in English, an "alexandrine").[2] It is in fact the commonest line in French poetry, being the standard form for classical tragedy and most serious verse of all kinds. "Par où sera jamais ma douleur apaisée?" is a typical alexandrine. As compared with this successful French line, the English counterpart is a graceless creature indeed, thanks to the ponderous accents that characterize our language. Pope demonstrated the fact neatly in the *Essay on Criticism* with the following lines, the second of which is an example of the English iambic hexameter:

A needless Alexandrine ends the song,
That, like a wounded snake, drags its slow length along.

[2] Sometimes the English iambic hexameter is also called an alexandrine, since it normally contains twelve syllables.

The next most frequently encountered line in French is the *décasyllabe*. It was used in the medieval *chansons de geste* and is presently employed in many kinds of verse. An example is the line, "S'il avait su quelle âme il a blessée." The *octosyllabe*, which was the standard line of much medieval narrative verse, sometimes also appears alone in light poetry, and sometimes is used in conjunction with the alexandrine, as in these lines from André Chénier's "Iambes":

> Comme un dernier rayon, comme un dernier zéphyre
> Animent la fin d'un beau jour,
> Au pied de l'échafaud j'essaye encor ma lyre.
> Peut-être est-ce bientôt mon tour.

Of the lines with odd numbers of syllables, the *pentasyllabe* with five and the *heptasyllabe* with seven are the most common. Like the *octosyllabe*, they are used sometimes alone and sometimes in combination with lines of other lengths. Their slightly disjointed effect was often exploited by certain poets of the nineteenth century. In Baudelaire's "Invitation au voyage," for example, lines of five and seven syllables are combined in the same stanza:

> Mon enfant, ma sœur,
> Songe à la douceur
> D'aller là-bas vivre ensemble!
> Aimer à loisir,
> Aimer et mourir
> Au pays qui te ressemble!

It would be foolish to assign specific functions (other than traditional ones) to any of the possible lines, but the reader should certainly take them into account as part of the poem's meaningful structure. To do so he must be able to determine the length of any given line, which is a matter of counting syllables. This is not quite so simple an operation as it appears to be, since some syllables are counted in French poetry even though they are not pronounced in ordinary speech. The reason for this is that the so-called "mute" *e* (which is not always mute) is treated in poetry as though it were being pronounced, unless it occurs in one of two kinds of position: either directly before or after a vowel (or mute *h*), or at the end of a line. Mute *e*'s are the *e*'s not carrying a written accent which normally remain silent in spoken French or else are pronounced very colorlessly, as in the words "le," "de," "robes," "médecin," and "tombera." (Although the two *e*'s in *effet* have no written accent, they are not mute *e*'s, since the first is pronounced like an *e aigu* [*é*], and the second like an *e grave* [*è*].) If a mute *e* occurs in verse just before or after another vowel it is not counted, because the other vowel absorbs it. Thus in the line "Cette *oie* ne sera pas assez

grasse demain" the *e* at the end of *cette* will not count or be heard, because it is absorbed by the following *oi* sound; and the *e* at the end of *oie* will also not count, because of the preceding *oi*. The *e* at the end of *grasse* will be counted, however, as will the *e* of *demain*, because they both occur between pronounced consonants. A mute *e* at the end of a line, does not count; it merely serves to make the rime feminine, as we have seen.

Once the question of which *e*'s do or do not count is clear, all one has to do to determine the number of syllables in a line is to total the pronounced vowel sounds (including counted mute *e*'s), since each will be part of a different syllable. In the line "Qui, contre les cha-leurs, por-tent aux champs a-rid(es)" the twelve vowel sounds are italicized. It takes two written letters to represent the *eu* sound of *chaleurs* and the *au* sound of *aux*, but the two letters stand in each case for a single vowel sound, and it is the sounds that we are counting, not the written symbols. The *e* of *portent* is a mute *e*, and it is truly silent in *spoken* French, since the -*ent* ending of verbs in the third person plural is normally not pronounced. In this line, however, it will be counted and heard, as it falls between audible consonants (the two *t*'s of *portent*, the second of which will be pronounced in liaison with the following vowel sound, *au*). The *e* of *arides* is not counted because it comes at the end of a line. (The final plural *-s* is silent and therefore disregarded.)

The following two lines represent the typical situations that arise: "L*a sour-ce de mes jours* comm(e) *eux* s'est *é-cou-lé*(e)," and "S*a* lè-vr(e) *é-cla-*t(e) *en* ri-*res sous les* branch(es)." The first line contains twelve syllables, the second ten. In the first line the *e* at the end of *source* is counted, though it would be silent in spoken prose, and the *e* of *comme* is not counted, since it is followed directly by the vowel sound *eu* which absorbs it. The last *e* of the line (the third *e* of *écoulée*) is of course not counted. In the second line the second *e* of *lèvre* is absorbed by the immediately following *é* of *éclate*, and the final *e* of *éclate* is in turn absorbed by the nasal vowel sound, *en*; but the *e* of *rires* is counted, though it would be silent in prose speech. The final *-es* of *branches* is not counted, being at the end of a line with no audible sound after it.

One more example should suffice: "L*a* gai(e)-*té de la* fêt(e) *et la* sé-ré-ni-té. . . ." Here again we have an alexandrine with its twelve syllables. The unaccented *e* of *gaieté* is absorbed by the preceding *ai*; the *e* at the end of *fête* is absorbed by the *e* of *et* (pronounced *é*); the final *é* of *sérénité*, although it ends the line, is counted since it is not a mute *e*. It makes the line masculine and must enter into a masculine rime.

It is reasonable to assume that a French poet never errs in his syllable-count, so that any apparent irregularity is almost certainly illusory. A little practice in counting the syllables in the lines quoted elsewhere in this book will soon overcome any initial difficulties. For example, every line in Rimbaud's "Tête de faune" contains ten syllables, and every line of

Mallarmé's "Le Vierge, le vivace et le bel aujourd'hui" has twelve.

Sometimes an apparent error in counting will turn out to be the result of misinterpreting a diphthong involving the semi-vowels *i* or *u* and a vowel following directly in the same word. In cases of this kind the diphthong may be counted as either one or two syllables. Thus a word like *rien* may be pronounced *ri-en* in two syllables or *ryen* in one. In modern poetry such words are normally counted as monosyllables, but splitting them into two syllables may sometimes help the poet out of a difficulty. In the line "Le vier-ge, le vi-vac(e) et

le bel au-jour-d'hui," the *ie* of *vierge* is counted as one vowel and pronounced like the *ye* of the English word "yet," not like the *ē-ĕ* of "the end." The *u* of the final -*ui* is a semi-vowel like the *i* of the -*ie*- diphthong we have been discussing; it therefore makes a single syllable in the combination -*ui*.

This may at first appear to be excessively complicated, but it seems less so when one realizes that learning to pronounce verse correctly is ultimately a matter of feeling. One way to develop the feeling is to read lines aloud, actually pronouncing the "mute" *e*'s that are counted. The ones that would be silent in prose should be pronounced gently and given the sound of the *e* in *le*, *de*, or *me*. If the reading is done smoothly, so that each syllable is allotted the same time span, the number of syllables should be felt fairly distinctly. The feeling will be stronger if stressable syllables are clearly accented, as this breaks the line into smaller, more easily perceptible units. An alexandrine such as "Le vierge, le vivace et le bel aujourd'hui" will permit a stress on *vier-*, *va-*, *bel-*, and -*d'hui*, breaking the over-all unit of twelve syllables into smaller groups of two, four, three, and three, thus:

"Le *vier*-ge, le vi-*va*-c(e) et le *bel* au-jour-*d'hui*."

Though the *ge* of *vierge* will be audible as a separate syllable, the *ce* of *vivace* will coalesce with the word *et* to form one syllable pronounced *cé* ("say").

When a French actor recites poetry aloud he may handle the mute *e*'s in either of two possible ways, according to his feeling about the nature of the given case. He may pronounce very lightly the counted mute *e*'s, especially if omitting them would create an undesirable cacophony. More often he drops them (thereby making them truly mute), while compensating for their absence by a slight lengthening of the preceding syllable. When possible he lengthens the consonant sound that directly precedes the mute *e*, so that a phrase such as "En une peine extrême" is pronounced: "En unnn(e) pei-n(e) ex-trêm(e)." Only five syllables are heard, but the elapsed time is almost exactly the same as though he had said: "En u-ne pei-n(e) ex-trêm(e)," thereby clearly enunciating all six counted syllables. Naturally, when the consonant preceding the mute *e* cannot be prolonged, the vowel preceding the consonant will be lengthened if the *e* is dropped. In such a line as "Femme, plus claire que le jour," the *mm* of *femme* can be prolonged to compensate for not pronouncing the following *e*, but the *r* of *claire* cannot be treated the same way. Here the *ai* sound will have to be extended, so the line will be heard as "Femmm(e), plus claaiir(e) que le jour," with only six of the eight counted syllables audible, but with two of them almost doubled in length. In such a line as "Chevaliers de la Table ronde," the *e* of *Table* would have to be clearly pronounced. Otherwise a very ugly cacophony would result from the *blr* combination: "Che-va-liers de la Taaa-blrond(e)." This would be ghastly; the correct reading should be "Che-va-liers de la Ta-ble rond(e)."

Only two other details need be mentioned regarding the correct recitation of French verse. The first has to do with *liaisons*. A *liaison* occurs when the final consonant of a word is pronounced because the next word begins with a vowel. For example, the *s* in *vous* is silent in *avez-vous*, but it is pronounced (like a *z*) in *vous avez* to avoid the hiatus between *ou* and *a*. In normal speech many such *liaisons* are not made, but in verse they are always at least theoretically audible. Some reciters eliminate a few of them even in poetry, but in principle the *t* of *donnent,* for example, would be heard in a phrase such as "Ils vous donnent un cadeau" if it occurred in verse.

The second point has to do with French verse which is literally sung. In the lyrics of vocal music all the rules applying to the reading of French verse remain in effect with one exception: the final mute *e* of a feminine line is actually sung, a fact which is normally obvious since the *e* is likely to have a musical note all to itself. For the same reason, of course, all counted *e*'s will be clearly pronounced, never dropped. The line "Chevaliers de la Table ronde," quoted above, is actually part of a song, and the *e* of *ronde* does have a note of its own. Therefore the line, which would be read in eight syllables, is sung in nine: "Che-va-liers de la Ta-ble ron-de."

There are now available many excellent recordings of French verse read by native Frenchmen. Listening to such recitations while following the text is one of the best ways to improve one's skill at reading.

Lines of verse are frequently grouped into what is the equivalent of a prose paragraph, and if the grouping is done purely in accordance with the sense of what is being said the resulting arrangement is commonly called a "verse paragraph." If, however, the lines are arranged in a pre-established pattern with a fixed rime scheme we usually speak of a stanza (*une strophe*). Stanzaic forms may be dictated by the conventional fixed form adopted by the poet, as in the case of the sonnet; or the poet may design his own stanza in a way that will suit the other elements of the poetic structure. If stanzas consist entirely of lines of one length they are called isometric; if the component lines vary in length the stanza is heterometric. The stanzas of a French sonnet are isometric, the lines being alexandrines as a rule. (Compare Mallarmé's sonnet, "Le vierge, le vivace . . . ," quoted above.) But the following fable of La Fontaine contains heterometric stanzas in which the variations in the lengths of the lines conform to shifts in the tone or attitude expressed by the poem, or are actually imitative of the denotation:

LA GRENOUILLE QUI SE VEUT FAIRE AUSSI GROSSE

QUE LE BŒUF

Une grenouille vit un bœuf
Qui lui sembla de belle taille.
Elle, qui n'était pas grosse en tout comme un œuf,
Envieuse s'étend, et s'enfle, et se travaille
Pour égaler l'animal en grosseur,
Disant: "Regardez bien, ma sœur,
Est-ce assez? Dites-moi. N'y suis-je point encore?
—Nenni. —M'y voici donc? —Point du tout. —M'y voilà?
—Vous n'en approchez point." La chétive pécore
S'enfla si bien qu'elle creva.

Le monde est plein de gens qui ne sont pas plus sages:
Tout bourgeois veut bâtir comme les grands seigneurs;
Tout petit prince a des ambassadeurs;
Tout marquis veut avoir des pages.

Stanzas in both English and French are named for the number of lines they contain, beginning with the single line (*un vers*), and proceeding through the couplet or distich (*un distique*) to the three-line tercet and four-line quatrain, which have the same names in both languages. The stanza of five lines is a cinquain in English and *un quintain* or *quintil* in French. Beginning with stanzas of six lines, one obtains the French name by adding the ending *-ain* to the corresponding cardinal number, thus: *sixain, septain, huitain, neuvain, dizain, onzain, douzain,* etc. As can be seen, the *f* of *neuf* changes to *v* and all final *e*'s are dropped before the ending is added.

The shape of a stanza is governed not only by the number and type of lines it contains, but also by the arrangement of the rimes that occur at the ends of these lines. This arrangement may conform to a predetermined pattern or it may be simply a scheme invented by the poet for the particular poem. If the pattern is inconsistent, and therefore unpredictable, one speaks of free or mixed rimes (*rimes libres* or *mêlées*). In the fable of La Fontaine just quoted, for example, the rime scheme is *ababccdede, fggf.* The shift in the middle of the first stanza to a couplet rime (*cc*) lends variety to the development, and the use of embraced rimes (*fggf*) instead of alternating rimes (*abab*) in the second stanza sets off the moral of the fable from the illustration. Even when he is using a free rime scheme, the poet usually places his riming words close to one another so that the listener will not lose track of the pattern. A reader unfamiliar with the poem might well miss the repeated identical sounds if eight or ten lines intervened between them. Consequently, the poet writing in mixed rimes tends to fall back on certain simple schemes while shifting frequently and unexpectedly from one such arrangement to another, as in the fable of La Fontaine.

The simplest possible pattern occurs when all the riming words of a stanza end in the same sound. This is usually indicated by the notation *aaaaaa*. A stanza based on one rime is likely to be monotonous, but that may be desirable at times for special effect. A modified form of this technique was used in the medieval *chansons de geste,* where all of the stanzas (called *laisses*) were constructed on one assonance. In the following *laisse* from the *Chanson de Roland,* which dates from the eleventh century and is written in Old French, every line ends in an assonance involving the sound *i:*

> Guenes respunt: "Pur mei n'iras tu m*i*e.
> Tu n'ies mes hom ne jo sui tis s*i*re.
> Carles comandet que face sun serv*i*se,
> En Sarraguce en irai a Mars*i*lie;

Einz i ferai un poi de leger*ie*
Que jo n'esclair ceste meie grant *ire*."
Quant l'ot Rollant, si cumençat a r*ire*.[3]

Among the more common rime schemes in French are couplet, embraced, and alternate rimes, all of which are exemplified in La Fontaine's fable, "La Grenouille qui se veut faire aussi grosse que le bœuf."

Couplet rimes (*rimes plates*) have the scheme *aabbccdd*, with the inevitable alternation between masculine and feminine pairs. This is the standard pattern of classical tragedy as exemplified by Racine's *Andromaque*, which begins:

ORESTE:

Oui, puisque je retrouve un ami si fid*èle*,
Ma fortune va prendre une face nouv*elle*;
Et déjà son courroux semble s'être adou*ci*,
Depuis qu'elle a pris soin de nous rejoindre *ici*.
Qui l'eût dit, qu'un rivage à mes vœux si fun*este*
Présenterait d'abord Pylade aux yeux d'Or*este*?
Qu'après plus de six mois que je t'avais per*du*,
A la cour de Pyrrhus tu me serais ren*du*?

Embraced rimes (*rimes embrassées*) enclose a rimed couplet between two other riming lines, the scheme being *abba, cddc*, as in Victor Hugo's poem, "Écrit au bas d'un crucifix":

Vous qui pleurez, venez à ce Dieu, car il pl*eure*.
Vous qui souffrez, venez à lui, car il gu*érit*.
Vous qui tremblez, venez à lui, car il sou*rit*.
Vous qui passez, venez à lui, car il dem*eure*.

Alternate rimes (*rimes croisées* or *alternées*) are so arranged that two pairs of riming words are intertwined. The

---

[3]"Ganelon replies: 'You will not go in my place. / You are not my vassal, and I am not your lord. / Charles commands that I do his service: / I shall go to Marsile in Saragossa; / But I shall commit some folly there / Before I calm my great anger.' / When Roland hears him, he begins to laugh."

pattern is *abab, cdcd,* as in Lamartine's "Lac," which begins:

> Ainsi, toujours poussés vers de nouveaux riv*ages,*
> Dans la nuit éternelle emportés sans ret*our,*
> Ne pourrons-nous jamais sur l'océan des *âges*
>   Jeter l'ancre un seul j*our?*

> O lac! l'année à peine a fini sa carr*ière,*
> Et près des flots chéris qu'elle devait rev*oir,*
> Regarde! je viens seul m'asseoir sur cette p*ierre*
>   Où tu la vis s'ass*eoir!*

The rime scheme of La Fontaine's fable about the frog was, as we saw: *ababccdede, fggf.* He begins with a pair of alternate rimes, adds a couplet, and concludes the stanza with another pair of alternate rimes. The rimes of the second stanza are embraced. Thus La Fontaine's rimes are mixed, as opposed to our other examples in which the same scheme is maintained throughout the poem.

In all these cases the individual rime never involves more than two lines. If three or more lines rime with each other the rime scheme is called redoubled (*redoublée*), as in Hugo's "Djinns," which begins thus:

> Murs, v*ille*
> Et p*ort,*
> A*sile*
> De m*ort,*
> Mer g*rise*
> Où b*rise*
> La b*rise,*
> Tout d*ort;*

and ends with the stanza:

> On d*oute*
> La n*uit.* . . .
> J'éc*oute:—*

Tout f*uit*.
Tout p*asse*;
L'esp*ace*
Eff*ace*
Le br*uit*.

Here the rime scheme is *ababcccb*.

Blank verse (*vers blancs*), a succession of unrimed lines in iambic pentameters in English, is a device rarely used in French since, as we have seen, rime in French poetry is almost essential for determining aurally the length of the lines.

Poems using any of the rime schemes we have discussed need not necessarily be split up into stanzas. It is possible to write a thousand lines in alternate rimes without a break, though it is customary to divide very long poems into large sections which are sometimes called cantos (*chants*). As a rule, if a poet uses stanzas he invents his own form, but there are a few common conventional arrangements that are worth mentioning.

Terza rima (sometimes called *rime tiercée* in French), the scheme used by Dante in *The Divine Comedy*, consists of a succession of tercets rimed *aba, bcb, cdc, ded,* etc. The rimes are redoubled since three lines end in the same sounds. The middle line of each tercet rimes with the first and third lines of the following tercet, thereby creating an interlocking arrangement. A nice refinement consists in having the middle line of the last tercet rime with the first and third lines of the very first tercet of the poem, so that the circle is finally closed. More commonly, the final stanza of the poem is a quatrain printed as a tercet followed by a single line and rimed *yzy, z,* as in "La Tête du comte" by Leconte de Lisle, which ends:

A mon haut bout sieds-toi, cher astre de ma *race*!
Par cette tête, sois tête et cœur de *céans*,
Aussi bien que je t'aime et t'honore et t'emb*rasse*.

Vierge et Saints! mieux que l'eau de tous les o*céans*
Ce sang noir a lavé ma vieille joue en f*lamme.*
Plus de jeûnes, d'ennuis, ni de pleurs mals*éants*!

C'est bien lui! Je le hais, certe, à me damner *l'âme*!
Rui dit; —L'honneur est sauf, et sauve la m*aison*,
Et j'ai crié ton nom en enfonçant ma *lame.*

Mange, père! Diego murmure une o*raison*;
Et tous deux, s'asseyant côte à côte à la *table,*
Graves et satisfaits, mangent la ven*aison,*

En regardant saigner la Tête lamen*table.*

Note the prodigality of rich rime in the best Parnassian tradition!

The tail rime stanza (*rime couée*) commonly has the rime scheme *aabccb*, the riming *b* lines being shorter than the *a* and *c* lines, as illustrated by the first strophe of Victor Hugo's "Tristesse d'Olympio":

Les champs n'êtaient point noirs, les cieux n'étaient pas
        mornes;
Non, le jour rayonnait dans un azur sans bornes
        Sur la terre étendu,
L'air était plein d'encens et les prés de verdures
Quand il revit ces lieux où par tant de blessures
        Son cœur s'est répandu.

We have already noted the verse paragraph, which is simply a section of text set off by a space from the preceding and following passages, like the ordinary stanza. It differs from the stanza in having no clear formal organization, such as a rime scheme or a set number of lines. The length of the verse paragraph, like that of the prose paragraph, is determined merely by the sense of what it has to say. A related technique involves the use of the *verset*, which bears a closer resemblance to a line than to a stanza. It is a free verse line with an indefinite number of syllables, intended to reproduce something of the effect of Biblical verses. Because a single *verset* may require several lines of print it occasionally resembles a verse paragraph, although it is usually intended to be read in one breath like an ordinary line. *Versets* are usually unrimed, since a rime would serve almost no purpose other than that of indicating breathing points. The technique has been used extensively by such twentieth-century poets as Paul Claudel and Saint-John Perse.

As a general rule, a poet will fit the shape of his poem to his material, adopting a rime scheme, a stanzaic form, and a type of line that seem most appropriate to the expression of what he wishes to say. The form of the poem is born simultaneously with its meaning, so that a unified structure results. Sometimes, however, a poet will use a conventionally fixed form, such as the sonnet. The school of poets called *Les Grands Rhétoriqueurs,* which flourished at the end of the fifteenth and beginning of the sixteenth centuries, invented or adopted extremely complicated fixed forms whose difficulty was sought after for its own sake. Many of these forms failed to survive the early Renaissance, but a number of rather complicated types, such as the rondeau, continued into the seventeenth century and reappeared in the nineteenth, at moments when the game aspect of versification once again came to the fore.

The most celebrated of the fixed forms is undoubtedly the sonnet, which in French poetry is of the Italian (Petrarchan) type. It is composed of two quatrains rimed *abba, abba,* followed by two tercets rimed variously; *ccd, ede* or *ccd, dee* are common schemes. We have seen several examples earlier, such as Mallarmé's "Le vierge, le vivace et le bel aujourd'hui," or the sonnet in monosyllables. Poets do not always observe the form strictly; there are many free sonnets in Baudelaire's *Fleurs du mal,* for example, but only four strict sonnets. The free sonnets usually have alternate (instead of embraced) rimes in the quatrains: *abab, abab.*

Other set forms range from the eight-line *triolet* through the thirteen-line *rondeau,* the fourteen-line *rondel,* and the nineteen-line *villanelle,* to the twenty-four-line *rondeau redoublé,* the thirty-six-line *sextine* (sestina), and the *chant royal, ballade,* and *pantoum,* which are of indefinite length. All of these are described in detail in the Glossary at the end of the book, and since space does not permit illustrating each of them here, a few examples must suffice.

Perhaps the most consistently popular form after the sonnet is the rondeau. It shares with many of these fixed forms a minimal number of rimes and a recurrent refrain. The rondeau is normally composed of three stanzas of five, three, and five lines respectively. There are only two rimes, the scheme being *aabba, aab, aabba.* Just to make the problem more challenging, the first four syllables of line one are repeated as a refrain at the end of stanzas two and three, preferably in such a way that the meaning or tone of the phrase differs slightly on all three occasions. The following rondeau is by the seventeenth-century salon-poet, Vincent Voiture:

> Ma foi, c'est fait de moi: car Isabeau
> M'a conjuré de lui faire un rondeau,
> Cela me met en une peine extrême.
> Quoi! treize vers, huit en eau, cinq en ème!
> Je lui ferais aussitôt un bateau.
>
> En voilà cinq pourtant en un monceau,
> Faisons-en huit, en invoquant Brodeau,
> Et puis mettons par quelque stratagème:
>   Ma foi, c'est fait.
>
> Si je pouvais encor de mon cerveau
> Tirer cinq vers, l'ouvrage serait beau.
> Mais cependant je suis dedans l'onzième,
> Et si je crois que je fais le douzième,
> En voilà treize ajustés au niveau:
>   Ma foi, c'est fait!

The pantoum is a form which originated in Malaya. It contains an indefinite number of stanzas, each a quatrain rimed *abab*, with a curious further provision: the second and fourth lines of each stanza must be repeated as the first and third lines of the following stanza; and as if that were not enough, the second and fourth lines of the last stanza should be the first and third lines of the first stanza reversed, so that the poem ends with the same line with which it began! Baudelaire wrote a beautiful pantoum in which he chose to ignore the last-mentioned restriction; all of the other requirements, however, are met:

HARMONIE DU SOIR

Voici venir les temps où vibrant sur sa tige
Chaque fleur s'évapore ainsi qu'un encensoir;
Les sons et les parfums tournent dans l'air du soir;
Valse mélancolique et langoureux vertige!

Chaque fleur s'évapore ainsi qu'un encensoir;
Le violon frémit comme un cœur qu'on afflige;
Valse mélancolique et langoureux vertige!
Le ciel est triste et beau comme un grand reposoir.

Le violon frémit comme un cœur qu'on afflige,
Un cœur tendre, qui hait le néant vaste et noir!
Le ciel est triste et beau comme un grand reposoir;
Le soleil s'est noyé dans son sang qui se fige.

Un cœur tendre, qui hait le néant vaste et noir,
Du passé lumineux recueille tout vestige!
Le soleil s'est noyé dans son sang qui se fige . . .
Ton souvenir en moi luit comme un ostensoir!

In all such complex forms as these the game element leaps to the eye. The poem in all but the most skillful hands may degenerate into a feeble excuse for the elaborate technique and become a mere display of empty virtuosity. The less difficult the special device is, the less this risk is incurred. Thus François Villon was probably not much troubled by the attendant difficulties when he set up an acrostic in the *envoi* of his "Ballade pour prier Notre Dame":

> Vous portâtes, digne Vierge, princesse,
> Iésus régnant, qui n'a ni fin ni cesse.
> Le Tout-Puissant, prenant notre faiblesse,
> Laissa les cieux et nous vint secourir;
> Offrit à mort sa très claire jeunesse;
> Notre Seigneur tel est, tel le confesse,
> En cette foi je veux vivre et mourir.[4]

The first letters of the first six lines read down spell the poet's name. The last line is a refrain and does not count in the acrostic. Here the artifice is easy, but it becomes less so when, for instance, the entire poem is constructed in the form of an emblem, a shaped design in which the printed words are so distributed on the page that a visual image emerges. This type is called a "carmen figuratum" in English literature, and has been exemplified in French by the *Calligrammes* of Guillaume Apollinaire. The game element, which here is almost supreme, probably approached the culminating point in the seventeenth century when a fashionable pastime was the proposing of sets of detached rime-words (*bouts-rimés*) to one's guests, the trick being to write appropriate verses to fit them. The resulting "poems" rarely left the drawing-room in which they were written, and for that we may probably be thankful.

In general, a simple shape is best, since it does not imply

---

[4] The original fifteenth-century spelling has been modernized. A literal translation would be: "You bore, Virgin, worthy princess, / Reigning Jesus, who has neither end nor cessation. / The Almighty, taking on our weakness, / Left the heavens and came to help us; / He offered unto death His very fair youth; / Our Lord, such He is, such I confess Him to be, / And in this faith I wish to live and die."

that the poet may be merely a clever technician, a skillful versifier, and not truly a poet. It is really just as heretical to permit the "form" to become the focus of attention as it is for the "content" to be the only element that matters. In either of these cases we have verse, but not poetry. Poetry is a total structure in which all the elements are equally engaged. Some forms, such as the sonnet, lend themselves to a poetic structure; other more elaborate and eye-catching conventional types are all too often intricate masks concealing a void where there should be a poem.

The problem of where verse ends and prose begins has really been with us only since the advent of free verse. Exactly how regular a rhythm must be before it turns what would be bad prose into verse is impossible to say. A perfect alexandrine in French prose is often quite as offensive as a lilting, bouncy rhythm is in English, whether consciously employed or accidental. If that last sentence seemed awkward, the fault may have lain partly with the thirteen successive trochees that made up the second half. Free verse, as exemplified by the *verset*, rarely uses such strict rhythms as the excessively trochaic sentence before last. In free verse the rhythms are usually far looser, and may be so vague as to be almost prosaic. This was, however, not so true of the poems by one of the "first" *vers-libristes* in the modern manner, Jules Laforgue. In the following extract from his "Simple Agonie" there is an alexandrine (line two), an octosyllable (the last line), and four successive hexasyllables (lines six through nine):

Oh! que
Devinant l'instant le plus seul de la nature,
Ma mélodie, toute et unique, monte,
Dans le soir et redouble, et fasse tout ce qu'elle peut
Et dise la chose qu'est la chose,
Et retombe et reprenne,
Et fasse de la peine,
O solo de sanglots,

Et reprenne et retombe
Selon la tâche qui lui incombe.
Oh! que ma musique
Se crucifie,
Selon sa photographie
Accoudée et mélancolique! . . .

Rhythm is, of course, never so regular in French verse as it is in English—but that is a question we must reserve for another chapter.

Before we turn to the question of genre, it may be appropriate to pause here for a brief summary of what has been said about the shape of a poem. We have seen that the three governing factors that determine shape are the length of lines, the length of stanzas, and the rime scheme. In French, lines are characterized by the number of syllables they contain, not by their number of stresses; and these syllables are all indicated by the way in which the line is pronounced. When a mute *e* is not clearly enunciated, for example, a compensating prolongation of the preceding syllable will indicate to the ear that the syllable containing the mute *e* is in fact present. Although a stanza may contain lines of varying length, they will usually follow a pattern, such as two alexandrines succeeded by an octosyllable, and then two more alexandrines and an octosyllable. Similarly, the rime scheme is usually fashioned according to a fixed design. The result is that a threefold recurring pattern should be detectable by the ear as well as by the eye in poems which are formally versified. If these patterns are conventionally used in conjunction with one another, the poem is said to be written in a fixed form. More often, the poet will use, for example, a conventional rime scheme (such as alternating rimes) but will choose independently the lengths of the lines and stanzas. Or he may vary the rimes or the line lengths unpredictably. If he goes to the limit of his freedom the result will be free verse, in which not even the length of any given line will conform to a set standard. The problem, in short, is first to "hear" the line lengths (even when reading silently), note the stanzaic form, and perceive the rime scheme, and then to determine in what way these properties of the poem work in conjunction with each other and with sound and rhythm to affect the structure of the poem as a whole.

Although a discussion of genre and the related problem of distinguishing poetry from non-poetry would appear to remove us rather far from the problem of "shape" with which this chapter has been primarily concerned, it seems wise to try to shed some light on these matters now. The question of genre and the nature of poetry form such an obvious parallel with the question of fixed forms and the nature of verse that it would be senseless to reserve one of the two topics for later treatment. Indeed, the very fact that the two problems tend to be so frequently confused is a strong argument in favor of juxtaposing them in such a way as to underscore the distinction between them.

As a general rule, generic classifications are of little importance to our understanding of the poem, except that in so far as they are conventional they may place certain thematic limitations upon the poet, and theme is a very important consideration in analysis. The difficulty with generic terms is that they are often open to very loose interpretation. They also tend to change meaning fairly radically from generation to generation, as outmoded conventions die out and are replaced by others. Genres sometimes spring up, bloom, and wither in a very short period of time. To attempt to list all of the generic terms in common use would require a great amount of space and would not be particularly helpful.

As we have seen, it is the theme, or tone, or sometimes the mode of hypothetical presentation that usually characterizes a given genre. By "hypothetical presentation" is meant the manner in which the poem is theoretically supposed to be conveyed to the listener, as by an actor in a theater, or by a

singer, or by the printed page. Often the mode of presentation is in fact a purely conventional fiction. This is true, for
example, when the poet pretends to be writing a verse-drama
but actually expects his poem to be read in a book, as in the
case of Victor Hugo's *Cromwell.* The criteria of theme, tone,
and manner of presentation may by their nature impose certain restrictions on the shape of the poem, but this is a purely
secondary effect.

Among the major generic categories into which poems
have been traditionally divided are the epic, didactic, dramatic, satiric, narrative, and lyric types. Each of these classes
contains almost unlimited numbers of subcategories. Epic
poems, such as the *Chanson de Roland* or Ronsard's unsuccessful and unfinished *Franciade,* are in fact extended narrative poems, but endowed with such special characteristics
that they are usually thought to constitute a separate genre.
They are distinguished according to their subject, which
normally involves the exploits of a national hero whose deeds
of war often reflect superhuman powers. Didactic verse, as
exemplified by Voltaire's *Discours en vers sur l'homme,* is
characterized by its tendency to try to communicate ideas,
usually moral injunctions. Dramatic poems are presented as
though they were to be declaimed from a theater stage,
though this presentation often involves nothing more than a
conventional understanding and a special, formal appearance
of the poem in print. Thus the term "dramatic monologue"
is used for any poem that expresses the words of a single
person who reveals by what he says both his own character
and the nature of the dramatic situation in which he finds
himself. Narrative poems, such as ballads, relate a story,
while lyric poems tend to be relatively brief descriptions of
an emotional state, and thus resemble the verbal aspect of a
song. Strictly speaking, a lyric poem is one written as though
it were to be sung to the accompaniment of the lyre, though
such a definition shows how far generic conventions may

depart from literal reality. The mere fact that the mode of presentation of a poem is hypothetical does not mean that it is unimportant, however. The lyric poem, as exemplified by most of the quotations in this book, is so planned as to suggest that the poet is singing to himself (or to some other fictional character) and that we, the readers, are permitted to eavesdrop on the song. This mode of presentation avoids the suggestion that the poet is attempting primarily to communicate a "message" directly to us.

Subcategories of genres may depend simply on theme, as in such classifications as "anacreontic verse" (written in praise of Epicurean pleasures), *"ubi sunt* elegies," such as Villon's "Ballade des dames du temps jadis" (based on the "Where are the snows of yesteryear?" refrain), or *"carpe diem* poems" like Ronsard's "Mignonne, allons voir si la rose . . ." (centered on the "Gather ye rosebuds while ye may" motif). Sometimes the category is established in terms of subject and form of presentation, as exemplified by the apologue, an animal fable of the Æsop or La Fontaine variety; or it may be a function of tone and attitude, as is the case in satire, the kind of poetry in which persons, types, or ideas are ridiculed. It can be seen from this latter example that still further subdivisions of classes are possible. If the technique of the satire consists of handling an elevated subject in a trivial manner, as illustrated by Scarron's version of the *Æneid,* the poem is a burlesque; if a trivial subject is treated in an exalted, noble style, as in Boileau's *Lutrin,* the result is a mock-epic. If the subject of the satire is another work of literature the poem becomes a parody or a pastiche or, if the treatment is broad or grotesque, a travesty.

The medieval troubadours and trouvères developed a wealth of highly organized generic types, many of which, perhaps happily, soon disappeared. Much more recently, surrealistic automatic writing appeared in the poetic domain, and someday it too may be felt to constitute a genre. Clearly, since these categories call attention to potential groupings of related poems, they are primarily of use in helping us to generalize from specific texts that share some common characteristics. On the other hand, they are of small assistance in the analysis of single texts. The fact that a poet calls a poem an "elegy" tells us little; we shall still have to study the text to see precisely what he means by that term.

We noted that lyric poetry differs from didactic poetry in maintaining the convention that the poet is not directly addressing the reader. In didactic poetry he does seem to speak to his public, and that fact may give trouble to an unskilled poet, because poetry is grounded more on the expression of attitudes than on the statement of propositions. It does not portray reality but "meta-reality," a reconstructed or transposed reality. Many unskilled efforts in verse are not poems precisely because they are statements of ideas which have been "ornamented" by rime and rhythm. Here the "form" is indeed a disposable container for the "content," and therefore we are not in this case dealing with poetry. When, as may sometimes happen, the same thing is true of didactic verse, that is, when only the idea really matters and "tout le reste est littérature," we are not concerned with poetry but with versified prose.

Sometimes when we read certain allegories (e.g., parts of the *Roman de la rose*) we find that the idea being conveyed and its manner of expression are separable, so that we do not enter into the scene being portrayed; we merely rationalize about it. In these cases poetry has vanished and left us with a page of exceptionally effective verse. It is not intended here to suggest that all apparently didactic verse is unpoetic. Seemingly propositional statements may in fact be nothing more than imitation propositions; they may be what Northrop Frye calls "hypothetical" ideas. When Pope, for instance, or Boileau, states a rule about the writing of verse, the *way* in which he states it may be as important or more important than *what* he says. The manner of presentation of the idea may make it esthetically effective, so that we read Pope and Boileau with pleasure even if we have little specific interest in the basic thoughts they are expressing. They are transposing or reconstructing the reality they seem to be describing, and this remaking of reality is an aspect of poetry.

We see, then, that poetry and verse are two radically different concepts. By analyzing the structure of the poem we may hope to arrive at conclusions that will help us to determine where the poem falls on the scale which runs from undoubted poetry to definite non-poetry. And in order to make the analysis complete, we must also take up the matter of versification. But these two problems are quite distinct from one another. The question of verse involves the "physical" aspect of the poem: its sounds, shape, and rhythm. The question of "poetry versus non-poetry" cannot arise until we have also considered the poem's language and imagery and the total structure of connotations established by the interaction of all of these levels of meaning. Now that we have addressed ourselves to the poetic significance of sound and shape, we have only to deal with one remaining element, rhythm, in order to make our analysis of the verse aspect of a poem complete.

6
Rhythm and Pace

From what was said in the last chapter it may not have been obvious why the length of a line in French verse should be of any profound importance in the analysis of a poem. Why should the mere fact that a poet writes in alexandrines make his poem essentially different from what it would have been if he had written it in octosyllables? The reason has primarily to do with rhythm.[1] The length of the line (or even of the stanza) has no immediate bearing on what the poet says; it does, however, directly influence the kinds of rhythm he may use, and the rhythm in turn can affect the connotations evoked by the language of the poem. Rime is not essen-

[1] It seems only fair to warn the reader that this is yet another technical chapter; however, it deals with matters that cannot be overlooked by anyone concerned with reading poetry in French. Nothing is more exasperating than having to describe sound phenomena in print, unless it is having to read such descriptions. The only excuse that can therefore be offered is that it has to be done. The job of the reader, at least, can be made less onerous if he is in a position to listen to recordings of good readers of French poetry while thinking about the phenomena of rhythm described here. A single example is worth a thousand words, and many of the remarks made in these pages will be far clearer if they can be tested on the home laboratory called a record player. A partial list of available recordings of French poetry will be found in the Bibliography at the end of the book.

tial to verse, though in French it is very nearly so. Rhythm, on the other hand, is so vital that even modern poets do not try to dispense with it, no matter how much they may soften or disguise its effect.

We have already noted that the recurrence of stresses is less regular in French verse than it is in English. In standard English metrics there will normally be one stressed syllable per foot, so that a perfect iambic pentameter will contain five accented syllables:

$$\breve{\ } \ / \ \breve{\ } \ / \ \breve{\ } \ / \ \breve{\ } \ / \ \breve{\ } \ /$$

"For *fools* rush *in* where *angels fear* to *tread.*"

Needless to say, if the poet when constructing iambic pentameters confined himself to a relentless hammering out of this same rhythmic beat the result would be monotonous if not maddening. He therefore varies the pulse from time to time by substituting some other foot for one of the iambs. He may reverse the iambic foot, thereby making it a trochee, as in the first word of the line,

$$/ \ \breve{\ } \quad \breve{\ } \ / \ \breve{\ } \quad / \quad \breve{\ } \ / \breve{\ } \ /$$

"*Silent* u*pon* a *peak* in *Darien,*"

or he may introduce a foot with three syllables instead of two (usually an anapest), as in the second foot of this line:

$$\breve{\ } \quad / \ \breve{\ } \ \breve{\ } \quad / \ \breve{\ } \ / \ \breve{\ } \ / \ \breve{\ } \quad /$$

"With *ravishing sound* of *his* melodious *harp.*"

If, in fact, the *-ious* of "melodious" is pronounced in two syllables another anapest appears as the last foot of the line. In such ways as these, the poet in English breaks the over-perfect regularity of his rhythm and plays against the pattern his reader has learned to expect.

Much the same effect is found in French verse, though there the rhythmic irregularity is far greater to begin with. We have observed that despite the fact that French verse has no feet governed by heavy accents like those of English verse, there are slight stresses (which are essentially changes of musical pitch) in the French line. A "stress," as we shall call

it for short, falls on the last syllable of a word that stands at
the end of a "sense group," the strongest accent occurring
normally at the end of a clause or sentence. Thus in the following alexandrine there are four stresses (as marked), of
which the strongest is the last, the next strongest is the second,
and the weakest are the first and third:

/ // / ///
La *sour*-ce de mes *jours* comme *eux* s'est é-cou-*lée*.

The musical pitches of the twelve syllables of the line might
be indicated as follows:

A slight pause will follow each of these accented syllables,
varying in length in direct proportion to the amount of stress
placed on the syllable itself.

It is a general rule that there must be a stress on the last
syllable of any French line, and this syllable will be followed
by a pause. The alexandrine and the ten-syllable line also
require a secondary pause in the interior of the line, and the
syllable preceding it is likely to be slightly stressed. This
secondary pause is called the caesura (*la césure*), and in the
alexandrine it almost always falls directly after the sixth
syllable, splitting the line in half. In the following quotation
from Racine's *Phèdre*, the caesuras are marked with a slash:

On dit qu'un prompt départ / vous éloigne de nous,
Seigneur. A vos douleurs / je viens joindre mes larmes.
Je vous viens pour un fils / expliquer mes alarmes.
Mon fils n'a plus de père; / et le jour n'est pas loin
Qui de ma mort encor / doit le rendre témoin.
Déjà mille ennemis / attaquent son enfance.

The effect of the caesura is to divide the alexandrine into two parts, called hemistichs, each containing six syllables. The question of how long one should make the pause when reading aloud depends entirely on the sense of the line, and the same is true of the degree of stress (if any) on the preceding syllable. In the passage just quoted the greatest stress and pause will occur in the fourth line because of the semicolon. The stress and pause will be the least in line six, since they separate a subject from its verb.

In the decasyllabic line the caesura usually falls after the fourth syllable, though it may follow the sixth. The following lines illustrate the two respective types:

> A ton oubli / je vais m'accoutumer.
>
> . . . .
>
> Je t'obéis enfin; / sois sans alarmes.

Lines of less than ten syllables have no caesura.

The rule about the position of the caesura in the alexandrine and the ten-syllable line is not, of course, inviolable, though it was very rarely broken before the nineteenth century. Since then, especially for special effect, poets have shifted the position of the pause in both types of line. Victor Hugo popularized, but by no means invented, what is sometimes called the Romantic trimeter. Here there are two caesuras instead of one. They occur after the fourth and eighth syllables of the alexandrine, thereby dividing it into thirds, as in Hugo's line, "Tantôt léger, / tantôt boiteux, / toujours pieds nus!" That Hugo was not, contrary to what is sometimes said, the first to come upon this rhythmic variation can be seen by Corneille's parallel construction which is two hundred years older: "Toujours aimer, / toujours souffrir, / toujours mourir." Similarly, it is possible to split the ten-syllable line in half by putting the caesura after the fifth syllable. The result is a strange lilting effect quite appropriate for representing a dance, as in "Les Elfes" of Leconte de Lisle:

Couronnés de thym / et de marjolaine,
Les Elfes joyeux / dansent sur la plaine.
Du sentier des bois / aux daims familier,
Sur un noir cheval, / sort un chevalier.

This position of the caesura in a decasyllabic line is very rare.

Apart from the regularly recurring caesura and the break at the end of the line, other internal pauses may occur but their position is not fixed. They are usually caused by a lightly stressed syllable that may be followed by a very brief hesitation which the French call *une coupe*. These stresses are floating accents, that is, they occur wherever the sense of the line happens to require them. In general, there are two floating accents with accompanying *coupes* in an alexandrine, one of them appearing in each hemistich. The decasyllabic line is more likely to have one, normally in the section which contains six syllables. Lines of nine or less syllables have no fixed caesura, and may contain two, one, or no *coupes* depending on the length and syntactical nature of the line.

The rhythm of a French line, then, is a function of the position of the caesura and of the number and arrangement of the *coupes* (if any). An alexandrine may be perfectly quartered, with a *coupe* after the third syllable, the caesura after the sixth, another *coupe* after the ninth, and the final pause following the twelfth. For example:

/ // / ///
Pour un *cœur* / généreux // ce trépas / a des *charmes*. ///

Here the stresses and pauses go hand in hand: the greatest stress and longest pause are at the end, the next degree of intensity is at the caesura, the weakest stresses and shortest pauses are the remaining pairs at the *coupes*. The same applies to the following line.

/ // / ///
Qu'il est *peu* / de nos *fils* // qui ne *soient* / vos neveux! ///

Alexandrines such as these sound almost like anapestic tetrameters in English. Compare: "Pour un cœur généreux ce trépas a des charmes," with " 'Twas the night before Christmas, and all through the house. . . ." These particular examples have been chosen because the disparity between their respective tones is symbolic: the rhythmic resemblance between them conceals a far more important difference. What makes the English line an anapestic tetrameter is the fact that it conforms to a strict rhythmic pattern; what makes the French line an alexandrine is the fact that it contains twelve syllables. There is a world of difference between these two criteria. The lines succeeding this English line, with only an occasional exception, will also have stresses on the third, sixth, ninth, and twelfth syllables:

$$\overset{/}{\quad}\qquad\overset{/}{\quad}\qquad\overset{/}{\quad}\qquad\overset{/}{\quad}$$

"Not a *crea*ture was *stir*ring, not *ev*en a *mouse.*"

But the six lines that follow the French line, which was taken from Corneille's *Horace,* do not conform to the anapestic tetrameter rhythm at all. All that can be counted on in an alexandrine will be a stress (followed by a pause) on the sixth and twelfth syllables. Any other accents will be floating; they may occur anywhere (or nowhere) in the line. Thus, in the passage from *Horace* just alluded to we find this pattern:

HORACE:

Pour un coeur / généreux // ce trépas / a des charm(es); ///

La gloi- / -re qui le suit // ne souf- / fre point de larm(es), ///

Et je le re-ce-vrais // en bé-nis-sant / mon sort, ///

Si Rom(e) / et tout l'État // per-daient moins / en ma

mort. ///

CURIACE:

A vos a-mis / pour-tant // per-met-tez / de le craindr(e); ///

Dans un si beau trépas ⫽ ils sont les seuls à plaindr(e.) ⫻

There are other possible readings of these lines, but this one seems legitimate and demonstrates what will be found in almost any sample of French alexandrine verse. If we diagrammed a series of anapestic tetrameters in English according to the number of syllables in a foot, i.e., the number up to and including each stressed syllable, we would arrive at a series of notations in the form 3–3–3–3. Thus " 'Twas the night before Christmas, and all through the house . . ." has the rhythm: "one-two-*three* one-two-*three* one-two-*three* one-two-*three*." Sometimes an iamb might be substituted for an anapest, in which case one of the three's would become a two: "The stockings were hung by the chimney with care" has a 2–3–3–3 rhythm: one-*two* one-two-*three* one-two-*three* one-two-*three*. Otherwise there would be little variation. But if we do the same for the French passage just quoted, the result is:

$$3–3–3–3$$
$$2–4–2–4$$
$$6–4–2$$
$$2–4–3–3$$
$$4–2–3–3$$
$$6–6$$

No two of these lines have exactly the same rhythm. And the possible variations are far from exhausted; here, for example, is a 1–5–4–2 line from the same scene of *Horace*:

"Rom- / -e, quoi qu'il en soit, ⫽ ne se-ra point / su-jett(e). ⫻

The nearest approach in French to the English concept "foot" is the *mesure*. A *mesure* is a group of syllables occurring between pauses or stresses. In our diagram of the French rhythm the figures represent the number of syllables in each *mesure*. The stress will always fall on the last syllable of the series. In this respect the *mesure* differs from the foot, since the number 3 in our English diagram does not tell us whether the foot is, for example, an anapest (with the accent on the last syllable) or a dactyl (with the stress on the first syllable). It could be either, since both anapests and dactyls contain three syllables. What is more, there is no standard English foot with four, five, or six syllables.

French rhythm, then, differs in certain fundamental respects from English rhythm, though the two also agree on many points. The basic characteristic of any rhythm is the regularity of recurrence of the pulse. In English the pulse is essentially a matter of intensity: a stressed syllable is pronounced more forcibly than an unstressed syllable. In French it is a question of a change in pitch, combined with a very slight increase in volume and a following pause that is often almost imperceptible.

Whatever its nature may be, the pulse must recur with regularity if there is to be a detectable rhythm. On the other hand, if the pulse recurs with *perfect* regularity the rhythm will soon become annoying, jingly, boring, and ultimately stupefying. What is needed is a regular pattern that sets up an expectation in the listener's mind, together with enough deviation from that pattern to keep the mind alert. English solves this problem by varying the type of foot from time to time; French deals with it by having fewer fixed stresses than English and by separating them with more syllables, while at the same time equalizing their rate of recurrence in time. In the case of the classical alexandrine, the listener is certain to hear a beat and a definite pause every twelve syllables, that is, at the end of each line. With only the rarest exceptions, he can also count on hearing another pulse followed by a slight pause at the sixth syllable of each line. These two regular, constant beats and rests set up the basic pattern of expectation. The variety will be guaranteed by the unpredictable position of the two floating accents and *coupes* that may (or may not) appear anywhere else in the line.

In the decasyllabic line, the basic pattern is established only by the final stress at the end of the line. The caesura will usually fall after the fourth syllable, but this expectation can be pleasantly disappointed by placing it after the sixth. Notice what a balanced effect Baudelaire achieves by switching the rhythm from the normal 4–6 to the 6–4 pattern in the third line of this tercet:

> De ses cheveux / élastiques et lourds,
> Vivant sachet, / encensoir de l'alcôve,
> Une senteur montait, / sauvage et fauve.

Lines of less than ten syllables depend entirely on their final syllable to establish the basic rhythm, and secure their variety by the irregular placement of any number of lighter stresses from zero to two in the interior of the line.

Even this system would tend to produce a somewhat choppy effect, however, if all the syllables were pronounced at equal intervals of time. If we took exactly two seconds to read each of the six alexandrines quoted above beginning with "Pour un cœur généreux ce trépas a des charmes" we would hear a pulse every second: at the mid-point and at the end of every line. But we would also hear secondary pulses at irregular intervals during the course of these two seconds. The first 3–3–3–3 alexandrine would give us pulses at the half-second points, but the next line, with its 2–4–2–4 rhythm, would give us a beat one third of a second after the line began and one third of a second after the caesura, leaving two intervals of two thirds of a second unfilled. To test this effect we have only to count to twelve perfectly evenly six times, placing a stress always on the numbers six and twelve, but adding other stresses according to the diagram we made of the six successive alexandrines from *Horace*. The result would be:

$$1 - \mathbf{2} - 3 - \mathbf{4} - 5 - \mathbf{6} - 7 - \mathbf{8} - 9 - \mathbf{10} - 11 - \mathbf{12}$$
$$1 - \mathbf{2} - 3 - \mathbf{4} - 5 - \mathbf{6} - 7 - \mathbf{8} - 9 - \mathbf{10} - 11 - \mathbf{12}$$
$$1 - 2 - 3 - 4 - 5 - \mathbf{6} - 7 - 8 - 9 - \mathbf{10} - 11 - \mathbf{12}$$
$$1 - \mathbf{2} - 3 - 4 - 5 - \mathbf{6} - 7 - \mathbf{8} - 9 - 10 - 11 - \mathbf{12}$$
$$1 - 2 - 3 - 4 - 5 - \mathbf{6} - 7 - 8 - 9 - 10 - 11 - \mathbf{12}$$
$$1 - 2 - 3 - 4 - 5 - \mathbf{6} - 7 - 8 - 9 - 10 - 11 - \mathbf{12}$$

Clearly, if every syllable is given the same time interval, the rhythm is jerky and difficult to grasp. After all, rhythm is regular recurrence in time. The solution is to read the lines so that the *stressed* syllables have nearly equal time intervals between them. Then if we read the total alexandrine in two seconds we will have a pulse approximately every half a second, but some pulses will have more syllables between them than others. A line with a 2—4—2—4 rhythm will be read so that the first two syllables are pronounced relatively slowly, at about a quarter of a second each, while the next four syllables are spoken almost twice as fast, at about one eighth of a second each. In that way the beats will all be nearly regular and the choppiness will disappear. But we must not exaggerate: if we were perfectly regular in this timing the choppiness would simply be transferred from the pulses to the individual syllables. A compromise is needed. The answer is to accelerate *slightly* the *mesures* that contain more than three syllables, and to slow down *slightly* those with less than three syllables. The stresses will not then be perfectly evenly spaced, but perfection in this case is not desirable anyway. The stresses on the sixth and twelfth syllables will be absolutely regular; the others will be only approximately regular. And that is exactly the effect to be sought: the rhythm will be detectable but not monotonous. We are speaking here of the norm, the "standard" reading of the line; in a versified play, however, there will of course be changes in phrasing and pacing that the actors will introduce in order to represent variations in the personality and mood of the different characters.

The basic principle of French rhythm, in short, is that lines of the same length are read in approximately the same length of time, so that the last accented syllables (which are usually rimes) will recur at equal intervals. This sets up a basic pattern. Furthermore, long lines such as the alexandrine and the decasyllable have another essentially fixed accent that will also return at equal intervals. This is necessary because of the difficulty in keeping track of patterns involving large numbers. It would be very hard to detect in a series of alexandrines, for example, the regularity of a pulse that recurred every twelve syllables; but it would be much easier to feel a beat falling on every sixth syllable. Beyond that, the units of six in an alexandrine are usually divided roughly in half by the floating accents which, with a little skill on the reader's part, can be made to reappear very nearly at the mid-point between the beginning of the line and the caesura, or between the caesura and the end. The approximate timing of these light floating accents insures the necessary variety in the over-all rhythm of the line.

Thanks to the device known as enjambement, rhythm can be made to strengthen the meaning of a text by imitating its denotation or by calling attention to a particular word. An "enjambement" or "run-on line" is a construction in which a word or several words belonging to a syntactical unit that has been begun in one line are carried over into the next line:

> Et le char vaporeux de la reine des ombres
> Monte. . . .

In this phrase from Lamartine's "Isolement" the verb whose subject is *le char vaporeux* appears in the following line with an effect of greater emphasis. The words that are run on to the second line are called *le rejet* in French. *Contre-rejet* is the process of beginning a proposition at the end of one line and giving over the entire next line to the completion of the statement. Thus *contre-rejet* is the reverse of enjambement. Victor Hugo was fond of *rejet à l'hémistiche* which differs from *contre-rejet* simply in that the extension to the second line runs only through the first hemistich, not through the whole line:

> Non, elle continue, invincible, admirable,
> Entre dans l'invisible et dans l'impondérable,
> Y disparaît pour toi, chair vile, *emplit l'azur*
> *D'un monde éblouissant*, miroir du monde obscur. . . .

Rhythm is regularity of recurrence; pace is the rate of that recurrence. Changes in pace are a very important aspect of rhythm. We have already noted the changes in pace caused by the number of syllables in a *mesure*. An alexandrine with a 2—4—2—4 rhythm will be read so that the *mesures* with two syllables occupy roughly the same time interval as those with four syllables. This means that the syllables in the first and third *mesures* of the line will be pronounced at a slow rate compared with those of the second and fourth *mesures*. As a general rule, the more syllables there are in a *mesure* the faster its pace will be. Therefore a line with just two *mesures* will generally occupy less time than one with six. Compare these two alexandrines:

"Dans un si beau trépas ils sont les seuls à plaindre."
"Il pense, il règle, il mène, il pèse, il juge, il aime."

The second line will almost inevitably take longer to recite than the first. In short, the absence of *coupes* in a line is apt to accelerate the pace, while a multiplicity of *coupes* and stressed syllables will tend to slow it down.

There are a number of other non-metrical influences on pace, such as repeated sounds (alliterations, internal rimes, etc.) which tend to speed the recitation, whereas clusters of consonants or numerous mute *e*'s will decelerate it. Note how the mute *e*'s check the reading of this description of trees: ". . . Aux longues branches langoureuses." In modern poetry pace is often slowed by isolating single words as independent lines, or by introducing unexpected spacings into or between lines. We may also note that (surprisingly enough) *elaborate* rime tends to accelerate pace, whereas profuse punctuation, italics, capital letters, and the like decelerate the rate of speed at which the text is read.

Almost all that we have said here about rhythm has had to do with regular verse. The rhythm of free verse, called "cadence," tends to follow the rhythms of speech, which are arranged by the poet into highly complicated patterns. An intermediate stage favored by some modern poets consists of the use of verse which is regular except for the fact that mute *e*'s which are silent in normal prose speech are not counted. An example is the (irregular) "alexandrine": "C'était une belle peinture du quartier latin," in which the final *e*'s *of une, belle,* and *peinture* are disregarded. Another variation is the elimination of the central caesura: "Il a raconté le conte absurde en riant."

The elements we have been discussing in the last three chapters—sound, shape, and rhythm—have in common the fact that they do not in themselves convey the kind of meaning that can be paraphrased in prose. They are vital, however, in enriching the meanings expressed by the text, and in that sense they are part of its meaning. They operate not alone but in conjunction with many other elements of the poem in evoking connotations, the meanings that extend beyond the purely propositional sense of the words and phrases of the text. It is never enough simply to identify these "physical characteristics" of the poem; the problem is always to see how they coöperate with other elements to express a meaning that could not be conveyed by prose.

Perhaps no better demonstration of the importance of rhythm could be found than this magnificent sonnet of Baudelaire, in which the use of mute *e*'s, enjambement, punctuation, variable *coupes,* and displacement of the caesura provide the changes in pace that give the poem its unforgettable cadence:

RECUEILLEMENT

Sois sage, ô ma Douleur, et tiens-toi plus tranquille.
Tu réclamais le Soir; il descend; le voici:
Une atmosphère obscure enveloppe la ville,
Aux uns portant la paix, aux autres le souci.

Pendant que des mortels la multitude vile,
Sous le fouet du Plaisir, ce bourreau sans merci,
Va cueillir des remords dans la fête servile,
Ma Douleur, donne-moi la main; viens par ici,

Loin d'eux. Vois se pencher les défuntes Années,
Sur les balcons du ciel, en robes surannées;
Surgir du fond des eaux le Regret souriant;

Le Soleil moribond s'endormir sous une arche,
Et, comme un long linceul traînant à l'Orient,
Entends, ma chère, entends la douce Nuit qui marche.

7

Diction and Rhetoric

Let us consider a well-known piece of French verse that is written entirely in nonsense syllables. It is the Gallic equivalent of our own traditional method of selecting the child who is to be "it" in games of Tag or Hide-and-Go-Seek: "Eeny Meeny Miney Moe."

> Am stram gram
> Pic et pec et comégram
> Bouré bouré ratatam
> Am stram gram.

If we were to analyze this anticipation of the Dada tradition with appropriate scholarly solemnity, we could call attention to the fact that the heterometric quatrain, which is constructed on a single rime, is composed of two heptasyllabic lines embraced by a trisyllabic refrain characterized by internal rime, the effect of which is enriched by consonance in line two and a repeated word in line three. We might even feel that such a lucid and impressive sounding explication would mark the first step in accounting for the unusual success this jingle has had over the years with small children. It would not, on the other hand, inspire us with sublime and penetrating insights into the rich inner fabric of the poem's meaning—principally because it has no meaning. It is simply a shape, a frame, a body without a mind. And as a body cannot live without a mind, so this bit of verse is poetically dead.

This is not to say that shape is unimportant in poetry. Intelligence cannot survive without a body any more than a body can live without a brain. But we tend to feel that if a hierarchy of values is called for, the mind should be granted more central importance than the body that supports it. In the same way, we may well assume that the principal function of a poem's verse form is to support the less mechanical aspect of the poem, which is its meaning. It is time then that we turn our attention more directly to what we may think of as the mind of the poem.

A poem's meaning is to be located first in its language, in the denotations and connotations of words. We have recognized that although we cannot look up connotations in a dictionary, we certainly cannot ignore them either. They are often more important in poetry than the denotations which are much more easily identified. Sometimes the connotations of a particular word are so perfectly attuned to a central theme which the poet is developing that the word immediately strikes us as the *mot juste;* no synonym would serve the same purpose so effectively. Another reason for feeling that the poet has chosen precisely the right word may be its etymology. The original sense of the word, especially when combined with the meaning it had developed at the time the poem was written, may suggest a particular nuance that is more appropriate to the context than any overtone that a synonym could provide. The word *superbe,* for example, when used of a person, may be apt because it suggests haughtiness as well as grandeur. (*Superbus* in Latin meant haughty.)

Since the French language is derived from Latin, many French poets, particularly in the sixteenth and seventeenth centuries, were very conscious of the original Latin sense of the terms they used and dwelt upon their etymological meanings, either in preference to the more modern ones or in conjunction with them. Correspondingly, the more Latin we know, the richer our feeling about the connotations of French words will be. An etymological sense may even save us from such an anachronistic reading as would result if, for example, we interpreted the word *généreux* as used by Corneille in terms of the modern sense of generosity (munificence). When Corneille writes: "Pour un cœur généreux ce trépas a des charmes," he is giving *généreux* its etymological sense of "magnanimous" (having the attitude appropriate to a person of noble birth or spirit).

Because he was a classical tragedian, Corneille tended to make abundant use of such words as *généreux*, which were considered in the seventeenth century to be noble and poetic. We have already noted the term *courroux* as a synonym of *colère*, and *coursier* replacing *cheval*, both of which are encountered constantly in classical tragedy. Certain words were banned from the poetic lexicon of that period as being low or prosaic; other terms which were felt to be elevated and aristocratic were highly encouraged. The result is that a number of stock expressions turn up in classical drama with what to us may seem to be almost unbearable frequency. For example, an outraged nobleman almost never speaks simply of his *courroux* or of his *colère*, it is always his *juste courroux* —as though the rage of a Cornelian prince could possibly be anything but "just" in his own eyes!

The term "diction" is used to refer to the choice and arrangement of words in a poem, and the sort of language we have just described may be called "restrictive diction." When a poet uses restrictive diction he is rejecting certain words from the poetic vocabulary as unsuitable. In contrast to this, most modern poets favor a "permissive diction," in which any word is acceptable if it suits the purposes of the moment. Archaic diction is, of course, restrictive. It is far rarer in French than in English, because modern French poetry is largely an outgrowth of the Romanticism of the nineteenth century that rejected Classical restrictions (at least in theory). As a result of this repudiation, most poets since the eighteenth century have been more concerned with the novelty of their diction than with any attempt, like that of Coleridge in "The Ancient Mariner," to imitate the language of an earlier age. Neologistic diction, the application of new meanings to old terms, or the use of nonce-words invented for the particular occasion, was also quite rare in French until the twentieth century. Now poets such as Henri Michaux and Jacques Prévert, born respectively in 1899 and 1900, are quite capable of creating such verbs as *andromaquer* (from *Andromaque*, "Andromache") and *majusculer* (from *majuscule*, "capital letter"). On the other hand, the conscious use of barbarisms (the use of deformed or non-existent words) or solecisms (deviations from standard usage, particularly in matters of syntax), for the purpose of setting a certain tone has been fairly common since the mid-nineteenth century. Notable illustrations can be found in the regional poetry of Tristan Corbière in which he imitates the rough language of Breton sailors; in these lines from "La Fin," for example, he refers to drowned seamen:

> Allons! c'est leur métier: ils sont morts dans leurs bottes!
> Leur *boujaron* au cœur, tout vifs dans leurs capotes . . .
> —*Morts* . . . Merci: la *Camarde* a pas le pied marin;
> Qu'elle couche avec vous; c'est votre bonne femme . . .
> —Eux, allons donc: Entiers! enlevés par la lame!
> Ou perdus dans un grain . . .

Any of these forms of diction may help to set up a tone that reveals a great deal about the poet's attitude. The harsh, proud, caustic tone of the lines just quoted from Corbière are indicative of his attitude toward Victor Hugo's sentimental, landlubberly poem, "Oceano Nox," which is here under attack.

While precision, as exemplified in the *mot juste,* is one of the most obvious characteristics of good poetic diction, it does not exclude controlled ambiguity from the list of acceptable

poetic devices. As we have seen, connotations, which are of
the essence of poetry, are themselves ambiguities in William
Empson's sense of the term. They mean more than the literal
denotations of the words which evoke them. Any controlled
ambiguity which makes a word effective in more than one
way at a time has inevitably enriched the poetic value of
the word. Consider, for example, this rather obscure poem
by Mallarmé:

SALUT

Rien, cette écume, vierge vers
A ne désigner que la coupe;
Telle loin se noie une troupe
De sirènes mainte à l'envers.

Nous naviguons, ô mes divers
Amis, moi déjà sur la poupe
Vous l'avant fastueux qui coupe
Le flot de foudres et d'hivers;

Une ivresse belle m'engage
Sans craindre même son tangage
De porter debout ce salut

Solitude, récif, étoile
A n'importe ce qui valut
Le blanc souci de notre toile.

This poem was first read on the occasion of Mallarmé's elec-
tion as "Prince des poètes"; from his place of honor at the
banquet table, he lifted his champagne in this toast (*salut*
means "toast" as well as "salvation," "greeting," "bow," etc.).
The word *écume*, denoting the frothy bubbles of the champagne, also refers to the poem (*vierge vers*). *Coupe,* apart
from the technical use to which, as we have seen, it is sometimes put in versification, also means "shape" and "champagne
glass." The *ivresse* mentioned in line 9 is undoubtedly poetic

intoxication as well as a further allusion to the toast in champagne, and the word *blanc*, in addition to being the normal color of a ship's sail, is also Mallarmé's symbol for poetic sterility, since it is the color of a blank page. There are many other such ambiguities in the poem, all contributing to the possibility of interpreting it in a variety of ways.

There are, of course, ambiguities that merely confuse, instead of enriching poetic meaning. But no specific technique of ambiguity may be safely assumed to be valueless or bad; its effect must be judged from the individual case. The obvious sort of ambiguity which is produced by verbal looseness ("I watched her weeping": who was weeping?) or by the multiple meanings of words ("I slipped on the pike": did I step on a fish, trip over a medieval weapon, or fall on the highway?) is called an amphibole. But many subtler kinds of ambiguity or vagueness can be exploited by the poet. William Empson's *Seven Types of Ambiguity* deals so exhaustively with the subject in a way which is immediately applicable to French literature that little further development is necessary here. We need only observe that in general there is no waste in good poetic diction. The tension and compactness of poetry are characteristics that distinguish it obviously from prose. Controlled ambiguity is a way of getting the most work out of the least number of words, and it thereby contributes to the density which is a true requirement of poetic language.

One of the clear signs of technical incompetence or lack of care and craftsmanship on the poet's part is the habit of "padding," the introduction of unnecessary words into a text merely for the purpose of filling out a line or permitting a rime-word to be used. The French use the term *cheville* to refer to such superfluous words and rightly condemn the practice of using them, despite the fact that even the greatest poets sometimes stoop to it. We may reasonably overlook a few such lapses, so long as they do not prove to be habitual. At times what appear on first inspection to be *chevilles* turn out to be calculated risks on the poet's part. The same may be true of tautologies or pleonasms. André Chénier appears to have perpetrated a pleonasm (the unnecessary addition or repetition of a word in expressing an idea) when in "Le Chant d'Alonzo" from "L'Amérique" he writes the line: "Que je m'élève au ciel comme une flamme ardente." Since *ardente* here means simply "burning," we have only to consider whether Chénier really needed to rule out the image of a non-burning flame as a possible source of misunderstanding before we condemn the end of the line as a *cheville*. Furthermore, the fact that *ardente* rimes with the word *brûlante* ("burning") in the next line seems to compound the felony, until we notice that throughout the fragment the poet is balancing and contrasting two kinds of imagery: light, purifying heat, and swift motion through air, as against darkness, chill, and encumbering solidity. In order to intensify to the utmost his heat imagery, he has permitted himself the redundant expression "flamme ardente." And while we cannot consider the fragment a masterpiece, we may find it possible to forgive the poet this verbal excess in terms of the effect of the total passage.

Up to this point we have been addressing ourselves primarily to the subject of individual words, but we noted earlier that syntactical constructions are also capable of producing connotations or of setting a tone which may reveal something about the poet's attitude. The commonest types of construction intended to have this sort of effect are the rhetorical figures, also called figures of speech. They are modes of expression that focus our attention, intensify our emotional experience, or have some other strong effect upon us. Many of these devices have been in fairly constant use since classical antiquity, and some of them have Latin or Greek names of formidable length. It is not, of course, strictly necessary to know these names, which are merely a longish sort of "shorthand" intended to avoid having to redefine the device every time it happens to be referred to. Students who need to call attention to these figures will find their names useful, but others have only to recognize the constructions as they occur. They are important to note because of their ability to charge poetic language with the kind of meaning that cold-blooded neutral prose cannot convey.

Perhaps the most important class of figures of this kind is the one that includes all the techniques for expressing meaning obliquely. Statements made with the aid of a device in this category are "oblique" in the sense that they say something other than what they mean. Ambiguity in the usual sense is clearly a synonym for oblique expression, and amphiboles of the type already alluded to constitute the first entry in this list.

The second principal type of oblique expression is irony, and specifically ironic statement. The word "irony" itself is an amphibole, since it is used in two entirely different senses. An "ironic statement" is one that is intended to convey a meaning different from the one it professes to give. Thus, in these free-verse lines taken from Jules Laforgue's "L'Hiver qui vient" the poet, speaking of the "joys" of winter, inquires:

> Mais, lainages, caoutchoucs, pharmacie, rêve,
> Rideaux écartés du haut des balcons des grèves
> Devant l'océan de toitures des faubourgs,
> Lampes, estampes, thé, petits-fours,
> Serez-vous pas mes seules amours! . . .
> (Oh! et puis, est-ce que tu connais, outre les pianos,
> Le sobre et vespéral mystère hebdomadaire
> Des statistiques sanitaires
> Dans les journaux?)

Ironic statements when used consistently create an ironic tone that can pervade an entire poem. The ambiguous nature of the word "irony" results from its use in the expression "ironic situation," referring to a situation in which just deserts are not appropriately rewarded or in which the character's total or partial ignorance is combined with the spectator's or reader's full knowledge. This type of irony is not our present concern, but ironic statement, since it is a form of non-explicit-ness, falls clearly within the category of oblique expression.

There is obviously a very close connection between ironic statement and understatement, which is sometimes called "meiosis." Several types of irony specifically involve under-statement, such as "antiphrasis," the designation of a person or thing by its opposite, as when Baudelaire refers in "Les Petites Vieilles" to decrepit old women as Vestals, Madonnas, and Eves. In the *Oresteia* of Æschylus, similarly, the Furies are referred to as the Eumenides ("The Gracious Ones"). The effect here, of course, is not ironic but rather euphemistic. Related to antiphrasis is "antonomasia," the substitution of a proper name for a common noun, or vice verse, as in Rim-baud's description of Customs officers: "Ils empoignent les Fausts et les Diavolos." The effect of this figure may be an understatment or an overstatement, depending on the con-text and the exact term used. A form of irony with a specific effect of understatement is the device called "litotes," which consists of affirming something by denying its opposite; thus when Corneille's Chimène says: "Va, je ne te hais pas," she means: "I love you." In French the word *litote* has been extended to cover all forms of understatement.

Technically each of these figures is an example of "periph-rasis," or "circumlocution," or "euphemism," all of which mean the avoidance of plain terms. Euphemism is specifically a softening of the harsh or brutal effect that the use of direct language could provoke, whereas the other two words imply a side-stepping of such language. In elevated poetic dis-course circumlocution (or periphrasis) is commonly used to avoid "vulgar," i.e., ordinary, diction. In Racine's *Phèdre*, the heroine is referred to as "La fille de Minos et de Pasiphaé," thereby avoiding the use of her actual name, though in this case the chief point is to call attention to her ancestry. The term "hypocoristic language" (from "hypocorism," a diminu-tive or "nickname") is sometimes used to designate language that makes extensive use of euphemistic expression, particu-

larly endearing terms, as in Baudelaire's tendency to refer
to his "Douleur" as "ma chère."

We have already alluded to overstatement; the commonest
device employing it is "hyperbole," an exaggerated description of persons, things, ideas, or feelings. Thus Lamartine,
referring in "L'Isolement" to the recent death of the woman
he loved, wrote:

> Que me font ces vallons, ces palais, ces chaumières,
> Vains objets dont pour moi le charme est envolé?
> Fleuves, rochers, forêts, solitudes si chères,
> Un seul être vous manque, et tout est dépeuplé!

Here the poet has been carried away by his emotion, but in
other situations he may use hyperbole with ironic effect.

The second major category of rhetorical figures, coming
directly after the group characterized by oblique expression,
is the class involving paradox. Cleanth Brooks believes paradox to be at the heart of poetry, since paradox sets up an essential structural tension between conflicting attitudes which
are held in suspense, harmonized, but not resolved. The figures that express meanings indirectly are also involved in
tension to the extent that what they say plays against what
they mean. But paradox goes further; it takes the form of a
seemingly self-contradictory statement which in fact contains
a basis of truth. It is this underlying truth that reconciles
the apparent opposites. The form of paradox called "antithesis" is a rhetorical figure in which sharply opposed ideas
are expressed in a balanced syntactical arrangement, as in
"Eat, drink, and be merry, for tomorrow you die." A reduced
form of the same technique is illustrated by the device called
"oxymoron," the use in a sentence of two apparently contradictory terms which seem to express a paradox reduced to the
minimal number of words, as in the English cliché "conspicu-
ous by his absence," or the phrase in which Valéry has his
temple columns speak of their "antiques jeunesses," or Mallarmé's description of a closed fan as "ce blanc vol fermé."

An effect similar to that of paradox is produced by "hysteron-proteron," a verbal putting of the cart before the horse. This sets up a tension of expectation in the listener's mind, since the element that should logically be expressed first is placed at the end. A common French use is illustrated by the construction: "Qu'elle est svelte et jolie, cette femme!" This is close to the device of "anastrophe," the deliberate inversion of normal word order. Since inversion is such a common syntactical arrangement in French, however, it usually has no very noticeable effect.

Paradox is also at the root of the figure called "catachresis." Though that term is sometimes used to denote the misuse of a word in the manner of Mrs. Malaprop, it also refers to any strained or tortured figure of speech, with special reference to the metaphoric association of two material things, as in Mallarmé's "blancs bouquets d'étoiles parfumées."

Wit is often based on paradox, as in the "aphorism," a short, pithy expression of some truth. Under the heading of wit we might mention the forms of paradox involved in grammar (or in lack of grammar—which is itself a kind of paradox). The term "syllepsis" denotes what happens when one word links two constructions each of which implies a slightly different meaning of the yoking word, as in the phrase: "In my office we labor under a tyrant and a leaking roof." This is grammatically correct, as opposed to "zeugma," in which the connecting term is properly related to only one of the dependent words, as in the famous Shakespearean example: "Kill the boys and the luggage," where the purpose of the expression is to suggest uncontrolled emotion. In general, the use of ungrammatical constructions in poetry serves to point up the intensity of the speaker's emotional state, as in the case of "aposiopesis," an abrupt breaking off in the middle of an utterance so that the thought remains only half expressed:

> Blocus sentimental! Messageries du Levant! . . .
> Oh, tombée de la pluie! Oh! tombée de la nuit,

> Oh! le vent! . . .
> La Toussaint, la Noël et la Nouvelle Année,
> Oh, dans les bruines, toutes mes cheminées! . . .
> D'usines . . .

The same purpose sometimes underlies the use of "anacoluthon," an ellipsis in which the correlative of a word is omitted, usually because the structure of a sentence is changed abruptly in mid-stream:

> Ainsi, triste et captif, ma lyre toutefois
> S'éveillait, écoutant ces plaintes, cette voix,
>   Ces vœux d'une jeune captive. . . .

Here the words *triste* and *captif* are intended to refer to the poet; they require the sentence to continue with the word *je*. Instead, Chénier shifts to the personification "ma lyre," leaving the masculine singular adjectives dangling in mid-air.

The term "paronomasia" refers to the illogical, hence paradoxical, association of one word with another as a result of a similarity in their sounds. It includes everything from the pun to the Freudian slip. In the former case, at least, wit is normally at play.

Just as it is possible to suggest strong emotion by means of aposiopesis or anacoluthon, so one can render it directly by exclamation ("O rage! ô désespoir! ô vieillesse ennemie!") or by apostrophe. "Apostrophe" consists of an abrupt break in the development of the text, at which point the speaker turns aside and speaks either to an absent person or thing, or to a personified abstraction. "Personification" (or "prosopopoeia") is the addressing of inanimate objects or abstract entities as though they were alive. Thus Lamartine cries out in "Le Lac":

> O lac! rochers muets! grottes! forêt obscure!
> Vous que le temps épargne ou qu'il peut rajeunir. . . !

Baudelaire is rather given to personifying abstractions, as in the famous lines from "Au lecteur":

C'est l'Ennui! —l'œil chargé d'un pleur involontaire,
Il rêve d'échafauds en fumant son houka.
Tu le connais, lecteur, ce monstre délicat,
—Hypocrite lecteur, —mon semblable, —mon frère!

Another device which often implies strong emotion is "anaphora," the repetition, in successive clauses or lines, of a word or construction. We can find an example of it in Lamartine's poem mentioned above, "Le Lac":

Eh quoi! n'en pourrons-nous fixer au moins la trace?
Quoi! passés pour jamais? Quoi! tout entiers perdus?

Finally we may mention "chiasmus," the balancing of the two halves of a phrase so that the terms of the second half correspond to those of the first half, but in reverse order. This can create various effects ranging from wittiness to the dirge-like finality evoked by the magnificent opening of Chénier's "Jeune Tarentine":

Pleurez, doux alcyons! ô vous, oiseaux sacrés,
Oiseaux chers à Thétis, doux alcyons, pleurez!

Perhaps this discussion of rhetorical devices may be clarified somewhat if we think of the customary uses to which these figures are put. Most rhetorical figures are intended to create one of five possible effects: irony, euphemism, wit, concentration, or strong emotion. The categories overlap, of course, as can be seen from the fact that both irony and verbal concentration are often aspects of wit. Furthermore, many of the figures can be properly placed in more than one category because of their natural versatility. With that understanding, however, we might divide up the figures as follows.

An ironic effect can be achieved, not only by means of ironic statement itself, but also by using understatement (meiosis) or overstatement (hyperbole). Antonomasia and litotes lead to understatement, and antiphrasis may represent either understatement or overstatement.

To express himself euphemistically, the poet may resort to circumlocution (periphrasis), including hypocoristic language. Here again, understatement in all its forms—antiphrasis, antonomasia, and litotes included—may be employed, this time with euphemistic instead of ironic effect.

Syllepsis, paronomasia, and catachresis may be used to suggest wit, and antithesis, oxymoron, catachresis, and ambiguity involve verbal concentration with or without overtones of wit.

Strong emotion is commonly expressed by means of exclamation, aposiopesis, anaphora, apostrophe, and personification (which also produces vividness), as well as by various ungrammatical constructions such as zeugma and anacoluthon.

The remaining figures—hysteron-proteron, inversion (anastrophe), and chiasmus—involve syntactical arrangements that may serve an indefinite number of highly varied purposes.

Whatever the device may be, the problem is to determine, as always, what effect it has in terms of the tone and attitude expressed by the lines in which it appears. The same may be said of the individual words. Their power may come from many sources: their etymologies, their sounds, their exactness for the expression of the thought, or their tendency to arouse the imagination and the senses. In the latter case, they are probably image-builders; but the matter of imagery is so central to poetry that it must be accorded a chapter of its own.

8
Image and Symbol

Unlike the language of mathematics, poetry is intended to engage more than the reader's mind; it also aims at stimulating his imagination—and the word "imagination" is here to be taken in its most literal sense. The imagination is, of course, the faculty that creates images. Poetry uses words in such a way that images are constantly burgeoning in the mind of the reader, which is another way of saying that the language of poetry is typically concrete. An abstract prose statement does not in itself generate images. When an arithmetician proclaims that $2+2=4$ his remark *in itself* evokes no image, because "two" is impossible to picture. We may, if we choose, imagine two apples added to two apples making four apples, but the arithmetician said nothing about apples; his statement would be equally applicable to skyscrapers, onions, or snowflakes. What the poet says, on the other hand, is not abstract but concrete. He *specifies* apples, skyscrapers, or snowflakes.

Concrete language affects the senses. The word "two" cannot do so, but the phrase "two apples," if suitably qualified, may be capable under certain circumstances of stimulating all five senses. Thus it would be possible, if not very poetic, to write: "As our teeth popped noisily through the skin and sank into the firm, moist flesh of the two glowing red apples, the scent of orchards flooded our nostrils and the sharp tang of fresh fruit filled our mouths." A gastronomic description like this is, of course, a prose sentence. What differentiates poetry from concrete prose is that the words of poetic language do more than merely represent things; they *re-present* them in the form of an image.

Words in poetry are not simply signs or tokens standing for something else; they have their own independent values, which are distinguishable from their denotative function. One of the most striking aspects of words as used by poets is that they are capable of calling forth (through the imagination) sensory reactions, thereby stimulating more than the reader's intellect. Thus the word "writhe," when used in an appropriate poetic context, may signify far more than what a dictionary definition would suggest. Part of its "meaning" might be located in the actual or incipient reaction of the reader's muscles to the word as he encounters it. In such a case the term would mean not only the concept "writhe" but also the physical reaction itself, and perhaps many other things as well if the word were thought of in the total context of the poetic structure. The language of poetry, therefore, because it is concrete, is also complex: it can create images that mean both themselves and something beyond themselves, so that they both represent (stand for) and re-present (regenerate a sensation).

An image, strictly speaking, is a picture; so the term "image" refers primarily to the visual sensations aroused by words (i.e., color, shape, and size). The word imagery, however, has been extended to encompass the other sensory reactions as well, thereby making it possible to speak of auditive, tactile, olfactory, and gustative images, as exemplified by the expressions: "strident trumpet," "rubbery skin," "acrid smoke," and "sour lemons." Critics even refer to "kinesthetic images," having in mind the kind of imagery which does not appeal directly to any of the five senses, but rather evokes memories of the muscular or nervous sensations that accompany physical movements or bodily postures. A phrase such as "quaking limbs" constitutes a kinesthetic image. Similarly, critics speak of thermal, pressure, static, and dynamic (or "kinetic") images, as well as of synesthetic imagery.

"Synesthesia" is the perception of different orders of sensations as a result of the stimulation of one sense. Some persons who are synesthetic see colors when they hear musical notes (or vice versa). Certain symbolist poets make great use of synesthetic imagery, mentioning, for example, the green notes of an oboe or black perfumes. Perhaps the most famous statement in French literature about synesthetic imagery is Baudelaire's sonnet, "Correspondances":

> La Nature est un temple où de vivants piliers
> Laissent parfois sortir de confuses paroles;
> L'homme y passe à travers des forêts de symboles
> Qui l'observent avec des regards familiers.
>
> Comme de longs échos qui de loin se confondent
> Dans une ténébreuse et profonde unité,
> Vaste comme la nuit et comme la clarté,
> Les parfums, les couleurs et les sons se répondent.
>
> Il est des parfums frais comme des chairs d'enfants,
> Doux comme les hautbois, verts comme les prairies,
> —Et d'autres, corrompus, riches et triomphants,
>
> Ayant l'expansion des choses infinies,
> Comme l'ambre, le musc, le benjoin et l'encens,
> Qui chantent les transports de l'esprit et des sens.

Whatever the type of imagery may be, it presents, as Ezra Pound has said, "an intellectual and emotional complex in an instant of time," for as we have seen, the image both represents something else and re-presents itself as a significant entity. Even the details of the setting of a poem may be more

than presentational; they may be representational, as in the
case of the stormy heath which, in *King Lear,* corresponds to
the state of mind of Lear himself. This technique of having
nature act in sympathy with a character's (or the poet's) mood
is what Ruskin termed "the pathetic fallacy." It is exemplified by the willows which weep for Ophelia in Rimbaud's
poem "Ophélie." As John Ciardi says in *How Does a Poem
Mean?,*[1] "Like words, images possess both denotation and connotation: they denote certain sensory (usually visual) iden-
tifications and they connote an emotional aura. Like words,
therefore, images in a poem tend to fall into overtone themes
united by either their denotations or their connotations." Thus
all images referring to a Provençal landscape are denotatively
linked, and when used together they establish what we may
call the Provençal-landscape motif. Through their connotations, images give rise to an emotional atmosphere, and all
images which (for example) suggest morbidity are connotatively related. Thus, the atmosphere of Baudelaire's first
"Spleen" is produced by the connotative associations attached
to such words as *Pluviôse, froid, ténébreux, pâles, cimetière,
brumeux, triste, frileux, sinistrement,* etc.:

> Pluviôse, irrité contre la ville entière,
> De son urne à grands flots verse un froid ténébreux
> Aux pâles habitants du voisin cimetière
> Et la mortalité sur les faubourgs brumeux.
>
> Mon chat sur le carreau cherchant une litière
> Agite sans repos son corps maigre et galeux;
> L'âme d'un vieux poète erre dans la gouttière
> Avec la triste voix d'un fantôme frileux.

---

[1] (Boston: Houghton Mifflin Company, 1960), p. 865. Many thoughts
expressed by Mr. Ciardi in his Chapter Six, "The Image and the Poem," are
so equally applicable to French poetry that it would have been impossible
to avoid paraphrasing or quoting them in this chapter. Though such borrowings are acknowledged in detail as they occur, the pervasive influence of
Mr. Ciardi's treatment of the subject has left its mark here in a general way
that must be gratefully recognized at this time.

Le bourdon se lamente, et la bûche enfumée
Accompagne en fausset la pendule enrhumée,
Cependant qu'en un jeu plein de sales parfums,

Héritage fatal d'une vieille hydropique,
Le beau valet de cœur et la dame de pique
Causent sinistrement de leurs amours défunts.

The possible scope of poetic imagery is enormous. Every concrete element of a poem, every name which (like *Pluviôse*) evokes a sensory impression, is an image. And from this level the types of imagery range out to include metaphors and metonymies, symbols, archetypes, and myths. All of these categories normally have two features in common: they produce concrete sensory impressions (as opposed to intellectual abstractions), and they involve "figuration" or "tropology." These terms refer to the method of oblique expression in which A is partly compared to B in such a way that our attention is called to connotations of A that would not otherwise be obvious. When I say that my love is like a rose, I am directing the reader's attention to the beauty and freshness of my love.

It can be said that there are two basic kinds of images, which in turn create two fundamental types of poetry. These two classes are distinguished by the manner in which items are compared; the first class is metonymy, the second metaphor.

"Metonymy," literally "name-changing," is the figure which results when the poet, instead of employing the term that directly fits the object he is describing, uses a logically or physically *related* term instead. Thus he may substitute the container for the contained, the cause for the effect, the sign for the thing signified, the possessor for the thing possessed, the abstract for the concrete word, the adjective for the noun it modifies; or he may employ the converse of any of these relationships. Examples are "the briny deep" (adjective, "deep," for noun, "sea"), "twenty greybeards," (part, "grey beard," for whole, "old man"), "Drink a cup!" (container, "cup," for thing contained, "tea" or "coffee"), etc. It should be noted that in metonymy the substitution of terms is based on a constant but unequal relationship between the two things signified. This relationship is logically or quantitatively analyzable. Metonymies may thus be described as figures of contiguity, since the association occurs within a single frame of discourse. A particular type of metonymy is called "synecdoche," the figure in which the relationship between compared objects is *internal*, e.g., the greater for the smaller, the part for the whole, the genus for the species, the material to represent the use to which it is to be put or the object made from it, or the converse of any of these. Several examples occur in the following lines by Racine (from *La Thébaïde*, Act I):

> Thèbes doit-elle moins redouter sa puissance,
> Après avoir six mois senti sa *violence?*
> Voudrait-elle obéir à ce prince inhumain,
> Qui vient d'armer contre elle et *le fer* et *la faim?*

The word *violence* represents the cause of which Thebes felt the effect. What the prince armed against her were not *iron* and *hunger* but people who were hungry and men with swords made from iron. The word *fer* as a substitute for "sword" was so dead a metonymy in the seventeenth century that Racine felt no hesitation about using the term *fer* for "swordsmen," thereby creating a double metonymy. It is obviously the swordsmen whom the prince arms, not the sword, much less the iron.

Kenneth Burke, in *The Philosophy of Literary Form*,[2] notes that in so far as any poem has surrealist content, i.e., to the extent that the text reproduces the raw materials of the unconscious mind as expressed in dream, this content is potentially subject to Freudian analysis. And Burke suggests that the two general categories for the analysis of the poem as "dream" are Freud's "condensation" and "displacement." "Condensation" is the coalescing of two or more images into

[2] (New York: Vintage Books, 1957), pp. 237–240.

a single image made up of parts of the original components. This condensed image, as Burke says, is synecdochic of the total original cluster. In the case of "displacement," the significance of one image is transferred to another image. Both of these processes are subject to logical analysis (though the results of the transfers themselves break the laws of logic); hence they are kinds of metonymy. In Freudian displacement, if a certain house becomes an image connoting terror, and the house is green, another object may displace the house and become a symbol of terror, simply because the other object is also green. In a sense, greenness becomes the symbol of fear. But by condensation it may be that, if the green object that displaces the house is a green automobile, what will cause fright will be the car's headlights (which are also lit windows in the green house). A literary example is to be found in these lines from Gérard de Nerval's "Artémis":

> Sainte napolitaine aux mains pleines de feux,
> Rose au cœur violet, fleur de sainte Gudule,
> As-tu trouvé ta croix dans le désert des cieux?

Here we have a case of condensation in line one, where an Italian sorceress who appeared as a character in Nerval's *Octavie* is associated with a statue of Saint Rosalie which the poet saw in the sorceress' house. In the phrase "sainte napolitaine" the two images are condensed. Displacement appears in line two, where Saint Rosalie, who was "crowned with violet roses," becomes momentarily the rose window in the Cathedral of Saint Gudule in Brussels, and the meaning originally attached to the condensed "sainte napolitaine" is displaced to the "flower of Saint Gudule."

The other basic type of image is the "metaphor," which consists of the substitution of one word for another, as in metonymy, the substitution being based in this case on an essential point of similarity or equality between characteristics of two items which *otherwise* are fundamentally different. "My love is a rose" is a metaphor. My love and the rose share a point of similarity (freshness, beauty), but they are otherwise quite unrelated. My love is not a plant, nor does she have thorns or green leaves, nor is she (we trust) bright red. Rather than association by contiguity within a single frame of reference, as in metonymy, we have here association by comparison, which joins a multiplicity of worlds.

The distinction between metaphor and simile is purely grammatical. Simile explicitly states that a comparison is being made, by the use of the words *like* or *as* (in French *comme* or *pareil à*, etc.). "My luve is like a red, red rose" is a simile, a direct comparison. (The French word for "simile" is *comparaison*.) If the word "like" is suppressed the simile becomes a metaphor, an indirect comparison. There is therefore no fundamental difference between simile and metaphor. When Rimbaud writes:

> Sur l'onde calme et noire où dorment les étoiles
> La blanche Ophélie flotte comme un grand lys . . . . ,

the word *dorment* in line one is metaphorical, whereas line two contains a simile.

Sometimes metonymy and metaphor are hard to distinguish. If there is logic or quantity naturally involved in the association of the two compared items the figure is metonymy, otherwise metaphor. The difficulty of differentiating the two often arises in the case of the use of a transferred epithet. A "transferred epithet" is an adjective that is applied to a noun to which it does not properly belong, since it really refers to another (usually unexpressed) noun. Thus if I say that I am playing a nostalgic song on the piano, I really mean that the song makes *me* nostalgic. I have used the word "nostalgic" to modify the song which arouses the emotion, not the person in whom the song has caused the effect. This is metonymy, the substitution of cause for effect. But if I say that I am playing a dreaming sonata, I may mean this same thing, and thus be using metonymy, or just possibly I am in effect *personifying* the sonata which, according to my image, is itself doing the dreaming. Then I have compared the sonata to a person who dreams—and that is metaphor.

As a glance at any poem will readily show, metaphor and metonymy are the very stuff of which poetry is made, metaphor being at present the more commonly encountered of the two devices. In metaphor it is usually the connotations which are shared between the two compared items; the denotations normally have nothing directly to do with each other, as can be seen from the case of my love and the rose.

If the poet forgets to maintain his metaphor and falls back upon the actual object being compared while talking in terms of the other object to which it is being compared he has perpetrated an incomplete metaphor. If, for example, I say that my love is a rose, and then describe the rose in terms that apply also to my love (as when I warn that its beauty will fade with time and that its petals will lose their color), I am on solid metaphorical ground. But if I speak of the rose's cheeks turning pale, I have failed to complete the metaphor, or else I have indulged in "catachresis," i.e., a strained figure in which I compare (ineptly) the rose's petals to cheeks. The term "catachresis" is used of any strained or tortured comparison, particularly the metaphorical substitution of one material thing for another, as cheeks for petals.

A mixed (as opposed to incomplete) metaphor occurs when the poet compares an act or an object with more than one other act or object at a time; for example, "The fires of my passion will melt away unless my love unlocks the burden of her heart to me." Fires do not melt away, and one does not unlock a burden.

When a metaphor has been overused it dies, of course. The true, live metaphor exists in its own right as well as for purposes of representation. When I describe a rose in terms that fit my love, I am presenting a rose which is an image in itself, apart from the fact that it also tells us something about my love. The metaphor stands in front of the thing it represents and means both itself and what it stands for. But dead metaphors, clichés, have no vitality of their own. Like zombies, they are active but lifeless. They make no impact upon the senses, being mere signs pointing to a concept. When someone says "Time flies," we do not visualize a beating of wings. It is often difficult, especially for a foreigner, to distinguish metaphors common to a generation or a school from brand-new live ones. Frequently, until we know a language well, we cannot tell whether what we are reading is an effective metaphor or a banality. To us it will be new and effective; to the more experienced reader in the language it will be a hackneyed, worn-out comparison that passes unnoticed. Thus, the novice might at first be struck by the "irons" and "flames" of which a seventeenth-century lover constantly boasts, but of course *fers* (meaning amatory "bonds") and *feux* (meaning "passion") were such trite expressions at that time that the word "amour" itself might almost have seemed more original.

It should be remembered that practically all words began either as metaphors or as onomatopoeias.[3] Language is built on metaphors, and it is thanks to them and to onomatopoeias that new terms can be coined. This is why etymology can be so fascinating: it brings long-dead metaphors back to life. The more we read in a foreign language, the more readily we will distinguish the live, vivid metaphor from the defunct one which is a mere token for a thought.

"Allegory" is essentially nothing more than extended metaphor in which ideas, feelings, moral, spiritual, or intellectual qualities or abstractions are personified (i.e., addressed as though they were persons). Any deliberate, prolonged, systematic use of people, animals, or inanimate objects to represent such qualities or abstractions (as exemplified by the constant recurrence of the fox as a personification of slyness) marks a case in which metaphor has been turned into allegory. *Le Roman de la rose* is the most famous example of the genre in French, as is *The Faerie Queene* in English.

[3] John Ciardi, *op. cit.*, p. 766.

A "symbol" may be described as a metaphor with the first term missing; e.g., if I refer repeatedly to roses in a certain way you may decide that the rose symbolizes my love, even though I neglect to say so. An image may be invoked once as a metaphor, but if it recurs persistently, both as a presentation (something significant in its own right) and as a representation (as a surrogate for something else), it becomes a symbol, perhaps even a part of a symbolic, allegorical, or mythical system. As Mr. Ciardi has noted, the persistent or recurring image which we call a symbol tends in general to stand for a wider area of meaning or experience than a simple metaphor can represent. A symbol is more conceptual (as in allegory); a metaphor is more sensory.[4] For this reason, a symbol need not necessarily be an image: "three," an abstraction, can function symbolically. Symbols usually have many referents, many meanings, each a little further away from the most central one, but all significant. For this reason it is unwise to attempt to place precisely or to list exhaustively all of a symbol's referents. The more a symbol is used, the more emotional expansion and intensity it is likely to have. Symbols often represent ambivalent meanings, equivocal possibilities of interpretation which are in conflict with one another. In short, a symbol is likely to be highly ambiguous. In Mallarmé's poetry, for example, *white* tends to represent sterility and *azure* usually stands for the ideal, but both colors occur here and there with other or richer meanings. As Mr. Ciardi has written,[5] symbols may be either specific devices introduced for the purpose (such as the swan representing primarily the poet in "Le vierge, le vivace et le bel aujourd'hui"), or they may be areas in which the writer remains deliberately vague in order to suggest some larger possible meaning that might not occur to the reader if the text were too precise and detailed. As Baudelaire seems to hint in "Correspondances," when we encounter "de confuses

[4] Ciardi, *op. cit.*, p. 866.
[5] *Op. cit.*, p. 711.

paroles" we may be on the edge of "des forêts de symboles."

Symbols may be parts of larger organizations of meaning called myths. Myths are narratives (as opposed to symbols, which are usually single objects or acts); indeed, the Greek word *mythos* essentially meant a "plot," or a "story." What distinguishes the mythical plot or story is its universal significance. A myth is a verbalization intended to dramatize directly or indirectly the most fundamental human concerns, and mythologies are therefore often theologically oriented. This need not be the case, however; political or cultural myths also occur in all civilizations. In so far as myth is rooted in theology it is connected with ritual. Rituals are dramatic representations that correspond to mythical narratives much as a play may correspond to a novel. As a rule, a ritual will die out long before the related myth ceases to be effective. Because there are a finite number of possible situations in which man may find himself, even though the specific details may vary greatly from case to case, myths tend to have a great diversity of possible applications and an equal variety of potential interpretations. Thus the myth of Œdipus can be thought of as representing man's impotence in dealing with the blind forces of the universe, or, on the contrary, we may look upon it as a demonstration of man's heroic capacity to gain knowledge through perseverance and sheer will-power despite the destructive power of uncomprehending, irrational Fate. Similarly, the ambiguity which is so central to myth is responsible for the flexible way in which the Prometheus legend has been handled in literature at various times. Myths, in short, stand for such basic and elemental ideas, situations, and values that because of their very antiquity they are usually authorless, or at least so publicly verifiable that authorship is insignificant. Occasionally, however, poets seem to have created them, as Hugo may be said to have done in parts of *La Légende des siècles,* or Baudelaire in his poetry about the Metropolis.

When myths are thought of as *patterns* of plot or character which evoke a "racial memory," i.e., a primordial image or structure, they are called "archetypes." An archetype may have entirely new details but a prehistorically traditional *ordering* of details. Some critics believe that these archetypal patterns exist in the subconscious mind as described by Carl Jung and that they appear in the patterns of poems as part of the shape of their narrative. Many examples suggestive of this possibility can be found in *Les Fleurs du mal* of Baudelaire where, in a number of poems, we find the poet imagining himself as a denizen of cellars or caves, or even of submarine grottos, or else embarked on mysterious voyages that extend beyond time itself. And these are but a few instances among many.

There are various ways of treating a poet's imagery. It is often possible, for example, to learn a great deal about a writer by tabulating his images and classifying them according to their concrete, denotative characteristics and according to their connotative values. Sometimes a unity of connotation in apparently disparate images will reveal facts about the poet's mental processes of which he may have been totally unaware himself. It may even be discovered that a poet unconsciously associates images that seem to have only tenuous denotative or connotative connections with each other, as Shakespeare has been shown to have done with his personal cluster composed of "candy," "melting," "licking," and "dog." Images, metaphors and metonymies, symbols, and mythical or archetypal elements are frequently the most direct source of enlightenment for the reader who wishes to explore the varied meanings which are implicit in the structure of a poem.

9
Synthesis: Theme, Tone, and Attitude

We have discussed a number of elements, which when fused together create the structure of the poem, but we have so far treated these elements in isolation. It is now time to see how they operate in terms of one another, and for that purpose we must have a concrete example. In an earlier chapter the little poem by Charles Cros called "Hiéroglyphe" was used to illustrate consonance, and it may serve again to demonstrate the total interaction of the various phenomena that enter into the poetic structure. It should be borne in mind, however, that because of its brevity, "Hiéroglyphe" cannot represent adequately every kind of event that is likely to occur in poetry. Any poem that could even approach doing that would be so long and complex that it would be more likely to cloud than to clarify the general principles being stated. But "Hiéroglyphe" will suffice as a simple example of the way in which poems tend to be organized.

HIÉROGLYPHE

J'ai trois fenêtres à ma chambre:
    L'amour, la mer, la mort,
Sang vif, vert calme, violet.

O femme, doux et lourd trésor!

Froids vitraux, cloches, odeurs d'ambre,
    La mer, la mort, l'amour,
Ne sentir que ce qui me plaît . . .

Femme, plus claire que le jour!

Par ce soir doré de septembre,
    La mort, l'amour, la mer,
Me noyer dans l'oubli complet.

Femme! femme! cercueil de chair!

The various poetic elements we have been concerned with in Chapters Three to Eight have been shown to fill one of two roles: either they enhance the meaning inherent in other areas of the poetic structure, or else they impart meanings of their own. Furthermore, most of these elements seem capable of establishing independent structures, apart from their engagement in complex relationships with one another. Sounds, as exemplified in such poems as Rimbaud's "Tête de faune" or Verlaine's "Clair de lune," may form patterns which can be studied independently of other aspects of the text they help to compose, but these patterns are not in themselves meaningful. Their effect is to increase, enrich, and broaden the meanings already implied (though not always clearly) by the words of which the sounds are a part. At the same time, the sounds create euphonies that are pleasant to the ear.

In "Hiéroglyphe" there are no such elaborate patterns of sound as are to be found in the other two poems just alluded to. Nonetheless, we may note, apart from the consonance whose effect is so obvious at the first reading, the echoing in other parts of the text of the vowel sounds in the three words that compose the consonance: "l'amour," "la mer," "la mort." The *ou* sound is repeated in the words *doux, lourd, jour,* and *oubli;* the open *e* sound in *fenêtres, vert, violet, plaît, claire, septembre, complet, cercueil,* and *chair;* and the open *o* in *vio-let, trésor, cloches,* and *doré.* Indeed, were it not for the fact that the "O" of "O femme" is a closed *o* we would have a perfect tonal chiasmus in the *o-ou-ou-o* sequence of "*O* femme, d*ou*x et l*ou*rd trésor." There is also, in the third line, a euphonious alliteration in *v* reinforced by a dissonance in *f*: "Sang *vif, v*ert calme, *v*iolet."

In our discussion of sound phenomena in an earlier chapter we observed that repetitions of sounds may do more than create harmonious effects; when skillfully handled, they are also able to point up connotations that might not otherwise catch the attention of the reader or listener. We may well question, therefore, whether the threefold consonance of "Hiéroglyphe," three times repeated, is not intended to be more than merely euphonious. Even at first glance it seems to be closely related to the way in which the shape of the poem has been worked out. Looking at the lines, we see that they fall into three classes. The basic line, if we may so describe it, is the octosyllable in a three-line stanza. Half of the lines in the poem fit this description, *viz.,* the first and third of each tercet. At one remove from this is the six-syllable line in the middle of each tercet, and perhaps even more at variance with the norm are the octosyllabic lines that are detached, one of them following each tercet. Clearly these changes in line length or in relationship of the line to the stanza are not meaningless. When the octosyllabic flow is interrupted by a hexasyllable, our attention is called to the unusual line by the rhythmic change. The same reaction is occasioned by the pause which sets off the three detached lines from the tercets. What is more, the consonance in the first hexasyllabic line is unmistakable at first reading, and we can hardly miss the fact that all three six-syllable lines contain the same three words in a different order: "L'amour, la mer, la mort," then "La mer, la mort, l'amour," and finally "La mort, l'amour, la mer." At each return of the hexasyllable the component words shift one place to the left, the first word circling around to the right end of the line. Thus, if the poem had continued for another stanza we would have come back to the arrangement we began with in the first tercet. This has an interesting effect on the rime scheme, which is *axbx, ayby, azbz*. The poet has established a total unifying pattern for the poem by having the first lines of the three tercets rime with *each other* (*chambre-d'ambre-septembre*) and by doing the same with the last lines of the tercets (*violet-plaît-complet*). He has also associated each detached line with the stanza preceding it by having it rime with the six-syllable line of that stanza. Thus the individual tercets are held together from the interior—and are in effect turned into quatrains—by the rime which links what we might call the two "odd" lines (the short one and the detached one), while the tercets are also fastened to each other by the triple rime that binds their first and last lines in an unbroken chain running through the poem. The result of this tight arrangement is that the *x*, *y*, and *z* rimes seem to *develop* by changing from stanza to stanza, whereas the *a* and *b* rimes suggest permanence and stability by remaining the same throughout the poem. The developing rimes, furthermore, are introduced on their first appearance by the three repeated words: *la mort, l'amour,* and *la mer,* in the first, second, and third tercets respectively. This order corresponds to the arrangement of words in the hexasyllable of the final stanza, so that this line seems almost to echo the progressive introduction of the rime words. Consequently the final word (*la mer*) of the hexasyllable of the last tercet serves to close two cycles: the *x*, *y*, *z* rime scheme and the final (and only remaining possible) permutation of the three words of the consonance.

Thus the sounds in combination with the line lengths and stanzaic pattern have established a kind of independent structure of their own. But it is not the structure of the poem: it is not even *in itself* a meaningful structure. What we must determine is how this shape coöperates with other elements of the poem to suggest meanings. Clearly the shape suggests several possibilities. It calls attention to the revolving words of the six-syllable lines, the three words which are associated with each other through consonance and with certain other words in the poem by means of assonance while at the same time each of them in turn becomes a rime word linking the six-syllable line to the following detached octosyllable. Obviously these must be the key words of the poem. They appear to be particularly closely connected with the separate octosyllabic lines, not only because of the rime, but also because these detached lines are the other "odd" lines of the text: they, too, are particularly emphasized by *not* being part of the stanzas. We may properly look, therefore, to see what meaningful relationships with one another these lines—the hexasyllables and the detached octosyllables—are engaged in. We should also bear in mind the structural finality of the last hexasyllable which, as we saw, closes two cycles at once. That fact may turn out not to be accidental.

Having looked at sound and shape, our next step is to give thought to the matter of rhythm. Rhythms too can be diagrammed and shown to have a separate, independent structure. In "Hiéroglyphe" they do not appear to play a very important role, though it should be noted that the tonic accents seem to fall with uncanny regularity on the words that contain echoes of the vowel sounds in *la mer, l'amour,* and *la mort*. This is partly the case because three of the twelve words at the ends of lines rime with the key words of the hexasyllables, but another three rime words (*violet, plaît,* and *complet*) have the same open *e* as *la mer,* even though they do not rime with it. In the interior of the lines, furthermore, we find stresses falling on such words as *fenêtres, doux, lourd, cloches,* and *claire,* all containing the significant vowel sounds: open *e, ou,* and open *o*.

We must also note the effect of pace in the poem. The mere fact that the three six-syllable lines are shorter than all the others makes us slow them down so that their total duration will approximate that of the octosyllables. The process is greatly facilitated by the commas, which always tend to retard the rate at which one reads. The result in this case is that the three key words are emphasized, pronounced distinctly, and slightly separated from one another. To feel the effect, first read the two opening lines of the poem as Charles Cros wrote them, and then compare the effect brought about by the following slight alteration:

> J'ai trois fenêtres à ma chambre:
> L'amour et la mer et la mort.

Commas (or exclamation marks) are also responsible for the special emphasis placed on the word *femme* which occurs four times, always followed by punctuation. Here again, the *em* sound of *femme* echoes the identical *am* sound of "l'*am*our, la *m*er, la *m*ort." We may well plan to devote special attention to the word "femme" also, since the primary purpose of all of these "physical" elements which we have been discussing is to call attention to connotations that might not otherwise emerge from the denotations of the text.

Much the same function is normally performed by rhetorical devices, which often depend for their effect on rhythm and patterns of repeated sounds (as in the case of anaphora or chiasmus, for example). The simplicity and brevity of the text of "Hiéroglyphe" preclude the use of rhetorical figures apart from the three exclamations which help to set the detached octosyllables off from the more reflective tercets. Otherwise, the condensation of the poem is such that only the first tercet even contains a normal, complete sentence, the other two depending on the optative (wishful) sense of the infinitive for their syntactical coherence.

Just as the words of the poem, which have both denotative and connotative significance, may have their connotations enhanced by the effects of sound, rhythm, pace, and rhetorical constructions; so the images, metaphors, metonymies, symbols, and even mythical narratives which the combinations of words create have both denotative and connotative significance, and all of the other poetic elements help to enlarge the number and add to the richness of these connotations. Thus the total structure of which all the elements are a part (and which is the poem itself) is meaningful, and the meaning is especially to be found in the connotations which the structure imparts.

As the title indicates, "Hiéroglyphe" is intended to be somewhat mysterious, and the obscurity is largely caused by the density and ambiguity of its symbols. In the very first line the poet says that he has *three* windows in his room, and the number three permeates the poem. There are three key words in the three hexasyllables, each word being repeated three times in the poem; there are three stanzas of three lines each, and three isolated octosyllables. There are also three developing rimes. Line 3 is a list of three colors, and line 5 contains three sensory images. That three has symbolic significance seems quite obvious. The poet, then, has three "windows" in his "room," and the colon at the end of line 1 implies that he will define them. He does—twice. First directly: "Love, the sea, death"; then in what we must suppose to be analogical terms, i.e., by means of images which are connotatively linked to the three concepts already mentioned: "bright blood, calm green, violet." Here a quasi-synesthetic association appears to be suggested between the three colors and the respective key words of the preceding six-syllable line. Next, after a pause, the woman is evoked: "soft and heavy treasure." Owing to the ambiguity of the word *femme*, the "woman" may in fact be a "wife." The biographical critic would leap to his reference works at this point in order to check on the marital status of M. Cros. The results of this research, of course, would have little if any bearing on the poem. Charles Cros, as far as the text is concerned, is a myth in the sense that there is no reason to suppose that if *femme* here means "wife" it therefore specifically means Mme Charles Cros.

The order of presentation in the next tercet is reversed: the connotatively linked images precede the key words instead of following them. This time the inventory lists cold stained-glass windows, a tactile-visual image for the sea; bells, an auditive image—suggestive, perhaps, of a tolling knell—for death; and odors of amber, an olfactory image associated with love. The verb *sentir* in the closing line of the tercet is also ambiguous; because of "odeurs d'ambre," the idea of "smell" presents itself immediately, but "feel" is the more plausible interpretation if it is necessary to choose. The point is that it is *not* necessary to choose. Both meanings may be operating at once.

In the last tercet the motif of death is ubiquitous. We are presented first with an allusion to autumn and to the evening, the times of death of the year and of the day. Then comes the consonance, with the word "death" in first place, followed by the expressed wish to *drown* in complete oblivion. And the woman returns for the third time, now as a "coffin of flesh." We see then that the special finality we decided to look for in the last four lines (because several cycles of physical developments in the text were concluded there so resoundingly) is indeed present. The last four lines have as their motif the ultimate finality, death itself.

The unity of these lines may suggest less obvious parallels in the two preceding groups of four. We saw that "death" was the first word of the last hexasyllable, and we know that the words of the hexasyllabic lines revolve. Perhaps, then, the first words of the other two hexasyllables establish the basic motifs that tie together the phrases in the two groups of four associated lines. Thus *l'amour* would provoke the exclamation, "O femme, doux et lourd trésor!" *La mer*, in turn, would be associated with "Femme, plus claire que le jour." As we predicted from our study of the physical properties of the poem, the word *femme* would thus be related to all three words of the consonance: *l'amour, la mort,* and *la mer*. The poet's chamber would have universal connotations: its three "windows," opening into the external, would reveal three aspects of Woman: love, the sea, and death.

It is understood, of course, that much of what we have been detailing would be felt on the first reading, at least vaguely. The first reading itself would indicate that the "physical" characteristics of the poem were particularly important and suggestive. What we are doing here is corroborating by inspection what we would first become aware of almost intuitively.

We have touched on all of the elements discussed in Chapters Three to Eight except diction, the poet's choice of words, especially key words. The connection between "woman" and "love" need hardly be insisted upon. The "sea," so often a symbol for the womb according to the psychoanalysts, is *la mer,* and the paronomasia it forms with *la mère* is even more obvious than the association between *claire* and *chair* suggested by the internal rime. The alliance between "woman" and "death," as reflected in such expressions as "femme fatale," is probably older than history. Furthermore, the three words of the hexasyllables are intricately interwoven with each other in a connotative manner. Not only do they represent the three great, traditional themes of lyric poetry (love, death, and nature), but death has often been associated with the act of love, as well as with the sea ("me *noyer* dans l'oubli complet"); the sea, apart from its archetypal association with the womb, is thought to be the place of origin of all life, as love is the specific source of individual lives, and death is life's end; and the sea is the supreme emblem of nature, its mightiest element, as love and death are two of its most obvious manifestations.

Thus we see that the connotations of the words and images (many of which are undoubtedly classifiable as symbols, since they are vaguer and broader than metaphors) are related to each other. They are also emphasized by the "physical" elements of the poem, which suggest affinities between them. These connotations are also representative of emotions and attitudes. Indeed, the total structure of any poem's implied meanings, or connotations, may be thought of as a structure of attitudes. The poem has a subject—which in the case of "Hiéroglyphe" is presumably "Woman, seen in relation to love, nature, and death"—and we may use the word "attitude" to refer to the way the poet looks upon this subject. At the same time, every poem has a "tone" which, as Robert Frost has said, represents the way "the poet takes himself"; we might express it another way and say that it suggests the way the poet wants the reader to take him.

The poet's attitude, which some critics call his mood, can range, for example, from awe-inspired through sympathetic, amused or patronizing to satirical or disgusted. The tone of the poem, on the other hand, may be wheedling, persuasive, accusing, scolding, or self-pitying. The tone and attitude of a poem will often correspond to one another, as when the poet admires his subject in a tone that invites us to do the same; on the other hand, he may present an admiring attitude while at the same time reprimanding the reader for *not* adopting the same stance. In any case, it is the poet's attitude that should concern us, not the subject that evokes it. The fact that Baudelaire wrote a poem about a putrefying carcass did not make the poem a success or a failure; it was Baudelaire's attitude towards his subject that determined the poem's value. The degree of technical perfection in the poem is also of secondary importance to its value as a poem. Occasional flaws are found in great poetry, and impeccable technique is sometimes present in poems that are clearly bad. Unless the poem is a tissue of blotches and blunders (in which case, as John Ciardi puts it, the poet has betrayed "an incompetent attitude toward the poem"),[1] the real test of its success will be our willingness to accept the poet's attitude.

In reality, what we are calling the poet's attitude is the poet's *attitudes*. Rarely will his stand remain consistent throughout the poem. Every paradox, antithesis, or ambiguity of any sort will suggest a multiplicity of potential attitudes; an adumbrated, implicit, or expressed point of indecision; a possibility that there may be various reactions to the subject of the poem.

The poem, then, expresses opposed attitudes, and these do

[1] *How Does a Poem Mean?* (Boston: Houghton Mifflin Company, 1960), p. 847.

not cancel each other out. Rather than being allowed to melt into a homogeneous state of compromise, they are kept separate, but in architectural harmony with one another. They are indeed unified, but not blended, for the unity of the poem is precisely that of the structure of tensions which is composed of these separate, conflicting attitudes. The point of analysis is to detect these tensions and to determine how they are produced and balanced. It is the attitudes in conflict that disclose the structure of the poem.

In the case of "Hiéroglyphe," we observe a progression of changes in tone and attitude from part to part, the development paralleling the succession of motifs suggested by the three words: *l'amour, la mer, la mort.* In order to describe these stages with any degree of precision, we would have to have determined what, for us, are the significant connotative overtones of the symbols in the poem. This we have not done. What we have said about "Hiéroglyphe" constitutes an almost mechanical description of certain dispositions of elements in the text, and this description may help us to see what images are particularly meaningful and how they are related to one another "physically"; but we have not attempted to locate the various specific connotations implied by the symbols, nor have we even tried to describe their resonances in a general way. In short, what we have said could have been set forth in much the same terms by anyone who took the trouble to look closely at the text. From this point on, insight, personal feelings, and extraliterary knowledge relevant to the significance of the symbols would have to intervene, and here we might find much variance in interpretation. The essential point to remember is that all of these insights and feelings might be "correct," "valid," i.e., in conformity with the text of the poem. The amount of possible variety in intelligent and perceptive reactions to the poem is often an index of its richness.

Let us note, simply, that the tone of the first four lines is essentially calm and informative, except for the exclamation in line 4. There is a domestic feeling provoked by the words *chambre* and *calme* and by the emphasis on the motif of love. The attitude toward *la femme* is already ambiguous, however; she is a treasure which is both *doux* and *lourd*. Heaviness, in the case of treasure, may be a sign of great value, but it also suggests a great burden. Many further possible implications about the complexity of love may be adumbrated by the symbols in these lines, notably the colors; but let us move on to the next group of four lines. Here a chill seems to descend, a sea-air comes in, and the tone is distinctly less suggestive of security. Line 7 could be felt to be regretful, or wishful, or even hopeful. The ambiguity of the infinitive is far more complex than the mere question of its two possible denotations indicates. The woman, "fairer than the day," is associated with the sea which, in turn, is related to cold stained glass. An expanded, less domestic sense of the significance of Woman seems to emerge. The last four lines are, as we have seen, final in a multiplicity of ways. The attitude is that of renunciation; the tone perhaps close to desperation. But, as usual, the attitude is complex. The poet seems to wish for death, the sleep of love perhaps, a total forgetfulness in any case. The death-wish is in itself paradoxical, and we may question whether the final line represents approbation and appreciation, or renunciation and despair—or both and much more besides.

The theme of a poem is to the notion of connotation what the subject is to that of denotation. The multivalences of the connotations of the poem imply different attitudes toward the subject. The "theme" is the general tenor of the over-all structure of opposed attitudes held in suspension. These attitudes have relevance beyond that of the specific, concrete subject (denotative meaning) of the poem. They constitute the total connotative meaning, a generalization of the subject concerning which attitudes are expressed. This larger intent grows out of the equilibrium of attitudes and is often revealed by symbols, archetypes, and mythical narrative structures. It is more abstract, more general than the specific subject of the poem from which it grows by implication. Thus, specific symbolic elements mean more than themselves, and correspondingly the poem as a whole means more than what it literally says. Since it is in the nature of poetry to be concrete, the general, more abstract theme is rarely stated except in the case of such didactic poetry as the allegory or the fable, where the "moral" may be added separately, sometimes to the detriment of the poem.

The theme of "Hiéroglyphe" could not be expressed in a few words, since to do so would involve omitting many possible rich implications of the text. Clearly, the notion of "Woman as seen by Man in the context of Love, Sea, and Death" has such elaborate ramifications that one could develop the inferences *ad infinitum.* Suffice it to say that the structure of this short poem is far more complicated than one might imagine at the first casual reading.

The word "theme" as generally used in literary criticism is ambiguous, as we might almost have expected after our experience of terms like "dissonance," "genre," "prose," and "poetry." In addition to the meaning we have just given to "theme," critics also tend to accord it a quite different sense. They use it to refer to types of character, verbal patterns, or kinds of situation that recur regularly in literature, art, and folklore, such as the sad clown, the *carpe diem* refrain, or the "Quest" plot. A better term for these recurring phenomena is "motif," which avoids confusing them with the connotational meaning of a poem as a whole.

Another ambiguous word is "mood," which may refer to the poet's attitude toward his subject or toward himself, or else to the atmosphere of the poem, the feeling engendered by the totality of the work. "Atmosphere" is here the safer, less ambiguous term. Setting and background, as well as rhythm and imagery, contribute to the establishment of the general, pervasive feeling we call atmosphere.

Theme, subject, tone, attitude, and atmosphere are far more difficult to generalize about than are the phenomena of sound, shape, imagery, diction, and rhythm, since the former depend so much upon the individuality of the particular poem. There are, as we saw when we spoke of genre, many ways of presenting a subject, each with its tendency to suggest a given tone or attitude or atmosphere. One can, of course, say that "The themes of serious poetry tend to center on the most basic concerns of Man: life and death, love, nature, etc." But this is essentially reducible to the tautological observation that serious poetry tends to be serious.

Though "Hiéroglyphe" is hardly a spectacular case in point, it should be recognized that even poems which are not specifically dramatic are likely to present some of the same elements that occur in overtly dramatic poetry, *viz.*, a speaker who reacts to a situation, a scene, or an idea; other characters, including the foils whose principal purpose is to give the major characters an opportunity to reveal more about themselves; a scene in which the events take place; episodes leading to a climax or (disastrously) an anticlimax; and an exposition to provide the reader with the information necessary for an understanding of the situation. In other words, the vocabulary of dramatic criticism is often applicable to poetry, most obviously to dramatic or narrative poetry, but often equally (if more subtly) to lyric poetry.

Different kinds of poems obviously call for different kinds of analysis. Recognizing the most relevant, crucial elements in the structure of the poem, determining how they give focus or intensity to its expressed or implied attitudes, and discerning how these attitudes achieve an equilibrium which gives a unified structure to the poem—all of these discoveries require perceptions, feeling, and insight. One reading will not suffice, though with practice even first readings will become sharper and will bear richer fruit. But it is always the rereading after the analysis that matters. (We might now reread "Hiéroglyphe" to see whether it has become more meaningful to us as a result of the analysis to which we have subjected it.) The point of analysis, we must never forget, is not to serve as an end in itself; it is merely a middle step between two kinds of readings, both of which are done for the sake of the poem.

10
Extraliterary Techniques

In the first part of this book we developed the idea that the analysis of poetry does not require it to be divorced from all extraliterary influences. It was agreed that the poem itself is central, and that it should be read and studied as a self-contained, coherent literary structure. The mere avoidance of the tendency to look upon poems as being essentially part of the subject matter of psychology, or history, or economics was not, however, meant to suggest that techniques borrowed from these disciplines could not be validly adopted as tools of literary method and applied to poetry. Indeed, to treat the poem in complete isolation would be absurd if it were not impossible. Even in this second part of the book, where our concern has been primarily with the organization of the poetic structure, we have found ourselves discussing in connection with imagery such psychoanalytic matters as Jungian arche-types and Freudian displacement and condensation. Thus we have implied that any accurate knowledge of psychology possessed by a reader might be put to profitable use in the inter-pretation of a text. The same implication extends to other areas of learning, as can be inferred from the performance of most modern critics when they confront a poem. Stanley

Edgar Hyman[1] has expressed it this way: "What modern criticism is could be defined crudely and somewhat inaccurately as *the organized use of non-literary techniques and bodies of knowledge to obtain insights into literature.*" (His italics.)

It has been assumed in the course of all that has been said here about the theory and criticism of poetry that the reader is not a professional critic or scholar of French literature, though he may be on his way to becoming one. Since it would be unreasonable to abandon that assumption now, it would be inappropriate to include in this chapter a complete discussion of the various techniques applied to poetry by full-time laborers in the literary vineyard. As we have seen, however, a certain amount of information of a non-literary kind often proves to be very helpful to the reader who has it and is willing to use it. Even though the non-professional student can hardly be expected to engage in research in such areas as anthropology, psychoanalysis, linguistics, esthetics, or Marxism for the express purpose of reading poetry, many non-specialists are familiar with Frazer's *The Golden Bough*, certain writings of Freud and Jung, and some of the principles of contemporary sociology. All such information, whether acquired as a result of formal education, general reading, or even professional experience, can often be turned onto a poem with very fruitful results, provided that the principle of the poem's centrality is constantly observed. When annotated editions of texts are used, a certain amount of the background work will already have been done for the reader, and still more insight can often be gained by consulting the better critics, who have a full arsenal of methodological weapons to turn on the poem. Otherwise, the more general reader has only to use what lights he has at his disposal, secure in the knowledge that the brighter they are, the further he will see.

Without attempting to be exhaustive, we may still provide

[1] *The Armed Vision: A Study in the Methods of Modern Literary Criticism* (2nd edition; New York: Vintage Books, 1955), p. 3.

a few examples here of ways in which critics can apply non-literary techniques and knowledge to the study of poetry, if only to give a hint of the variety of methods that one may find in their books and articles. It is possible to divide these methods into two categories, the first including those techniques or frames of reference that have their source in some intellectual discipline that is essentially non-historical in nature, and the second comprising the historically oriented approaches to poetry. Perhaps the most important of the non-historical bodies of knowledge that are sometimes brought to bear on literary works (including poetry) are linguistics, psychology, philosophy, anthropology, and sociology.

The first of these disciplines, linguistics, is capable of being applied in many ways to criticism; some of the most recently developed techniques involve the "programming" of electronic computors which can "remember" vast amounts of information about the kinds of syntax, imagery, diction, and rhythm that have been used by a given poet. When linguists supply a calculator with a large amount of information of this kind, the machine may be able to judge whether or not a given poem was in fact written by the author to whom it has been attributed. It does this by comparing the style of the poem with the style used by the poet in works that he unquestionably wrote. Linguistics provides the methods by which the language of the poet is reduced to the kind of unit the computor can "absorb" and manipulate for purposes of making comparisons.

On the level of textual analysis, the branch of linguistics called phonetics makes possible the detailed analysis of the sound texture of a poem by reducing the sounds to their distinguishing characteristics. Thus, if we classify the sounds of Mallarmé's sonnet "Le Vierge, le vivace et le bel aujourd'hui" according to their basic characteristics, we discover that the poem contains an extraordinary number of fricative consonants (i.e., consonant sounds, such as *f, v, s,* and *z,* which are produced through a greatly narrowed but not altogether closed oral passage) and front vowels (i.e., vowels articulated far forward in the mouth). This fact may help to explain more clearly why the poem seems to have a highly unified texture when read aloud.

We saw in Chapter Eight some applications of Freudian psychological concepts to poetry; the theories of other schools, such as Gestalt psychology or Jungian psychology, have also been used in literary criticism. It might, for example, be possible to shed light on a good deal of the poetry in Baudelaire's *Fleurs du mal* if one believed, as some critics do, that he anticipated Jung's theory of the collective unconscious. This approach could help to elucidate many poems (e.g., "La Vie antérieure" or the second "Spleen," which begins with the suggestive line: "J'ai plus de souvenirs que si j'avais mille ans") not to mention Baudelaire's distinction between ordinary dreams and what he called "grands rêves," which would, according to this theory, represent respectively the purely personal as opposed to the archetypal dream. Of course, when psychology is handled principally in terms of the *author's* psyche it becomes an aspect of biography and thus begins to shade off into the historical category (critical biography being essentially historical in nature).

Philosophy has contributed many criteria applicable to the ideological aspect of literary criticism. Aristotle's *Poetics* has always been a major source of dramatic theory and has often been applied to French classical tragedy; Platonism, sometimes considerably colored by Christian mysticism, has been influential, directly and indirectly, in various periods of French poetry, but most especially in the Renaissance where we find it (for example) in the poetry of Maurice Scève and the members of the school called the *Pléiade*. Philosophical criteria ranging from Kantian categories to existentialist postulates can be and have been applied to poems; whatever the theme of the poem may be, it is always possible to consider it in terms of some larger framework of philosophical thought.

Anthropology is usually related to literature in terms of folkloric, or primitive ritualistic, or even archetypal concepts, the central notion being that certain fundamental beliefs, rhythms, or ritual gestures of primitive man still find expression in advanced civilizations "disguised" in the form of works of art. Thus the structure of a poem may correspond to the structure of a myth or a ritual that anthropologists regard as naturally common to all men, perhaps because it appears in civilizations that are not known ever to have been in contact with one another. Frazer's *The Golden Bough,* a major source of early information about such myths and rituals, is still quite useful, and Chrétien de Troyes' romances illustrate many legends that can be traced back to very primitive sources.

Perhaps the most widely known socio-economic approach to literature is Marxist criticism, which tends to see literature as just one more factor in an entirely materialistic universe. Literature is thought of by the Marxist critic as a symptom of social change, a reflection of events in the economic world, or even a manifestation of revolutionary or counter-revolutionary political developments. It might be argued, for example, that Victor Hugo's *Ruy Blas,* with its theme of the valet who falls in love with a queen ("ver de terre amoureux d'une étoile") testifies to the progress made by the French Revolution over the strictly hierarchized society of which a much earlier representation would be found in the tragedies of Corneille and Racine; certainly in those plays a proletarian hero in love with a queen would be hard to imagine. Other uses to which sociological and economic knowledge can be put in literary criticism tend to be more useful to the criticism of literature itself, but they are inclined to merge with the historical approach to criticism.

From the examples just given it can be seen that there is no end to the variety of ways in which non-historical bodies of knowledge can be made to contribute to the criticisms of a poem. They may, as in the case of the example involving phonetics, make our analysis of the text more complete, or they may help us to relate the matter of the poem to relevant external data. It will perhaps have been noticed that in the course of our analysis of "Hiéroglyphe" in the preceding chapter, though our principal concern was with technical matters, we nonetheless became involved with such extraliterary areas as psychology (in connection with the archetypal association between sea and womb and with the death-wish implicit in the closing lines), and even our study of images and sounds was on a limited scale a study in linguistics and phonetics.

In general, however, the application of extraliterary knowledge and techniques to a poem is intended to situate the poem within a larger, usually historical framework. Literary scholarship, as distinguished from literary criticism, is very largely (though not exclusively) oriented towards history. Obviously, our understanding of a poem can be deepened and our feeling for it can be enriched by the fruits of scholarly research and, indeed, of historical knowledge in general. There is really no conflict between our thinking of the poem as a structure of connotations that must be inspected analytically to be fully understood and our placing that structure in its historical context. It is exclusive devotion to either of these enterprises in isolation from the other that is almost certain to diminish our appreciation and falsify our understanding of the poem. No amount of biographical information about, for example, Gérard de Nerval will suffice to tell us about the essential structure of "El Desdichado," but on the other hand, no amount of analysis of "El Desdichado" performed in a complete historical vacuum could fully explain the meaning of various important elements of the poem's structure. For example, the famous opening lines,

> Je suis le ténébreux, —le veuf, —l'inconsolé,
> Le prince d'Aquitaine à la tour abolie . . . ,

gain in richness if we know that Gérard Labrunie (which was the poet's real name) thought that he was the descendant of a noble family whose armorial bearings consisted of "three towers argent." Thus the family "tower" was, indeed, "abolished" by the French Revolution. (Marxist critics take note.) But while knowing this fact helps us to see better some relevant connotations of the poem, if we assume that having thus "placed" the words *tour* and *abolie* we have thereby "explained" them, we are sadly mistaken. Within the structure of the poem itself they develop other meanings that are relevant not to Gérard de Nerval alone but to a much broader and more universal theme. The symbolic meanings of these two words go far beyond the contexts of the Labrunie family and of the Revolution. So we can see that analysis without historical knowledge can be as limiting to our view when applied to a poem as scholarship without criticism. A scholar need not be a critic—his work may be valuable for other reasons or may constitute a prelude to criticism by someone else; but no critic can safely avoid being a scholar and, as such, an historian. It is because the uses of historical knowledge are so manifold in criticism that the third part of this book is devoted entirely to history. First we will concern ourselves with the rôle played by history in criticism; second, with the principal developments in the history of French poetry.

PART III
HISTORY

11

The Historical Context

As we saw at the end of Chapter Ten, the most important type of non-literary information available to the reader of poetry is undoubtedly history, including biography. History, in relation to literature, differs from linguistics, semantics, philology, religion, economics, philosophy, and the other disciplines mentioned in Chapter Ten in the fact that while all of these may be of use in the reading and study of poetry, only history seems potentially capable of becoming a purely literary study in itself. This is because it appears possible—though as yet exceedingly difficult—to write a history of literature. By "history of literature" is *not* meant a history of taste, or a history of poets, or a history of ideas, or a history of social changes as reflected in literature, or a chronologically arranged series of critical impressions, or a history of manners. All of these have often been undertaken, but none of them really constitutes literary history. As René Wellek and Austin Warren put it, "Most leading histories of literature are either histories of civilization or collections of critical essays. One type is not a history of *art;* the other, not a *history* of art." [1] A true history of literature, if it existed, would consti-

[1] *Theory of Literature* (2nd edition; New York: Harcourt, Brace and Company, 1956), p. 243.

tute a purely literary study, because it would represent a particular way of *organizing* literary materials and would not therefore involve the introduction of extraliterary elements into the operation, a process which invariably occurs even when literature is treated in terms of close relatives, such as semantics or linguistics.

The question is often raised, however, whether true literary history is possible, i.e., whether it can be simultaneously literary and historical. For it to be literary, it must concentrate, not on society, nor on the poet's biography, nor on the author's personal evaluation of the works under discussion, but on the internal literary structure itself. To be historical, it must show that the developing changes in internal literary structures are subject to systematic study and treatment in terms of chronology. This would mean recognizing that while individual works of art are discrete they are nevertheless not discontinuous, because they are part of a total body, literature itself, which grows and undergoes change in time.

A total history of literature conceived in this way is as yet unimaginable, and even the history of national literatures, or parts of them (such as poetry) can hardly be undertaken now, because there has not been enough preliminary work done in the analysis of literary structures. Since a proper history of literature as art would depend on detailed knowledge of formal literary properties, we need much more information about the nature of existing verbal structures than we presently have. In the meantime, literature continues to be treated by historians in terms of phenomena external to itself. The closest that anyone has come to real history of literature is the history of certain *parts* of literature—but that results, precisely, in partial history. Much work has been done in the area of sources and influences, but the resulting discoveries rarely establish a real basis for the study of literary evolution; instead they usually tend to bog down in misunderstanding about the nature of literary conventions and the nature of originality. The history of literary content, of course, turns out invariably not to be literary history, but rather the history of ideas, or of attitudes, or the like. Therefore, while we may hope for an eventual history of literature, we had better not stop reading and thinking while doing so— the millennium is not yet at hand.

Even though we must still regard history as an extraliterary approach, we may certainly use it in the way we use psychology and other disciplines: as an aid to our analysis of structures. Though it would be a fallacy to attempt to treat a work exclusively in terms of its original historical setting, or in terms of the criteria of judgment prevalent in its day, we have at least recognized that certain kinds of anachronistic readings are wrong ones, and it is clear that a knowledge of literary conventions operating in given periods may help us to evaluate with greater accuracy the novelty of certain devices. The history of taste and of criticism may be useful to us in determining which poets to read first, and other kinds of historical knowledge will often assist us in elucidating references found in various kinds of texts. The point is that historical information must be used with discretion; but if we are careful not to slide inadvertently into fallacies, whatever historical knowledge we have should be of great service to us.

One of the most valuable contributions that historical knowledge can make to our understanding and appreciation of a poem is the enrichment that comes from seeing the poetic structure in terms of a larger framework. We have already considered some ways in which historical knowledge can add important connotations to various elements of a poem. The meanings of the words *tour* and *abolie* in the first two lines of Gérard de Nerval's "El Desdichado" are enriched when we recognize the particular reference he was making to what he believed to be his own family's origins, though it must always be remembered that these are not the only meanings of those words in that particular poem. But the contribution that historical knowledge can make to our appreciation of a poem is not limited to expanding the possible denotations and connotations of the text itself. The poem, properly understood, may acquire even greater resonance, its degree of univeral appeal and symbolic relevance may expand even further, when we consider it in the light of the larger historical traditions and frames of reference in which it may significantly be placed.

A poem can scarcely escape being part of some sort of literary tradition, and it may be revealing to consider it in terms of other members of the same historical stream. Knowing the literary sources from which a given poet derived some measure of his inspiration often permits the reader to judge and enjoy more fully the unique step forward the poet took in conceiving and producing a given work. Similarly, appreciating the nature of the literary conventions within which framework the poet operated will often prevent the reader from criticizing unnecessarily the poet's seeming inability to handle some detail of his poem in a different way. The poet may simply have acceded to a traditional restriction and then tried, within that limitation, to handle his material as effectively as possible. If he was great, he probably made the restriction look more like a handy support. Rime and versification are themselves conventional, self-imposed restrictions within which the poet tries to manoeuvre as gracefully and effortlessly as possible. He establishes his skill in part by the ease with which he overcomes a self-imposed obstacle.

Historical frameworks need not be limited to one national literary tradition; the comparison of poems written in French in a given literary period, such as the early nineteenth century, with poems written in, say, England in the corresponding literary period may often illuminate the distinct and particular contributions made by poets on both sides of the Channel, and thereby enhance the feeling one has for specific writers in each national tradition. The comparison may also suggest wider meanings for such a term as Romanticism and thereby enlarge the context within which the reader considers a particular poem born of that tradition or, indeed, in revolt against it.

Not only the history of literature but that of other arts as well may often shed light on a poem. Either directly or through his association with a school or a movement, a poet may be strongly influenced by literary theories or practices that originated in some other branch of the arts. Guillaume Apollinaire and some of the later Surrealist poets were much influenced by the early Cubism of Picasso and other painters (and there have been many cases in which painting has been influenced by literature).

Aside from the matter of literary history itself, the social and political climate in which a poem was written has sometimes played an important role in its genesis, and knowing something about the nature of that climate may permit us to consider the poem in a special light. That light, strictly speaking, does not so much illuminate the poem directly as it throws into relief the *relationship* between the poem and events outside itself. But that relationship can be very fascinating to contemplate, and the attitude we take towards the structure of the actual poem may be affected, not by changes in the value of the structure brought about by external events, but by differences in the perspective from which we consider the poem. The structure of certain of Chénier's "Iambes" is not altered by the fact that when their author wrote them he was about to be guillotined in the French Revolution. Nonetheless, a knowledge of that fact may, by changing the perspective from which we consider the "Iambes," enhance our appreciation and enrich our understanding of them. And this particular perspective would be a valid one from which to criticize the "Iambes" if it were clear that we were looking at them from this point of view, and if we were careful not to attribute to the structure of the "Iambes" themselves meanings or resonances that are not there in fact, merely because we would like to see them there.

We can see, then, that all forms of history—literary, artistic, biographical, social, or political—may validly be put to use as we give our critical attention to a French poem.

Despite its title, the next chapter makes no pretence of

being either true literary history or any other sort of proper history. It is merely a compilation of information chronologically arranged, and the criteria governing the amount and kind of such information to be included are purely utilitarian. Since the non-expert in the critical reading of French poetry is probably a non-expert in the history of French poetry as well, he may be able to put to some practical use a few indications concerning the generally recognized major poets of French literature: who they were, when they wrote, the kind of poetry they chiefly produced, and what are usually thought to be their literary affiliations. Despite the fact that only a hazy idea of these details can be presented in a few pages, even a very schematic account may help to orient the reader who is essentially unfamiliar with the history of French poetry. With the aid of the Bibliography at the end of the book, it should be easy to develop further the information provided in the brief account which follows.

12

A Brief History of French Poetry

Since the evolution of Latin into French was a slow and gradual process, it would be folly to attempt to assign a date to the origins of French as a distinguishable language. We can, however, affirm with some display of precision that the history of French poetry spans 1,083 years as of this writing, having begun in 881 A.D. Long after spoken Old French had clearly differentiated itself from Latin, the latter tongue remained the only medium of written communication and literary art. One spoke in Old French but wrote (if at all) in Latin. Therefore, the first example of poetry which has come down to us written in the "vulgar" idiom (the anonymous "Cantilène de sainte Eulalie") is of such late date that it is unmistakably composed in French, and we may use it as the point of origin of French poetry.

It need hardly be said that the French language underwent a considerable evolution during the course of the 1,083 years with which we are concerned. The dividing line between Old French and present-day speech cannot be fixed

[1] For the events listed in this chapter I have relied on a number of sources, all of which are listed in the Bibliography under the heading "Histories of French Literature."

with any accuracy, but for practical purposes we may say that the first major poet who can be read in the original by those who have not made a special study of the early language is probably François Villon (1430?–1463?), and even he presents considerable difficulties that are best circumvented by using a thoroughly annotated edition of his works. Much of the poetry written prior to the time of Villon can still be read with pleasure in translation, and the best (because closest) form of translation is modern French. But since pre-sixteenth-century poetry is the kind least likely to be perused by the English speaking reader, the following account of medieval poetry will be kept as brief as possible.

The earliest French poetry was primarily religious: hymn sequences adapted directly from Latin, an account of the Passion, and lives of the saints, of which the best is undoubtedly the *Vie de saint Alexis* written about the year 1040 in assonanced decasyllables. (The use of assonance in place of rime was common to virtually all the verse of this period, and the two standard lines were the decasyllable and the octosyllable.)

Though religious poetry continued to flourish in the eleventh century, it soon had a popular rival, a new secular genre inspired by the idealization of the warring knight, the defender of his lord, his (local) country, and the faith. This new literary development consisted of a series of *chansons de geste* (songs of historic deeds), written in "cycles" (groups of related epics) centering on the deeds of valor performed by knights associated with such heroes as Charlemagne and William of Orange. The success of these epic poems, which were sung by minstrels called *jongleurs,* was enormous, and they proliferated remarkably. They began to degenerate in quality in the thirteenth and fourteenth centuries, however, and died out soon thereafter. The most famous of the *chansons de geste,* probably the oldest, and certainly the best is the *Chanson de Roland,* a fragment of which was quoted in an earlier chapter. The *Chanson de Roland* is marked by a simplicity and directness of language which makes up in power what it loses in refinement. Scenic description is reduced to a minimum and is consistently calculated to suggest an atmosphere fraught with forboding and overtones of magic. Against a background battle portrayed entirely in terms of black and white (all Christians are virtuous, all pagans demonic), a central dramatic conflict is waged between two Christian heroes: Roland, the reckless and dauntless warrior who risks the lives of the soldiers under his command rather than lose face by calling for help when he is hopelessly outnumbered; and Olivier, the more sensible soldier by modern standards, who, being no less brave but a good deal more circumspect than Roland, would call for assistance when it was clearly required. It is significant that Roland emerges as the undoubted hero *par excellence;* in the eleventh-century epic view, valor is the better part of wisdom. Like the *Song of Roland,* the other *chansons de geste* are characterized by an almost exclusive preoccupation with the knightly ideal as represented by chivalric exploits set in a world in which women have no part.

The ladies' return to literature in the twelfth century was guaranteed by the advent of the *romans courtois* ("courtly romances"). Unlike the *chansons de geste,* the courtly romances were read aloud, not sung, and were much more consciously literary. Whereas the epics were usually composed in assonanced decasyllables, the romances were written in octosyllables rimed in couplets (*rimes plates*), with a good deal of attention paid to rhythm. Their audience was drawn primarily from the more aristocratic inhabitants of town and castle, as distinguished from the lower classes who avidly devoured the *chansons de geste.* Among the various kinds of *romans courtois* the most noteworthy are the *romans bretons* of Celtic inspiration, especially those of Chrétien de Troyes, who wrote, between approximately 1168 and 1190, his *Erec et Enide, Cligès, Lancelot, Yvain,* and *Perceval.* The themes of these "Breton romances" tended to revolve around the legends of Tristan and Isolde, King Arthur and the knights of the Round Table, and the quest of the Holy Grail. As a rule, the knightly exploits were accomplished in a general aura of magic and mystery for the sake of some god-like lady in whose service nothing was impossible.

Another group of poems whose source material originated on the other side of the English Channel was the *Lais*. The *Lais*, of which about a dozen can be attributed with some certainty to Marie de France, a French lady living in England, were short romances of a hundred to a thousand carefully rimed lines; they related tender, often delightful love stories.

A group of romances have come down to us that are quite distinct from the *romans bretons* because of their purely French and contemporary themes; it is customary to refer to them as *romans d'aventure*. (An example of the genre is the anonymous *Floire et Blancheflor* written about 1170.) Though their stories are still highly romanesque, the *romans d'aventure* are sufficiently close to the reality of the end of the twelfth century to give us some sense of life as it was then lived. The same may be said of *Aucassin et Nicolette,* a well-known work which is not actually a *roman d'aventure* but rather represents a unique form. It is called a *chante-fable*, being written alternately in prose and in verse, and is the only example of the genre in the French language. But although it is unique in form, *Aucassin et Nicolette* shares with many of the *romans d'aventure* the tendency to juxtapose the world of reality and the world of fantasy while relating, with delicacy and naïveté, a charming love-idyll.

While the epic and narrative genres which we have been discussing are essentially of northern origin, the lyric poetry that has come down to us from this period seems to have been primarily of southern inspiration. The language of the South of France at this time was Provençal, and the lyric poets who wrote in it were called *troubadours,* as distinguished from the *trouvères* of the North. The lyric poetry of Provence attained a brilliant development in the twelfth century, and the French poets tended to imitate their Southern colleagues until Provençal civilization was destroyed by the Albigensian crusade (1209–1218). Artistic refinement, subtlety, and conscious obscurity were the chief characteristics of Provençal poetry. The troubadours prided themselves on the difficulty of their poems, on the variety and ingenuity of their forms, and on their general technical virtuosity. A number of genres sprang up, such as the *chanson courtoise,* characterized by brevity and concentration on the inner struggles caused by passion (as opposed to the outward exploits); the *tenson* (Provençal *tenso*) and the *jeu-parti* (Provençal *partimen*), both involving debates between two poets, usually over some highly rarified question of proper amatory conduct; the *pastourelle* which portrays the wooing of a shepherdess by a knight or by the poet; the *chanson d'histoire* (or *de toile*) which tells the story of a girl separated from her lover with whom, finally, she is happily reunited unless, tragically, she learns instead of his death or infidelity; *chansons de mal mariées* (which constitute a sub-class of the *chanson d'histoire*), poems relating the complaints of wives regarding their husbands; the *serventois* (Provençal *sirventes*), based on moral or political causes and characterized by many pointed allusions to current events; *chansons de croisades,* crusade songs; *chansons d'aube,* sung by young lovers forced to separate at dawn; and various *chansons de danse.* Among the most famous troubadours we may cite William IX of Aquitaine, Marcabrun, the Bertrand de Born mentioned by Dante in the *Inferno,* and—the best, perhaps—Bernard de Ventadour. Of the Northern French trouvères note should be taken of Conon de Béthune, Guy de Coucy, and especially Thibaut IV of Champagne, who was King of Navarre from 1234 to 1253.

Almost all of this lyric poetry was composed in a style and on themes suitable to the aristocracy; but beginning with the thirteenth century, a more bourgeois type of realist and satirical poetry came to the fore. Its themes and forms varied, but its tone tended to be ironic and its subjects relatively plebeian. The most illustrious exponents of this poetic style were Jean Bodel, Adam de la Halle, Colin Muset, and the great Parisian, Rutebeuf. One of the more curious poetic efforts in the non-aristocratic vein, begun in the twelfth century and extending through the thirteenth, was the *Roman de Renart*. Fables had had a certain vogue as early as the eleventh century, but they now came to full fruition with the adventures of Renart the Fox, a vast epic to which many poets contributed and which actually caused the original French word for "fox," *goupil*, to disappear in favor of the modern word, *renard*. The vastness of the *Roman de Renart* makes it difficult to describe succinctly its literary importance; the *Roman* began as an animal epic, became (as more and more writers contributed to it) allegorical, then satirical, and finally metaphysical in nature. Thus different episodes, written in very different periods, aroused the interest of the public in a great variety of ways. Though attempts were made as late as the sixteenth century to prolong the history of Renart and his companions, Isengrin the Wolf, Chantecler the Rooster, and Noble the Lion, the original verve of the epic could by then no longer be recovered.

Two other bourgeois genres enjoyed considerable success in the twelfth and especially the thirteenth centuries: short anecdotal stories either of a religious nature (*contes dévots*) or of a comic and secular type (*fabliaux*). As opposed to the *contes dévots*, which were edifying tales usually calculated to point up a simple moral principle, the *fabliaux* are marked by crudity of plot and detail, Rabelaisian humor, usually inoffensive satire, and a general distrust of women, who are always shrewd, malicious, and plotting mischief.

Of medieval didactic and allegorical poetry we need say little. Apart from the lapidaries and bestiaries, the moral treatises and sermons in verse, the one major production in this category was the *Roman de la rose*, an immense poem in

two parts, the first written between approximately 1225 and
1230 by Guillaume de Lorris, the second and much longer
section having been continued by Jean de Meung, who picked
up in 1277 the thread which Guillaume had let fall forty-
seven years earlier. In the first part the poet (in a dream)
enters the garden of Love in which he finds a Rose. Love
pierces the poet's heart with an arrow and from that moment
on the poet's sole aim is to pluck the Rose; he is encouraged
by Welcome, Reason, Friend, and Frankness, but opposed by
the Rose's guardian, Danger. Finally he steals a kiss from
the Rose, but Danger (who has been alerted by Evil-Mouth
and Jealousy) drives him from the garden. Through this
allegory, Guillaume de Lorris presents a doctrine of courtly
love, and that is what makes the first part so different from
the second. In the second part Jean de Meung continues the
narrative, and the poet eventually succeeds in plucking the
Rose; but the significance of the allegory has changed completely. Now courtly love is under attack, and a doctrine of
love grounded in rationalism and naturalism is developed. In
the course of expounding his views, Jean de Meung touches
on much of the knowledge and many of the philosophical
concerns of his day. The influence of this monumental work
on subsequent allegorical and mystical literature and on such
poets as Guillaume de Machault, Jean Lemaire de Belges,
and Ronsard was enormous, but since it can scarcely be rec-
ommended now for the bedside table, the specially interested reader must be referred to the Bibliography which will
guide him to more information than can be furnished here.

The period we have been surveying up to now might be
called the apogee of the Middle Ages. The fourteenth and
fifteenth centuries represent an epoch of transition and, in
many areas, of decadence. A certain sterility becomes apparent as poets show themselves to be more and more totally
preoccupied with strict observance of the regulations governing such fixed forms as the *ballade,* the *rondeau,* the *triolet,*
and the *chant royal.* A few poets manage to escape the gen-

eral atmosphere of stultification however, notably Guillaume
de Machaut, Jean Froissart, Eustache Deschamps, Christine
de Pisan, Alain Chartier, and more especially Charles d'Orléans, several of whose *rondeaux* are justly famous.

Of all medieval poets the greatest by far is François Villon
(1430?–1463?). Hardly out of one scrape with the police before falling into another, Villon spent most of his short life
on the run, usually standing still only when constrained to do
so by iron bars in the shadow of the gallows. Not surprisingly,
therefore, he left only two thin collections: the *Lais* (lega-
cies," modern French *legs*), sometimes called the *Petit testament* (1456), in which he "bequeaths" his troubles to various enemies, and the more fully developed *Grand testament*
(1461) composed of 183 eight-line stanzas into which are
inserted sixteen *ballades* and three *rondeaux*. Among the
former are the "Ballade des dames du temps jadis" (which
was translated by D. G. Rossetti as the "Ballad of Dead Ladies") with its haunting refrain: "Mais où sont les neiges
d'antan?"—"But where are the snows of yesteryear?"

Much of the rest is a reflection of Villon's hectic existence,
and demonstrates why it has been said that if a term were
needed for the opposite of "sentimental," one could hardly
find a better word than "Villon." In verse that is as tough
as was his way of life, he proved capable of confronting
prison and probable execution with a display of humor that,
for all its irony and even sarcasm, had the virtue of preserv-
ing him from prolonged self-pity. He saw himself very much
as he was, not altogether bad but far from angelically good,
and therefore not too different from most other men. This
sharp insight he embodied in a work of remarkable power
and diversity; the combination of poignancy, realism, humor,
anguish, cynicism, clarity of vision, and lyric power in the
Grand testament as a whole has rarely been equalled in
French poetry.

We cannot abandon the Middle Ages without at least
glancing at the history of medieval drama. The theatrical

literature of the Middle Ages is commonly divided into two categories: religious drama and comic drama. Since the religious drama came first and the comic developed in part from it, we shall take up the two types in that order.

Medieval religious drama had its origin in the inherently dramatic liturgy of the Mass. The first step in its development was the introduction into first the Easter and then the Christmas liturgy of *tropes,* which were brief Latin paraphrases of sacred texts that helped to point up the dramatic significance of the particular feast being celebrated. They were sung in the manner of a dialogue and were eventually enhanced by a visible "stage-setting" involving such "properties" as the Christmas crèche or the Holy Sepulchre. The success of these short dramatic interludes in the monasteries was such that they were moved to the cathedrals and parish churches where they came to be sung partly in Old French (though direct scriptural quotations remained in Latin). Gradually, as the dramatic element began to surpass in importance the liturgical element, these "plays" were moved from the constricted area of the sanctuary to the outside of the church where they were performed against the background of the façade. Two Walloon Nativities, a fragment of a *Résurrection du Sauveur,* and the *Jeu d'Adam* have come down to us from the twelfth century. The typical verse-form of the period (eight-syllable lines rimed in couplets) is used in each case, and the language is simple, direct, and naïve. The *Jeu d'Adam,* the best-known twelfth-century drama, is composed in three parts, of which the first portrays Adam's temptation and fall, the second the murder of Abel, and the third a parade of prophets who announce the advent of the Redeemer.

The thirteenth and fourteenth centuries saw the development of the miracle plays, which were based on the lives of saints. As a rule, they involved an adventurous intrigue that only a miracle performed by the saint could unravel. Scenes from daily life were often freely mixed in with the legend, which was spectacular, romanesque, and expressed in a rather diffuse style. The versification consisted of quatrains of octosyllabic lines rimed *aaab, bbbc, cccd,* etc.

The early Christmas and Easter plays, after a slow development, fused into a single drama of the Redemption which, in the early fifteenth century, took the form of the mystery play. (The term "mystery" originated in a confusion between two Latin terms: *mysterium,* referring to the religious subject of the drama, and *ministerium,* meaning ceremony, service.) The production of mystery plays was in the hands of religious societies called Confraternities of the Passion, of which one was founded in Paris in about 1380. The production of mystery plays was an enormous enterprise; in effect the whole town took part. Actors were recruited from the corporations and confraternities; businesses were temporarily abandoned as crowds of people helped to construct elaborate galleries and "machinery" for special effects. The performances sometimes lasted over a period of several afternoons and the characters were frequently numbered in the hundreds. The whole universe was represented: heaven, earth, and hell were simultaneously displayed to the audience, and the drama might include episodes from the Old or the New Testament or both. The *Passion* composed for the Parisian confraternity by Arnoul Gréban, one of the most successful mystery plays, numbered 224 characters and was 34,574 lines long.

Eventually the mystery play, which had originally been a source both of edification and of entertainment, lost its religious framework and became a purely worldly, sometimes profane form of amusement. The result was that when the Church was touched by a breath of reform in the sixteenth century the mystery plays were found to be indecent and were formally suppressed by the *Parlement* of Paris in 1548.

Religious drama in its thirteenth-century aspect gave its external form to the first medieval comic drama. The same scenic conventions, versification, and even language appear in what may in fact have been originally nothing more than humorous scenes detached from religious plays (which usually contained a few comic episodes). The most noteworthy comic dramas prior to the fifteenth century are doubtless those of the thirteenth-century poet of Arras, Adam de la Halle. His *Jeu de la Feuillée,* a sort of *Midsummer Night's Dream* set in a tavern, combines fantasy with realism in a way that has reminded some readers of Aristophanes; his *Jeu de Robin et de Marion,* on the other hand, is a dramatic pastoral with overtones of satire, though it is not altogether clear whether what is being mocked is the code of courtly love or the man who refuses to submit to it.

In the fifteenth century there grew up in Paris and in the provinces groups of amateurs who formed what were known as *les sociétés joyeuses,* the comic counterparts of the confraternities of the Passion. In Paris there were two celebrated societies, that of the *Basoche* and that of the *Enfants sans souci,* each with its own forms of comedy. The *Basoche* specialized in morality plays; the *Enfants sans souci,* or the *Sots* (as they were also called), produced *soties* and farces. All three of these comic genres shared the same conception of man and of life, one in which a certain half-glimpsed ideal of humanity is contrasted with clearly perceived reality, and the result is laughter. The three forms were not clearly separated, and the morality play in particular was ill-defined. The morality play betrayed its religious origins by aiming, at least in theory, at the edification of its audience. Largely because it tended to assume the form of allegory, it disappeared about 1540 when allegory was no longer in fashion.

The *sotie* was a kind of satirical morality play consisting not so much of a plot as of a series of gibes at various kinds of *sots* and their political, moral, or social *sottises.* It, too, went rapidly out of fashion and failed to survive the morality play.

The farce consisted essentially of a scene from private life portrayed with the exclusive intention of causing laughter. It was short and often borrowed its material from the *fabliaux.* The best example and, indeed, the masterpiece of French

medieval comedy is the *Farce de Maître Pathelin,* written by
an unknown author in the 1460's. The influence of this farce
on Rabelais, Molière, Beaumarchais, and others testifies to its
remarkable qualities. Farce, unlike the morality play and the
sotie, has never died, though it diminished somewhat in favor
in the sixteenth and seventeenth centuries until Molière gave
it a magnificent fresh start. But that part of its history we
must hold in reserve until later.

We come now to the sixteenth century, a period in which
the French language reached a stage of development which
may be unhesitatingly called modern. The principal difficulty
—and it is not very grave—that the English-speaking reader
of French sixteenth-century poetry may encounter has to do
with spelling. Orthography was not properly settled at that
time, and certain words may therefore turn up in somewhat
unfamiliar garb. It will usually be found, however, that pronouncing such words aloud will immediately suggest the correct modern equivalent, as can be seen from the following list
of archaic spellings taken from Du Bellay's villanelle "D'un
Vanneur de blé aux vents" compared with the modern ver-
sions. The Du Bellay spelling is followed by the form used
today:

Troppe—troupe	*Icy—ici*
Legere—légère	*Freschement—fraîchement*
Aele—aile	*Œilletz—œillets*
Passagere—passagère	*Vostre—votre*
Doulcement—doucement	*Eventez—éventez*
Esbranlez—ébranlez	*Ce pendant—cependant*

If it is borne in mind that accents were treated in rather cava-
lier fashion at this time; that final *i* was often written as *y*;
that vowels now carrying a circumflex accent were then usually followed by an *s* instead; and that plural *s* was sometimes
written as *z*; few real problems will arise. One other rule
should be noted, however. At this time, and for a long subsequent period, the digraph *ai* was commonly written *oi* and

pronounced *weh* (*ouè*), notably in the endings of the imperfect and conditional tenses of verbs. Thus, *je savais* was written *je savois* and rimed with the word *bois* (pronounced *bouè*). We see a trace of this in the English spelling of *connoisseur*, as compared with modern French *connaisseur*.

Toward the end of the fifteenth century, French poetry came under the domination of a school of poets called the *grands rhétoriqueurs*, a group endowed with an immense reputation for and a unique concern with virtuosity. The themes treated by these poetasters remained those exploited by the courtly lyric poets of earlier centuries, but handled now with a greater emphasis on allegory and with an extravagant devotion to the most subtle, difficult, and elaborate forms of versification imaginable. It need hardly be said that the verse poured out by this school bore little resemblance to poetry, having more the features of a high-wire bicycle act. Nevertheless, two late disciples of the "rhetorical" tradition broke away from many of the limitations of their predecessors and helped to pave the way for the *Pléiade*. The first, Jean Lemaire de Belges (1473–1525?), introduced the Italian terza rima into France and exerted a considerable influence on the *Pléiade*. Despite his many weaknesses, including an inability to resolve the conflict between his essentially medieval background and an obvious enthusiasm for the Renaissance, he has been accurately described as an intelligent workman who helped to prepare the instrument of future poetry.

The second, Clément Marot (1496–1544), not to be confused with his father, Jean Marot, who was a pure *rhétoriqueur*, was probably the best French poet between Villon and Ronsard. He began in the rhetorical tradition to which his father never failed to adhere, and he never lost his predilection for puns, fanciful rimes, and unusual rhythms. Nonetheless, he established himself as a link between the poets of the Middle Ages and those of the Renaissance, while maintaining intact his own distinct personality. "L'Epître à Lion Jamet" (1525) and "L'Epître au roi pour avoir été dérobé" (1531) reveal his keen sense of humor and essential simplicity of style, and *L'Enfer* (1526) establishes him as one of the sharpest satirists of the day. He is equally famous for his translations of the Psalms which were promptly acclaimed by the Protestants in Geneva and show the unmistakable stamp of a true poet. The influence he exerted, quite apart from his introduction of the sonnet into France (in 1536), was remarkable; he was virtually the only poet of the Middle Ages or of his own day who continued to be read in the seventeenth and eighteenth centuries.

The development of poetry in the sixteenth century was of course fundamentally influenced by the humanistic concentration on Classical literature, as well as by the "discovery" of Italy, particularly in the person of Petrarch. The most important early propagator of the cult of Petrarch in France was Maurice Scève (1510–1564?), the leading member of the so-called *école lyonnaise*. The term "school" is something of a misnomer in this instance, since its "members" neither acted as a group nor recognized themselves as such, nor did they promulgate any doctrines. They were, however, all connected in varying degrees with Lyons society, and there are obvious parallels between their works. The dominant traits of the poetry produced by the *école lyonnaise*, as exemplified by Scève, are those of Petrarch with Platonic overtones. Scève's masterpiece, *Délie, object de plus haulte vertu* (1527?), still medieval in some of its characteristics, nonetheless established poetry as the recognized literary medium for the expression of the sublime. In the course of this collection of poems the poet struggles to free himself from a purely carnal response to the beauty of his lady and ultimately succeeds, after many relapses, in envisaging her as the incarnation of Platonic beauty uncorrupted by purely fleshly attractions. While no other member of the *école lyonnaise* achieved such artistic success as Scève did, Louise Labé (1525?–1565) deserves mention for her elegies and sonnets, which rank among the best love poetry written by any French poet of her sex.

The origin of another group which was destined later to eclipse the *école lyonnaise* may be placed in 1547, at which time a teacher of Greek named Jean Dorat became head of the Collège de Coqueret in Paris. This excellent teacher succeeded in surrounding himself with a notable collection of students devoted to the study of Hellenic literature. Among them were Pierre de Ronsard (1524–1585) and Joachim Du Bellay (1522–1560), both of whom had previously come under the influence of a humanist named Jacques Pelletier. As a result of the inspiration provided by Dorat and of the preaching of Pelletier, who advocated the enrichment of the French language and the imitation of Italy as a means of developing a new French poetry, Ronsard, Du Bellay, and a number of other aspiring poets at the Collège de Coqueret were set on fire. Volatile fuel was added to the flames in 1548 when Thomas Sébillet published his *Art poétique.* Sébillet's doctrine struck Ronsard and his fellow poets (who now called themselves the *Brigade*) as being at the same time too old and too new. To the extent that his ideas were medieval Sébillet was betraying the cause of Pelletier; in so far as he was modern he risked stealing the glory that the *Brigade* intended to garner for itself. The result was the publication of *La Deffense et illustration de la langue françoyse* (1549), signed with the initials of Du Bellay but obviously the fruit of a collaboration by the entire group. This burning manifesto promulgated a doctrine containing three essential tenets: that the French national language should replace Latin as the literary language and should be enriched with new words; that new poetic genres imitated from the Italians and Classical antiquity, along with new themes and techniques, should supplant the outmoded poetic forms of the Middle Ages; and finally that poetry should be recognized as being not a simple amusement but the proper means for expressing the highest form of human inspiration. While the *Deffense* was not truly original, it appeared at exactly the right moment and enjoyed an enormous success. Not only did it effectively establish the reputation of the *Brigade,* it set up the pattern on which *Renaissance* poetry was to model itself. Many of its specific injunctions regarding versification are followed even today.

By this time the *Brigade* had become so large that Ronsard felt it necessary to distinguish six of his best colleagues and himself with another name: *La Pléiade.* Of the seven members of this inner group, the two outstanding poets were Ronsard and Du Bellay.

In addition to the *Deffense,* Du Bellay produced in the memorable year 1549 the first edition of his collection called *L'Olive* containing fifty sonnets; his *Vers lyriques* consisting of thirteen odes; a *Recueil de poésie* of sixteen more odes; and a few other assorted poems. The second edition of *l'Olive* (1550) brought the number of sonnets up to 115 and established Du Bellay's ability beyond question. Despite the consistently Petrarchan and Platonic themes, the personality of the French poet is unmistakable and original. Among his other collections, *Les Antiquités de Rome, Les Regrets,* and *Les Jeux rustiques,* all published in 1558, are outstanding. Du Bellay's works, in which he shows himself to be less powerful but perhaps more delicate and sensitive than Ronsard are distinguished by a remarkable variety of tones, ranging from poignancy and tenderness to irony and even sarcasm.

As good as Du Bellay was, his sixteenth-century reputation never really approached that of Ronsard, who reigned supreme over the *Pléiade* in particular and over lyric poetry in general. Ronsard's production was immense, and only his greatest collections can be mentioned here. The earlier ones (the first five books of *Odes* and the first book of *Les Amours,* published in 1550 and 1552) betray an erudition that has not yet been brought under control, but the *Folastries* of 1553, the *Bocage* and the *Mélanges* of 1554, and the various continuations of *Les Amours* (1555–56) mark a turn in the direction of simplicity, grace, and lightness that resulted in prodigious popular success and, on the technical level, in the firm establishment of the alexandrine as the basic line for serious French poetry. In 1555–56 Ronsard produced two collections of *Hymnes* which placed him on the pinnacle of the poetic hierarchy. His prestige was such that he became the king's unofficial propagandist, guiding public opinion during the course of the civil war. With the exception of his unsuccessful attempt at a vast French epic (*La Franciade*), his last works, and most especially the *Sonnets à Hélène* (published in 1578), continued the level of perfection already achieved. Though his reputation was revived in the nineteenth century when the Romantics accorded him his rightful place among the greatest French poets, the seventeenth and eighteenth centuries ignored or reviled him. During his lifetime, however, his fame never dimmed, and one of the many kings he served is said to have remarked to him: "You and I are two crowned heads." So they were; one crowned with gold, the other with laurel.

During the course of the civil wars, Ronsard lent his tremendous weight to the Catholic cause, and on the Protestant side two poets made remarkable contributions. The first was Du Bartas, the second D'Aubigné.

Guillaume de Saluste du Bartas (1544–1590), the lesser of the two, is scarcely readable today. His tendency to pedantry far exceeded that of the early Ronsard, and his religious epics are inclined to be didactic and monotonous. Nevertheless, he was imitated more than once by Tasso, Milton, and Byron, and Goethe greatly admired him.

Agrippa d'Aubigné (1552–1630) is remembered primarily for his *Tragiques* (not published until 1616), a religious epic which is also a sermon, a satire, and a vision. In it he portrays in fiery tones the corruption of France and the persecution of the Protestants, calling down vengeance on his enemies and concluding with a terrifying picture of the Last Judgment. Despite occasional lapses into obscurity or monotony, he was unsurpassed in his generation when at his best.

By the time of Ronsard's death (1585), the noble genres favored by the *Pléiade* had begun to grow stale, and a touch of preciosity became apparent in much of French poetry, principally as a result of the close contact between poets and the worldly courts of their noble and royal protectors. The best poet representative of this phase was Philippe Desportes (1546–1606), though he never reached the heights attained by the *Pléiade*.

The renewed awareness of classical antiquity that exerted such a profound influence on the *Pléiade* had a corresponding effect on the development of French drama. The rediscovery of ancient drama inspired in the first half of the century a series of imitations, mostly in Latin, of classical tragedies. In 1552, at the *collège de Boncourt* in Paris, a group of young poets, including Etienne Jodelle and Rémy Belleau (both members of the *Pléiade*), created a center of dramatic production inspired by classical plays and by the recent developments in Italian drama. Jodelle's *Cléopâtre captive* (performed early in 1553) had a resounding success, though its effect was in some respects more lyric than dramatic. The playwright indulged in a somewhat clumsy alternation of ten-syllable lines with alexandrines, and his plot was open to criticism for its poverty of action, but there is no doubt that, along with several other contemporary successes, *Cléopâtre* represented a vital renewal of French drama. Of the comedies written by Jodelle and his colleagues (principally under the inspiration of classical and Italian sources and of the medieval farce), it may be said again that while their significance was largely historical, their importance should not be underestimated.

The publication at Lyons in 1561 of Aristotle's *Poetics* was followed by a wave of prefaces and treatises, the effect of which was to establish certain fundamental principles of construction applicable to "regular" tragedy and comedy. (The term "regular" as applied to tragedy and comedy refers primarily to the observance of the Aristotelian unities of time, place, and action, with greater liberty permitted in the comic than in the tragic genre. Several other "rules" having to do with the nobility of the language and with the question of what actions might be carried out on stage also served as criteria in determining the "regularity" of plays.) The "rules," however, were by no means universally accepted. Apart from contaminations caused by habits left over from earlier periods, many deviations were occasioned by the success of the Italian *commedia dell' arte* (a modernized form of medieval farce) and by other Italian and Spanish influences that gave rise to such non-classical genres as the tragi-comedy and the pastoral. It was long after the beginning of the seventeenth century that a truly classical theater was able to establish itself in France.

The most distinguished tragedian of the sixteenth century was Robert Garnier (1544–1590) whose tragedy *Les Juives* (1583) shows some affinity with opera in its lyric grandeur. Among the comic playwrights of this period, Pierre Larivey (1540–1611) was on the whole the most successful, though like his colleagues he was apparently unable to detach himself sufficiently from his (chiefly Italian) models. Both the tragi-comedy of Italian origin characterized by a complicated romanesque plot with a happy ending and the dramatic pastoral, marked by a worldly plot with comic overtones, an Arcadian setting, and a happy conclusion reached their peak of development in the early seventeenth century and need not detain us here.

Though the seventeenth century was the "splendid century," the age of French classicism, the period of Corneille, Racine, Molière, Descartes, La Rochefoucauld, Pascal, Mme de Lafayette, and Bossuet (to mention only the greatest), it was not an age of greatness for non-dramatic poetry. Boileau and La Fontaine are the only names of poets that may be appropriately added to the list of dramatists, philosophers, moralists, novelists, and orators just mentioned. Nevertheless, other talented poets appeared between 1600 and 1700, and in some instances their works can be ranked just below those of the masters.

The tendency of many people to associate the French seventeenth century exclusively with classicism sometimes leads them to overlook two other currents which were almost equally strong, and indeed at certain times stronger. One of these has been called the realist movement; the other is usually termed preciosity. The realist literature of the seventeenth century is characterized primarily by its espousal of libertine attitudes and its satirical tone. *Précieux* poetry, on the other hand, was inclined to be either too ingenious on the subject of love, or else not ingenious enough. Sometimes it was ingenious without any apparent subject at all. The only *précieux* poet who should be mentioned here is Vincent Voiture (1597–1648) whose rondeau, "Ma foi, c'est fait de moi," cited in Chapter Five, is typical of his work as a whole and reasonably characteristic of the movement in general.

The realist current produced two remarkable poets in the first quarter of the century: Mathurin Régnier and Théophile de Viau. Régnier (1573–1613) is known primarily for his *Satires* (1608–1613), and he may be said to have established the genre in France. Vigor was his hallmark; his liveliness and powers of observation were so strong that they overcame occasional failings in his style. For their picturesqueness and sharpness of detail his caricatures have been rightly compared to Callot's prints. Of Régnier's weaknesses, the chief one was an inclination to excessive freedom in both composition and subject matter, but his insistence upon liberty of inspiration and the right to exercise poetic imagination was no doubt a salutary antidote to the practice of some of his more pedantic contemporaries. Théophile de Viau (1590–1625), often called simply Théophile, was equally vehement in affirming the poet's right to the free exercise of fantasy in composition. His poetic doctrine emphasized simplicity, naturalness, and spontaneity, and he expressed it in a variety of poetic forms: odes, elegies, sonnets, epistles, epigrams, etc. His most frequently cited poems are two odes, "La Solitude" and "Le Matin."

The realist tradition was continued notably by Antoine Girard (sometimes called Marc-Antoine Gérard) de Saint-Amant (1594–1661), who contributed significantly to the introduction of burlesque poetry into France. Saint-Amant combined exuberance in verse with epicureanism in taste, and produced several remarkable poems, such as "Le Melon," "Les Cabarets," "Le Fromage," and "Le Tabac," certain of which are more than a little reminiscent of Flemish genre paintings.

During the rest of the century few, if any, notable realists appeared in the poetic domain. The principal mode of realist expression was prose, and what verse there was took the form of a relatively low order of burlesque.

Between the realist and *précieux* currents the movement we know as classicism gradually took form. Its first major representative in poetry was François Malherbe (1555–1628), whose poetic doctrine was expressed directly by the example of his verse, not by a formal treatise. Nonetheless, Malherbe's example established the rules of French versification in a form that prevailed for more than two centuries. He insisted upon a "purification" of the French language, from which all substandard forms of expression, all neologistic borrowings from Greek and Latin, and all conceits were to be eliminated. Enjambement, hiatuses, *chevilles*, and imperfect rimes were also banished, together with the vulgarities and fantasies of the realists on the one hand, and the extravagances and incomprehensibilities of the *précieux* poets on the other. Reason and order were Malherbe's watchwords, and they continued to be key values of the classical doctrine for the rest of the century. Among Malherbe's most famous poems are the "Ode à Marie de Médicis" (1600), the "Consolation à Du Périer" (1602), and above all the "Ode au roi Louis XIII allant châtier les Rochelois" (1627). The Malherbian doctrine was continued by a small number of disciples among whom the two most distinguished were François Mainard (1582–1646) and Honorat de Bueil de Racan (1589–1670).

By the middle of the century, the classical doctrine had been thoroughly expounded, but principally in scattered prefaces and treatises that no one had brought together in one work. Furthermore, a tendency toward pedantic formalism became more and more pronounced, with the result that poets were judged more by their strict observance of the "rules" than by their actual talent. This situation was at least partly rectified by the appearance of a great poet, Nicolas Boileau (1636–1711), the self-styled "legislator of Parnassus." Far from legislating new principles of classical prosody or taste, Boileau in fact simply formulated the rules that had been consistently followed by the better classical poets since Malherbe. Nonetheless, his influence was enormous. He began as a satirist in the tradition of Horace, Juvenal, and Régnier, defending good sense against what he conceived to be its various adversaries, and preaching reason and balance. From 1674 to 1683 he composed *Le Lutrin,* a poem in four cantos which reversed the fashion of the burlesque (in which a noble subject is parodied) by establishing the *héroï-comédie* (a mock-epic in which a trivial subject is treated with all the poetic apparatus associated with the epic). Then, in 1674, Boileau published *L'Art poétique,* also in four cantos, a combination of manifesto, satire, polemic, and treatise. Based on Horace, as well as on several seventeenth-century dissertations on poetics, the *Art poétique* was not very original. It was not even totally coherent. Nonetheless, it summarized the classical poetic doctrine with verve and concision, and exerted a great influence on the formation of taste. It remains a monument to the highest form of literary expression that was conceivable to the seventeenth-century mind.

The other truly great poet of the century was Jean de La Fontaine (1621–1695). A realist by instinct who nonetheless had a strong inclination toward fantasy, he made the best of both extreme currents, realism and preciosity, thereby proving himself to be in fact a classicist of the highest rank. Though he wrote in a variety of genres, he is primarily known for his *Fables* and *Contes*. Usually more interested in the illustration of the moral than in the moral itself, he portrayed the animals of the Æsopian world with a vividness and a sense of drama that turn what might have been moralistic verse into immensely successful poetry. Sainte-Beuve no doubt exaggerated in describing La Fontaine as the French Homer, but it is certainly true that none of the many later poets who tried to imitate him ever approached him in his own genre.

Before moving into the eighteenth century, we must glance back to the point at which we interrupted our tracing of the history of French dramatic poetry. The four genres (tragedy, comedy, tragi-comedy, and pastoral) which had begun to dominate the stage in the sixteenth century continued to be produced, in more and more irregular forms, in the early seventeenth century. Antoine de Montchrestien (1575–1621) and Alexandre Hardy (1569?–1631), despite some notable successes early in the century, did little to advance the cause of regular genres, but from 1628 on the situation quickly altered. The pastoral declined rapidly (it was dead by 1631) and comedy became "regular," thanks principally to Corneille's *Mélite ou les Fausses lettres,* the first example of "regular" comedy, which was followed by *La Veuve* and *La Galerie du Palais* (both slightly "irregular") and *La Suivante* and *La Place royale,* further examples of "regularity" in the genre. Tragi-comedy subsisted, but it tended more and more to become "tragedy with a happy ending," eliminating the obviously comic elements it had once displayed. The most important development of all this period was, however, the "regularization" of tragedy. The acceptance of the three Aristotelian unities (of time, place, and action) led in 1637 to the production of Corneille's *Le Cid,* after which the arguments regarding the structure of regular tragedy became limited merely to questions of detail involving taste and propriety. Pierre Corneille (1606–1684) was thus (along with others) instrumental in establishing the two dramatic genres, tragedy and comedy, most clearly illustrative of what was one day to be known as French classicism. Corneille's alexandrines ring out with a bronze-like authority that reflects the clarity and sublimity of the moral dilemmas he posed in his plays. His verse is grandiose, as were his concepts. *Le Cid, Horace, Cinna,* and *Polyeucte* must be numbered among the great examples of seventeenth-century dramatic poetry.

The brilliant comedy represented by Corneille underwent a decline in the middle of the century from which it was rescued by one of the greatest comic geniuses of all time, Jean-Baptiste Poquelin (1622–1673) who wrote and acted under the name of Molière. The author of *Tartuffe* and *Le Misanthrope* is too well known, and the space in which he can here be discussed is too limited, to make possible a detailed treatment of his work. Suffice it to say that his easy, supple, vigorous style was able to adapt itself to each character and to every situation with a mastery that has rarely if ever been equalled in the history of comedy.

Tragedy, too, went into a certain decline after Corneille's active career came to an end, and tragi-comedy, pastoral, and even "pastoral tragi-comedy" enjoyed a renewed vogue. In about 1660, however, the irregular genres lost favor definitively as the classical reaction took hold and tragedy reached its zenith. The apogee was attained with Jean Racine (1639–1699) who preserved the outer structure of the best Cornelian tragedy while profoundly altering the spirit that animated it. For the heroic discipline of reason he substituted the overwhelming force of passion, thereby inaugurating the expression of a new sensibility in the French theater. As a result, the poetic style of Racine became something quite different from that of Corneille; the eloquence, the bravura, the lucid sententiousness that marked the Cornelian style gave way in Racine to the more subtle revelation of dark emotions, often half-hidden before being permitted to show through in understated or deceptively simple language. No one in French literature has known better than Racine the secret of uniting grace with *élan,* simplicity with power. As *Phèdre, Andro-maque, Bérénice,* and the other great tragedies testify, Racine's verse has its own distinctive music, a music that is eminently suited to the self-expression of his brilliant and sometimes terrifying characters as they grope with their complex psychological involvements. This poetic, almost lyric style, combined with an architectural control of dramatic structure that never falters, marks Racine as the fitting exemplar of French classical poetry at its greatest.

As the seventeenth century drew to a close, the happy alliance of inspiration with formal discipline which marked the most successful classical works disappeared more and more from poetry. The various genres tended to be treated as rigid forms, into which the would-be poet poured whatever "content" he had at his disposal. As we have seen, there is no better way to insure that verse will *not* be poetry than to approach it in this way. Mediocrity, empty rhetoric, and insipidity, often clothed in the outer trappings of the ode, the epic, and the allegory, characterize much of the verse of the late seventeenth and most of the eighteenth centuries. The "Age of the Enlightenment" was perhaps too intellectually oriented for true poetic inspiration to come to life. Indeed, the eighteenth century witnessed a considerable development of anti-poetic feeling and produced few ardent defenders of the art. When we hear one of its rare apologists, Voltaire, define poetry as "a harmonious eloquence" it becomes obvious that the very nature of poetry has been lost sight of. Accordingly, the "game" aspect of light verse once again came into vogue, and elegance, virtuosity, and grace were its primary aims. The *épître,* the satirical epigram, madrigals, and ephemeral *pièces de circonstance* abounded, and in most cases the word "verse" proved to be the best descriptive term for what was clearly "non-poetry." As the eighteenth century progressed, the situation deteriorated: didactic poetry enjoyed an ever increasing vogue and led to works which one French critic, in an attempt at enthusiasm, described as written "not, sometimes, without a modicum of success." It seems fair, therefore, to say that only one eighteenth-century poet need be mentioned here: André-Marie Chénier (1762–1794).

André Chénier, the subject of Giordano's opera, *Andrea Chénier*, was born near Constantinople, the son of a Greek mother and a French father. He greeted the French Revolution with enthusiasm in 1790, but the violence of the immediate aftermath repulsed him, and he actually collaborated in the defense of Louis XVI. He was therefore arrested on March 7, 1794, and guillotined on July 20th, two days before the fall of Robespierre which would have saved him. The first incomplete edition of his works was published in 1819 and exerted an enormous influence on the Romantics. Chénier, perhaps partly because of his heredity, succeeded in bringing back to life the spirit of Alexandrian Greek poetry, while at the same time his natural ability to capture the picturesque in words resulted in a kind of neo-classical but genuinely personal touch that the early Romantics were quick to recognize as foreshadowing their own work. Much of Chénier's verse remained unfinished. Among his earlier poems were the "Bucoliques" (including the famous elegy, "La Jeune Tarentine"), and his last verse was composed chiefly of elegies, *épîtres*, odes (among which "La Jeune captive" is especially noteworthy), and the satirical "Iambes."

We may pass rapidly over the dramatic poetry of the eighteenth century, since the most successful theater of the period took the form of comedy, chiefly in prose. The tragedians tended generally to imitate Racine with but few innovations and only occasional moments of true poetic inspiration; Voltaire, Crébillon, and Piron were probably the best practitioners in the tragic mode at this time.

Since the principal trends of the eighteenth century continued relatively unchanged into the nineteenth, we need not linger over the period 1800–1820. But the century as a whole proved to be the greatest for poetry in the history of French literature. So many talented—and even great—poets wrote during these one hundred years that we must distinguish them by generations and movements.

The first group to be considered is the first Romantic generation, which includes Alphonse de Lamartine, Victor Hugo, Alfred de Musset, and Alfred de Vigny.

Alphonse-Marie-Louis de Prat de Lamartine (1790–1869) ushered in what was promptly recognized as a new poetic era when he published his *Méditations* in 1820. In this collection there was no absolute break with the past: the themes, diction, rhetorical figures, and images of most of the poems remained those of the eighteenth and very early nineteenth centuries. But the tone, attitude, and atmosphere were new. The pouring forth of the soul, the depth of feeling, and the aura of melancholy that pervaded such poems as "L'Isolement," "Le Vallon," and "Le Lac" revealed the dawn of a new kind of poetry. The volume was accordingly received with general acclamation, and Lamartine found himself famous overnight. In 1830 he entered the *Académie française* and published the *Harmonies poétiques et religieuses,* a collection of sixty-five poems, principally hymns to the deistic power which for him had replaced the Christian God. Of his many other lyric poems perhaps the best was "La Vigne et la maison" (1857) in which his mental torment turns at last into a melancholy resignation. Lamartine also inaugurated the romantic form of the philosophical epic, a genre later continued by Victor Hugo and Leconte de Lisle. Only two stages of what was to have been an immense poem covering the history of the world from before the Flood to after the Last Judgment were actually produced: *Jocelyn* (1836) and *La Chute d'un ange* (1838). While the whole of his vast production was uneven in quality, the influence of Lamartine on the subsequent development of French poetry was enormous.

Despite the quantity of his production, Lamartine was eclipsed in this and in all other aspects of his work by the greatest of the Romantics, Victor-Marie Hugo (1802–1885). After publishing volumes of *Odes* and *Ballades* which still owed a good deal to an earlier age, Victor Hugo established himself as leader of the new school with four outstanding collections: *Les Feuilles d'automne* (1831), *Les Chants du crépuscule* (1835), *Les Voix intérieures* (1837), and *Les Rayons et les ombres* (1840). In these remarkable volumes Hugo's emotional life was displayed side by side with the major public events of his generation in a style which revealed the poet as one of the great virtuosos of French literature. All of the major themes and motifs of romanticism are present in what are unquestionably masterpieces of lyric expression. The immensity of Hugo's visionary powers appeared with the publication of *Les Châtiments* (1853), a huge satire of Napoleon III; *Les Contemplations* (1856); and especially *La Légende des siècles* (1859–1883), a philosophical epic presenting a grandiose view of real and imaginary highlights of human "history."

Alfred de Musset (1810–1857) is primarily remembered as a poet for his *Nuits: La Nuit de Mai* (1835), *La Nuit de Décembre* (1835), *La Nuit d'Août* (1836), and *La Nuit d'Octobre* (1837), a series of lyric dialogues between the poet and his Muse in which the former's efforts, following his mistress' betrayal, to tear himself out of his despair and to return to poetry and life are poignantly detailed. This was his last truly successful poetry, written at the age of twenty-nine. Earlier he had provided fine examples of young romantic enthusiasm, whole-hearted in their display of personal emotions, though at the same time he was mocking the ideals and ideas of Victor Hugo's romanticism. His character was thus not as simple as it may at first have appeared to be. In any event, it was his analytical approch that saved much of his early poetry from being merely the self-centered effusions of a young man and that made his *Nuits* a major contribution to French lyricism.

Alfred de Vigny (1797–1863), whom Sainte-Beuve described as having returned early to his "ivory tower," was at the same time the most aristocratic and the most intellectual of the great Romantics. Vigny was not perfectly consistent in his expressed ideas, and that may help to remind us that he was really a poet and not a philosopher. He occasionally seems to have lost sight of that fact himself, and there are passages here and there that seem lifeless when measured against most of his work, probably because in writing them he was more concerned with expounding ideas than with re-creating the emotions which those ideas had evoked in him. But such lapses are rare; Vigny, in general, is rich both in ideas and in strong attitudes toward them, with the result that pessimism, stoicism, religious torment, idealism, and the social doctrine of the Positivists are found intermingled in his austere but often magnficent poems, of which the principal volumes are *Les Poèmes antiques et modernes* (1826) and the posthumous *Destinées* (1864).

A remarkable poet, who by birth but not by literary affilia-tion was of the same generation as Musset, must be men-tioned here. Gérard Labrunie, who wrote under the name of Gérard de Nerval (1808–1855), belonged to a group that has since been classed under the rubric of "romantic symbolism." His poetry is marked by an obscurity suggestive of Mallarmé and by a hallucinatory quality that reveal Nerval, not only as an early symbolist, but as a direct precursor of the sur-realists. He underwent periods of insanity from 1841 to the end of his life, and his mental illness left its stamp on his prin-cipal collection of sonnets, *Les Chimères* (1854), composed, as he said, "in a state of supernatural reverie." Probably his two most famous sonnets are "Artémis" and "El Desdichado." Although the nineteenth century proved to be so rich a period for lyric poetry, the fact that the greatest examples of roman-tic theater (e.g., Musset's *Lorenzaccio*) were written in prose attests to the decline of verse as the principal means of dra-matic expression.

Victor Hugo's *Hernani* (1830) and *Ruy Blas* (1838) re-main, however, as examples of their author's extraordinary ability to express himself effectively in verse in all possible circumstances. Despite many weaknesses of construction, artificialities of plot, and a frequent poverty of psychological depth, these dramas are often stunning for their poetry. Love duets are succeeded by lyrical meditations or by ringing Spanish tirades; epic or satirical tones follow passionate outbursts or evocative "arias." It has been said with some justification that Hugo's plays are made of a series of poems, only superficially connected, but admirable for their brilliance and variety.

The next major generation of French poets was that of 1850, including the members of the "Art for Art's Sake" school, whose leader was Théophile Gautier (1811–1872). The poems of Gautier's *Poésies* (1830) were in general too close to those of Hugo and Musset, but already distinguished by their tendency to resemble painting in words. His true originality became apparent with the publication of *Émaux et camées* (1852–1872), a volume in which the poet claimed to be treating minor subjects with as much perfection of detail as possible, like a miniaturist. Actually, the collection goes far beyond the confines of the enameller and represents a transposition of the plastic vision into verbal art in a manner that directly foreshadows the Parnassian movement.

The other chief representative of the same generation in poetry was Théodore de Banville (1823–1891), the advocate of rich rime as "le clou d'or" of poetry. A clown, virtuoso, and juggler with words, Banville resurrected the outmoded ballade, rondel, triolet, and chant royal, and created a new genre: *l'ode funambulesque.* His concern with perfect workmanship and unusual rhythms, his disdain of the bourgeoisie and passionate attachment to Greek beauty, caused him to be accepted by the Parnassians as one of their own.

The Parnassian movement, centered upon *Le Parnasse contemporain, recueil de vers nouveaux,* a serial anthology published in 1866, containing poems by Gautier, Banville, Baudelaire, Leconte de Lisle, Heredia, Verlaine, Mallarmé, and others, soon became as diffuse in doctrine as the list of its first adherents would suggest. Nevertheless, the basic ideal was clear and the term "school" is appropriate in this case. The essential position of the movement was anti-romantic, especially anti-Lamartine and anti-Musset. The goal was a synthesis of the Positivist spirit with the "Artistic" ideal, resulting in a solid, substantial poetry characterized by perfection of composition and endowed with plastic qualities like those of the "Art for Art's Sake" school. The lesser members of the group, Sully-Prudhomme, José-Maria de Heredia, François Coppée, Albert Glatigny, Léon Dierx, and others, were all outshone by their acknowledged leader, Charles Leconte de Lisle (1818–1894), whose principal collections were the *Poèmes antiques* (1852–1872), and the *Poèmes barbares* (1862–1878), and the *Poèmes tragiques* (1884). A certain impassivity combined with a fundamental but not unwavering pessimism, the whole expressed with remarkable craftsmanship, characterize the poetry of this writer who was strongly attacked later by the symbolists.

As there were four great romantics of the first generation, so we may speak of four great symbolists: Baudelaire, Verlaine, Rimbaud, and Mallarmé. Charles Baudelaire (1821–1867) remains one of the poets of the nineteenth century who live on almost as our contemporaries in the twentieth. His position in the literary history of his period was pivotal. *Les Fleurs du mal* (1857) shows traces of romanticism and the "Art for Art's Sake" ideal, while at the same time it advances the development of the symbolist technique. Tortured by contrary impulses toward beauty and evil, the poet attempts a series of "escapes" ranging from the "artificial paradises" of alcohol and drugs through blasphemy and perversion to death. Baudelaire's synesthetic imagery (which was related to his theory of "correspondances") exerted considerable influence on such poets as Rimbaud and Mallarmé; his myth of the metropolis can be seen again in Apollinaire; his interest in dreams points ahead to the Surrealists; and one could extend the list of influences indefinitely. Indeed, there are few major themes of twentieth century poetry that cannot be traced back, directly or indirectly, to *Les Fleurs du mal,* one of the most magnificent collections of poetry in the history of French literature.

Paul Verlaine (1844–1896), the musician in verse *par excellence,* reacted against the eloquence of some of his predecessors in favor of a fluid simplicity of line. The influence of Baudelaire upon him is primarily to be felt in the persistent aura of melancholy accompanied by a kind of emotional fatigue that permeates his best poetry. His verse is almost entirely suggestive, never assertive, and the half-tones of a verbal impressionism are expressed in song-like rhythms and vague images in his most successful collections, notably *Les Fêtes galantes* (1869), *Romances sans paroles* (1874), and *Sagesse* (1881).

Jean-Arthur Rimbaud (1854–1891) produced all of his poetry between the ages of twelve and twenty-one. The spirit of revolt (against virtually everything that could be called "established") was manifest in his earliest verse and increased progressively to the point at which, aged seventeen, he repudiated his own previous poems and all of the rest of contemporary literature, proposing to replace it with a poetry written in a new language capable of revealing a new vision of reality. According to his famous "lettres du voyant" the poet was to become a seer and prophet, a state of being that he would reach in part through a systematic "dérèglement de tous les sens" which would permit him to perceive himself and the world in entirely new ways. The attempt to do this led Rimbaud to moments of glorious hallucination that are reflected especially in his prose poems, but it also showed him that the imagination alone, no matter how far it is extended, cannot really transform reality in a fundamental or permanent way. Having failed to realize his own goal, he renounced literature definitively, probably at the age of twenty-one. His most celebrated poems are "Le Bateau ivre" and "Voyelles," followed by the prose-and-verse spiritual autobiography *Une Saison en enfer* (1873), and the magnificent collection of prose-poems,

Les Illuminations, all of which have exerted an immeasurable influence on modern poetry.

Stéphane Mallarmé (1842–1898) distinguished himself as the most absolute of the symbolist absolutists. His attempt to re-create reality through the power of *le verbe* (the poetic "Word" in somewhat the sense of the theological *logos*) led to poems of a sublime but often relatively incomprehensible purity and crystalline beauty in which syntax is disrupted and punctuation sometimes abolished. *L'Après-midi d'un faune* (1875) is no doubt the best known single poem of Mallarmé but not the most representative. "Le Vierge, le vivace et le bel aujourd'hui" quoted in Chapter Four is more typical of the obscure but lapidary and highly lyric poetry produced by this extraordinary "chercheur de l'idéal."

To this list of iconoclasts two names must be added: Tristan Corbière and Jules Laforgue. Corbière (1845–1875), in his *Amours jaunes* (1873) combined despair and cynicism with stunningly realistic evocations of the lives of Breton sailors. His difficulty for English readers derives chiefly from his nautical vocabulary and the abundance of colloquialisms that fill most of his poems; nonetheless he is well worth the effort needed to read him. The virility of his poetry makes it a perfect antidote to the more sentimental and "literary" effusions of the early romantics, whom he mocked directly in such poems as "La Fin." Jules Laforgue (1860–1887) was heavily influenced by Corbière and in turn exerted considerable influence on a number of twentieth-century poets, notably T. S. Eliot. In his *Complaintes* (1885), *L'Imitation de Notre-Dame la Lune,* and *Le Concile féerique* (1887) Laforgue, with the help of neologisms, slang, and free verse, expressed his despair of impotent humanity. His ironic and picturesque style give him a singularly modern appeal, and the influence of his free verse technique is obvious in much of the poetry written since his time.

The end of the nineteenth century was marked by a fragmentation of poetic inspiration that resulted in the formation of any number of "schools," none of which produced a really great poet. The *instrumentistes,* the symbolist school as officially constituted, the *école romane* of Charles Moréas, the *verslibristes,* and the various independent poets of the period need not detain us.

As we enter the twentieth century two names stand out above all others: Paul Valéry and Paul Claudel. Claudel (1868–1955), whose *Cinq grandes odes* (1910) represent him at his poetic best, invented the *verset* to express the products of his essentially Catholic inspiration. Through this form of free verse, in which the style of Biblical verses is at least partially reproduced, Claudel created a kind of poetry unique in French literature. A mixture of eloquence and of extremely concrete imagery and metaphor produce in his poems a somewhat diffuse effect. The Dionysian exuberance of his inspiration will tolerate no such careful planning and minute control as we find in the totally different poetry of Valéry.

Unlike Claudel, Valéry remained ever within the framework of classical French prosody; he was the last major poet to do so. Valéry (1871–1945) is best known for *La Jeune Parque* (1917) and *Le Cimetière marin* (1920), in both of which he shows the extent to which the symbolism of Mallarmé survived into our own century. Again in Valéry we find the Mallarméan sense of poetic language as a world in itself. And again we find the same type of obscurity. It should be noted, however, that this obscurity differs in a major respect from that of the Surrealists in that it represents in no sense a *random* use of language. Every detail is thoroughly and artistically controlled. The language is not that of day-to-day functional communication, but it does bear a definite relationship to reality conceived of as an organizable experience. Language for Valéry remains an *order,* not, as is the case for the surrealists, a deliberately chaotic expression of the disorder found in reality.

Before turning to the surrealists, we must mention Guillaume Apollinaire (1880–1918) whose *Alcools* (1913) and

Calligrammes (1918) represent the cubist and pre-surrealist period just prior to the First World War. Apollinaire was an experimenter who can be thought of as the precursor of any number of schools, none of which he really belonged to himself. His typographical experiments ranged from the first total avoidance of punctuation in a poem to the disposition of the words on the page in such a way as to produce a visual image (whence the name of his collection, *Calligrammes*). His style, or rather styles, were various and not always successful. While he was not a genius of the stature of Valéry, he nonetheless represented with extraordinary fidelity the diverse moods, ideas, and attempts at artistic experimentation that marked the period in which he lived, and many of his poems will no doubt remain long after those of his contemporaries have been forgotten.

The second quarter of the twentieth century was dominated by surrealism, which produced many excellent poets not all of whom remained members of the original camp for long. The surrealist position is a logical outgrowth of a tradition that can be traced back at least as far as the romanticism of Victor Hugo. It represents a basic dissatisfaction with the earlier attempts to grasp reality within the framework of the organized world. Victor Hugo avoids the issue by seeming to place God in *another* world; the Positivistic (Parnassian) realist shuts off our view of true reality in this world by accepting exterior, physical nature as the whole of reality; the symbolist (of the Mallarméan type) tries to break up the order of language so as to get away from the limited Positivistic view of external reality, but he does not break it up adequately: one can still construe a Mallarméan sentence with a little effort. All of these attempts to represent ultimate reality are therefore limited by their failure to escape from the known, physical, organized world which, according to the surrealists, is so clearly *not* reality. Since the only escape from the order of nature is *via disorder,* the surrealist position is opposed to order and logic. Chance, hazard, the unforeseeable and irrational become deified. In order to put the mind into contact with the irrational, the rational faculties must be eliminated in favor of the subconscious mind. Surrealist poetry, then, is the direct, illogical expression of the irrational content of the unconscious mind uncontrolled by voluntary effort of any kind.

André Breton (b. 1896), the leader of the movement, is perhaps the only writer who ever really followed its principles to the letter, and he is more of a prose writer than a poet. Paul Éluard (1895–1952) was perhaps the best poet produced by the surrealist tradition. His poetry was marked by a simplicity and direct sensuality to which surrealism added merely an element of mystery. Louis Aragon (b. 1897) was also one of the original surrealists, though after he switched his allegiance to Communism in 1930 he severed his ties with surrealism. Like Breton, he may well be better remembered as a novelist than as a poet. René Char (b. 1907) began as a surrealist but broke away from the movement in 1937 and has since developed into one of the best of contemporary French poets. His obscurity is more a reflection of his attempt to communicate complicated emotions than a deliberate effort in the direction of surrealism.

Among the "independents," one of the most easily accessible poets to the foreign reader is Jules Supervielle (b. 1884). He claims no literary affiliations and differs from the surrealists in his respect for life, his essential simplicity, and the over-all coherence of his writing. Pierre-Jean Jouve (b. 1887) is also a non-surrealist, though he shares some of the more nightmarish qualities of the members of that movement. His tone is often prophetic as he mixes, not always smoothly, Freudian techniques with religious themes in an effort to illuminate the "indissoluble conflict" which, in his opinion, characterizes Man. Of Henri Michaux (b. 1899) little is known, except that he is thoroughly unorthodox, highly original, essentially pessimistic, and endowed with a destructive sense of humor. His poetry seems intended primarily to exorcize the "surrounding powers of the hostile world," even if it sometimes becomes necessary to feed these powers in order to have something there to exorcize. Pierre Emmanuel (b. 1916) is a poet of essentially Catholic inspiration who shows clearly the influence of Jouve. His style, marked by an oratorical eloquence and a tendency toward apocalyptic imagery, has sometimes suffered from Emmanuel's enormous facility, while at other times it has shown promise of greatness.

Many other contemporary poets might have been mentioned here; indeed, the same can be said of all the periods we have touched upon. The point of this brief resumé has not been to try to treat exhaustively the history of French poetry but rather to provide, through a rapid, panoramic view, some idea of the scope and variety which have characterized French verse over the centuries. It is hoped that even such a fleeting glimpse as this will be of some help in "locating" the French poets whose names are most likely to be encountered by the reader, and that it will indicate in part what a wealth of material lies ready to be discovered by those who wish to explore the vast literary domain represented by the poetry of France.

APPENDIX

Appendix:
Questions to Ask of a Poem

It is obvious that there can be no mechanical "method" of analyzing a poem. Analysis requires insight, and insights are notoriously hard to mechanize. All the same, it is possible to call attention to aspects of a poem that are potential sources of insight, and that is the intended purpose of the following questions. Not all of these questions will be relevant to any particular poem. The only way to judge whether a specific question is appropriate to a given case is to note what kind of answer it elicits. If the answer leads to further questions pointed in the same direction, then the original question may be presumed to have been fruitful.

The order in which the questions are presented here is essentially arbitrary. Since the goal of analysis is to determine how various elements of a text operate together to produce a total experience, it is necessary at some point in the examination of the poem to try to envisage all of the essential elements simultaneously as they interact with one another. Which part of the text one begins with is therefore of secondary importance. The main point is to become conscious of the significant relationships between the various functional parts of the poem.

The ability to answer many of these questions accurately will often depend upon some preliminary knowledge of historical, biographical, or other extraliterary facts having to do with such matters as the author's life, milieu, tradition, period, and esthetic or ideological principles. It is hoped that having that information in hand, the reader will be able to see further into the text he is examining with the aid of thoughtful answers to whichever of these questions are appropriate to the case in question.

Preliminary Questions

1. On the basis of the first or second reading, how rich does this poem seem to be? Is it worthy of detailed analysis, and how thorough an analysis does it seem to require?
2. What particular insights or perceptions does the poem give rise to on first inspection (before you have begun to examine it systematically)?
3. Are there sections of the text which seem to be marked by exceptional intensity and therefore require special attention?
4. Are the denotative meanings of all the words in the poem clear?
5. Is the syntax of the poem fully understood? If not, will rearranging the order of the words make their grammatical relationships with one another clearer?
6. What references does the poet make to ideas, facts, events, persons, or things, real or imaginary, that exist outside the context of the poem? What are the denotative and connotative meanings of these references?
7. What is the subject of the poem; i.e., what is the poet ostensibly talking about?

Sound

8. At what point(s) in the poem do the following effects involving sound occur, and what is their function:
   a. Onomatopoeia?

     b. Extended onomatopoeia?

     c. Mimesis?

     d. Significant emphasis on euphonious or cacophonous sounds?

     e. Dissonance?

     f. Assonance?

     g. Consonance, including alliteration?

     h. Tonal chiasmus?

     i. Augmentation and/or diminution?

     j. Internal rime?

     k. End rime?

9. Do the poet's rimes tend to be predominantly rich, sufficient, or insufficient?

10. What characterizes the over-all verse texture of the poem?

11. Does the poet break the rule of hiatus?

12. What effect do the sound phenomena just mentioned have on other elements of the poem? (See No. 24, for example.)

Shape

13. What kind of lines does the poet use in this poem?

     a. If they are regular, are they commonly used lines or relatively rare ones?

     b. If the poet is writing in free verse, are the lines intended to be *versets?*

14. What type(s) of stanzas does the poet use in this poem?

     a. How many lines do the stanzas contain?

     b. Are the stanzas unusually long or short?

     c. Are the stanzas isometric or heterometric?

     d. If the poet is not using stanzas, does he write in verse paragraphs instead?

     e. Does the poet change the stanzaic pattern in the course of the poem?

     f. Has the poet used a standard stanzaic form such as terza rima or the tail rime stanza, or has he invented his own stanzaic form(s)?

15. What kind(s) of rime scheme is (are) used in the poem?

    a. Does the poet use a simple, standard type such as alternate, embraced, or couplet rimes, or does he employ a more difficult and complicated, perhaps redoubled, pattern?

    b. Are the rimes mixed?

    c. Is the poem written in blank verse?

    d. Is the rule of alternation observed or broken?

16. Has the poet adopted a fixed form, such as the sonnet, rondeau, or sestina?

17. Are special devices (such as acrostics or visual shapes) used in the poem?

18. In so far as the poet is operating within a tight, predetermined framework, how skillfully and easily does he manoeuvre "in harness"?

19. What role does the shape of the poem play in the total structure of connotations?

Rhythm and Pace

20. Does the poet use a free verse cadence or a regular rhythmic pattern?

21. If he uses a regular rhythmic pattern, what is it; i.e., what basic expectation does he establish in the reader's mind with regard to the regular recurrence of caesuras and/or stressed syllables followed by *coupes?*

22. How often, where, and in what way does the poet depart from the rhythmic norm?

    a. Where does he shift or eliminate the caesura?

    b. What variations does he use in the position of the *coupes,* thereby changing the time intervals between accented syllables?

    c. How many or how few *coupes* does he use, and what effect does this have on pace?

    d. What use does he make of *enjambement* and *contre-rejet,* and what is their effect on pace?

    e. Apart from the question of pace, what function do *enjambement* and *contre-rejet* perform in the poem?

Do they serve, for example, to accentuate a word, or to "imitate" the denotative meaning of a line?

23. What is the effect upon pace of:
    a. Alliteration, vowel and consonant sequences, internal and end rime?
    b. Mute *e*'s?
    c. Repetitions of words or phrases?
    d. Isolated lines or words, or unusual spacings?
    e. Special use of punctuation, capitals, italics?
    f. Elaborate rime?
    g. The denotations and connotations of the given passage?

24. What is the effect of rhythm and pace on other elements of the poetic structure?

DICTION AND RHETORIC

25. Are the connotations of the poet's words strongly felt?

26. Is the poet emphasizing the etymological meaning of any particular word, either in order to evoke a picture based on the root-metaphor from which the word sprang, or else in order to contrast the connotations evoked by the original meaning with those implied by the modern meaning?

27. Is the poet's diction essentially permissive or restrictive?
    a. If it is restrictive, what principle governs the choice of acceptable words?
    b. Has the poet invented terms (neologisms or nonce-words), perhaps through the adaptation of one part of speech to another?

28. Has the poet made unusually effective word choices?

29. Since it is generally recognized that nouns and verbs are the basic materials of most poetry, we may ask: Is the poet appropriately sparing in his use of adjectives and adverbs?

30. Does the poet use modifiers (adjectives and adverbs) purposefully and effectively?

31. Does the poet use ambiguity deliberately? How and why?

32. Are there unintentional ambiguities, *chevilles,* tautologies, or pleonasms in the poem?
33. Does the poet use ironic statement in the poem?
34. Does he use understatement (meiosis) or overstatement (hyperbole)? To create an ironic effect?
    a. Is understatement expressed by means of antonomasia or litotes? Is the effect ironic or euphemistic?
    b. Is antiphrasis used to express understatement or overoverstatement with euphemistic or ironic effect?
35. Does the poet employ circumlocution (periphrasis), including hypocoristic language, to express himself euphemistically?
36. Do syllepsis, paronomasia, or catachresis occur in the poem? With witty effect?
37. Are antithesis, oxymoron, catachresis, or ambiguity used for purposes of verbal concentration, with or without a witty effect?
38. Does the poet express strong emotion or vividness with overstatement (hyperbole), exclamation, aposiopesis, anaphora, apostrophe, personification, zeugma, or anacoluthon?
39. Do hysteron-proteron, inversion (anastrophe), or chiasmus occur in the poem? What function do they serve?
40. What effect do the diction and rhetorical devices in the poem have on other elements of the poetic structure?

IMAGE AND SYMBOL

41. To which senses do the images of the poem appeal?
42. In addition to the sensory images, are there kinesthetic, thermal, pressure, static, dynamic (kinetic) or synesthetic images?
43. Are the images united by their denotative or connotative meanings so as to form motifs? What are the motifs?
44. Does the poet use metonymy (including synecdoche)?
45. Are any metaphors mixed or incomplete?
46. Are the metonymies and metaphors alive or are they clichés?

47. Is the poem allegorical?
48. What symbolic elements are there in the poem?
    a. Is their presence suggested by deliberate vagueness on the part of the poet?
    b. Are they devices intended to serve specifically as symbols?
49. Are there mythical or archetypal elements in the poem?

THEME, TONE, ATTITUDE, ATMOSPHERE

50. What is the theme of the poem?
51. How does the poet cause the theme (the poem's connotative meaning) to develop from the subject (the poem's denotative meaning)?
52. What is the tone of the poem?
53. How is the tone affected by the poet's use of diction and rhetoric?
54. What attitude(s) is (are) implied in the poem?
55. What is the atmosphere of the poem?
56. How is the atmosphere affected by setting, background, rhythm, and imagery?

GENRE

57. Is the poem epic, didactic, dramatic, satiric, narrative, or lyric?
58. What conventions operating in the poem must be accepted by the reader?
59. What are the dramatic elements in the poem (characters, including the speaker; situation; exposition; episodes; climax; etc.)?
60. What can be said about the relationship between the thematic organization and the dramatic organization of the poem?

CONCLUSION

61. How do the elements of the poem require one another and operate together to produce a total, unified experience?

GLOSSARY

Glossary of Critical Terms

ABLAUT: See ASSONANCE.

ACCENT: See STRESS.

ACROSTIC (*acrostiche,* m.): A poem constructed in such a way that the initial letters of the successive lines spell a word or words when read down.

ADEQUATE RIME: See RIME.

AFFECTIVE FALLACY: The term used by W. K. Wimsatt and M. C. Beardsley in *The Verbal Icon* to characterize the error of judging a poem in terms of its effect upon the reader, as opposed to judging it in terms of its own inherent qualities.

ALEXANDRINE (*alexandrin,* m.): The commonest French line of verse, used for most serious poetry. It contains twelve syllables, usually divided by a central caesura (*q.v.*) into two hemistichs (*q.v.*) of six syllables each. The term "alexandrine" is sometimes applied to the English iambic hexameter, which also contains twelve syllables.

ALLEGORY (*allégorie,* f.): An extended narrative in which ideas, feelings, moral, spiritual, or intellectual qualities or abstractions are personified, so that a second level of meaning appears beneath the surface account of events.

ALLITERATION (*allitération,* f.): Sometimes called "head rime," alliteration consists of the repetition of the same consonant

214

sound at the beginning of several words in close proximity to one another. Alliteration is therefore a special form of consonance (*q.v.*).

ALLITERATION, MUTED: See MUTED ALLITERATION.

ALLITÉRATION SOURDE: See MUTED ALLITERATION.

ALLUSION (*allusion,* f.): Any indirect reference the poet may make to ideas, facts, events, persons, or things, real or imaginary, which the reader is expected to recognize from prior knowledge.

ALTERNANCE, LA LOI D': See RULE OF ALTERNATION.

ALTERNATE RIMES (*rimes croisées* or *alternées,* f. pl.): The rime scheme (*q.v.*) in accordance with which two pairs of riming words are interlocked with one another: *abab.*

ALTERNATION, RULE OF: See RULE OF ALTERNATION.

AMBIANCE: See ATMOSPHERE.

AMBIGUITY (*ambiguïté,* f. *équivoque,* f.): (1) Vagueness in the use of words; (2) multiple meanings expressed by single words or phrases (see AMPHIBOLE); (3) as used by William Empson in *Seven Types of Ambiguity,* any level of meaning beyond the strictly denotative meaning of a word, phrase, or passage.

AMPHIBOLE, -Y, -OGY, -OGISM (*équivoque,* f.): The kind of ambiguity caused by grammatical looseness or by the multiple meanings of words.

ANACOLUTHON (*anacoluthe,* f.): An elliptical (and often ungrammatical) form of expression in which the correlative of a word is omitted, usually as the result of an abrupt change in syntactical construction in the middle of a sentence.

ANACREONTIC VERSE (*vers anacréontiques,* m. pl.): Verse written in praise of Epicurean pleasures.

ANALYSIS (*analyse,* f.): The close examination of the structure (*q.v.*) of a poem.

ANAPEST (*anapeste,* m.), adj. ANAPESTIC: The English foot (*q.v.*) which consists of two unaccented syllables followed by an accented syllable ($\smile\smile/$), as in the word "indis*creet.*"

ANAPHORA (*anaphore,* f.): The repetition of a word or construction in successive lines or clauses.

ANASTROPHE: See INVERSION.

ANTIPHRASIS (*antiphrase,* f.): The designation of a person or thing by its opposite.

ANTITHESIS (*antithèse,* f.): A figure in which sharply opposed ideas are expressed in a balanced syntactical arrangement.

ANTONOMASIA (*antonomase,* f.): The substitution of a proper name for a common noun, or vice versa.

APHORISM (*aphorisme,* m.): A short, concentrated expression of a truth.

APOLOGUE (*apologue,* m.): A fable involving animals.

APOSIOPESIS (*aposiopèse,* f. *réticence,* f.): A sudden breaking off in the middle of an utterance so that the thought remains only half expressed.

APOSTROPHE (*apostrophe,* f.): A sudden break in the development of a speech, at which point the speaker turns aside and addresses either an absent person or thing or a personified abstraction.

ARCHAIC DICTION: See DICTION.

ARCHETYPE (*archétype,* m.): A primordial image or structure, thought by disciples of Carl Jung to exist in a "collective unconscious" or racial memory shared by all men.

"ART FOR ART'S SAKE" SCHOOL (*école* [f.] *de l'art pour l'art*): A group of mid-nineteenth-century poets led by Théophile Gautier, dedicated to art as an end in itself. The poems by members of the group tended to center on minor subjects visually portrayed in impeccable detail.

ASSONANCE (*assonance,* f.): Sometimes called "ablaut," assonance consists of the repetition of the same vowel sound in associated words without regard to surrounding consonants. Assonance sometimes replaces rime at the ends of lines.

ATMOSPHERE (*ambiance,* f.): Sometimes ambiguously called "mood" (*q.v.*), atmosphere is the general, pervasive feeling engendered by the totality of a passage or poem.

ATTITUDE (*disposition*, f.): Sometimes ambiguously called "mood" (*q.v.*), the poet's attitude is the way in which he looks upon his subject.

AUDITIVE IMAGE: See IMAGE.

AUGMENTATION: The term invented by Kenneth Burke to describe the repetition of a consonant cluster with the consonants spaced out on their second appearance, thus: "*gleaming gold*." The term can also be applied to a similar treatment of vowels. (See DIMINUTION.)

BALLADE (*ballade*, f.): A fixed form (*q.v.*) consisting usually of three stanzas and an envoy (*q.v.*). The customary rime scheme is *ababbcbC* in the first three stanzas and *bcbC* in the envoy. The capital letter stands for a refrain. Sometimes the refrain is doubled, the fourth line of each of the first three stanzas being repeated in the envoy as line 2, thus: *bBcB*. The ten-line (*grande*) ballade has the rime scheme *ababbccdcD* in the three stanzas and *ccdcD* in the envoy. Other forms of the ballade are also sometimes encountered.

BARBARISM (*barbarisme*, m.): The use of deformed or non-existent words.

BESTIARY (*bestiaire*, m.): A medieval treatise on animals in the form of didactic verse (*q.v.*).

BLANK VERSE (*vers blancs*, m. pl.): A succession of unrimed lines (in English, iambic pentameters).

BOUTS-RIMÉS (m. pl.): Sets of unattached rime words to which verses were prefixed as a fashionable pastime, particularly in the seventeenth century.

BRETON ROMANCE: See ROMAN BRETON.

BRIGADE, LA: The group of student-poets at the Collège de Coqueret who gathered around Ronsard, Du Bellay, and other members of the future *Pléiade* (*q.v.*) beginning in 1547.

BURLESQUE (*burlesque*, m.): A form of satire in which an elevated subject is treated in a trivial manner.

CACOPHONY (*cacophonie,* f.): The result of a succession of harsh, jarring, or not easily pronounced sounds. (see DISSONANCE.)

CADENCE (*cadence,* f.; *rythme,* m.): The rhythm of free verse which tends to follow the rhythms of speech while arranging them into highly complicated patterns.

CAESURA (*césure,* f.): A pause in the interior of a line occurring normally after the sixth syllable of an alexandrine (*q.v.*) and after the fourth syllable of a decasyllable (*q.v.*).

CALLIGRAMME: See CARMEN FIGURATUM.

CANTO (*chant,* m.): Major subdivision of a long poem.

CARMEN FIGURATUM (*calligramme,* m.:): A "shaped" poem which is so designed that it presents a visual image on the printed page.

CARPE DIEM POEM: A poem based on the theme: "Seize the day!" in which someone is exhorted to make the most of youth while it lasts.

CATACHRESIS (*catachrèse,* f.): A strained figure of speech, especially the metaphorical association of two material things.

CÉSURE: See CAESURA.

CHANSONS COURTOISES (f. pl.): Medieval lyric poems usually expressing the passion of a knight for his lady.

CHANSONS D'AUBE (f. pl.): Poems based on the farewell of lovers forced to separate at dawn.

CHANSONS DE CROISADE (f. pl.): Medieval songs supposedly sung by crusaders.

CHANSONS DE DANSE (f. pl.): Songs sung as accompaniment to a dance.

CHANSONS DE GESTE (f. pl.): Medieval epics, popular from the eleventh to the fourteenth century, in which the exploits of knightly warriors are recounted.

CHANSONS D'HISTOIRE (f. pl.): Also called *Chansons de toile:* songs which tell the story of a girl separated from her lover, with whom she is finally reunited or from whom she is permanently estranged because of his infidelity or death.

CHANSONS DE MAL MARIÉES (f. pl.): Medieval songs relating the complaints of a wife regarding her husband.

CHANSONS DE TOILE (f. pl.): See CHANSONS D'HISTOIRE.

CHANT: See CANTO.

CHANT-FABLE (f.): A medieval narrative written partly in prose and partly in verse, such as *Aucassin et Nicolette*.

CHANT ROYAL (*chant royal*, m.): A fixed form (*q.v.*) usually involving five eleven-line stanzas rimed *ababccddedE* and an envoy (*q.v.*) rimed *ddedE*, the capital letters indicating a refrain.

CHEVILLE (f.): A word or group of words inserted by the poet simply to fill out a line or to establish a rime, a process called "padding" in English.

CHIASMUS (*chiasme*, m.): The balancing of two halves of a phrase so that the terms of the second half correspond to those of the first half, but in reverse order.

CHIASMUS, TONAL: See TONAL CHIASMUS.

CINQUAIN (*quintain*, m.; *quintil*, m.): A five-line stanza.

CIRCUMLOCUTION (*périphrase*, f.:) The avoidance of a word or phrase by the use of an indirect statement, usually a descriptive phrase.

CLASSICISM (*classicisme*, m.): The movement, particularly in seventeenth-century France, which advocated (among many other things) reason, moderation, order, and discipline in the arts.

CLICHÉ (*cliché*, m.; *banalité*, f.): A trite, platitudinous, or hackneyed phrase. (See DEAD METAPHOR.)

CLOU D'OR (m.): Théodore de Banville's term for rich rime (*q.v.*), the "golden nail" that tacks the line in place.

COMMEDIA DELL'ARTE: A modernized form of Italian medieval farce.

COMMUNICATION: See HERESY OF COMMUNICATION; FALLACY OF COMMUNICATION.

COMPARAISON: See SIMILE.

CONDENSATION: The Freudian term referring to the dream-process whereby parts of two logically unrelated objects or situations are coalesced to form a single, new object or situation. A similar process sometimes occurs in the formation of poetic imagery.

CONNOTATION (*implication,* f.; *signification secondaire,* f.): The implied meaning of a word, phrase or allusion; all meaning beyond the literal meaning of the strict denotation (*q.v.*) is covered by the term. (See STRUCTURE OF CONNOTATIONS.)

CONSONANCE (*consonance,* f.): The repetition of identical consonant sounds in words in close proximity to one another, without reference to associated vowel sounds. Consonance is sometimes used at the ends of lines as a substitute for rime. (See ALLITERATION, ASSONANCE, RIME.)

CONTE DÉVOT (m.): A short anecdotal story of a religious nature, popular in the twelfth and thirteenth centuries.

CONTENT (*fond,* m.): A term often illogically used to refer to the ideas expressed by a poem. In this sense it is often opposed to "form" (*q.v.*). (See NOSEGAY FALLACY, HERESY OF PARAPHRASE, FALLACY OF COMMUNICATION, MESSAGE HUNTING.)

CONTRE-REJET (m.): The process of beginning a statement at the end of a line and giving over the entire next line to the completion of the phrase. It is thus the reverse of enjambement (*q.v.*). (See REJET A L'HÉMISTICHE.)

COUPE (f.): A brief pause or hesitation (mental if not physical) following an accented syllable in the interior of a French line of verse.

COUPLET (*distique,* m.): A pair of riming lines, also called a "distich."

COUPLET RIMES (*rimes plates* or *suivies,* f. pl.): The rime scheme (*q.v.*) in accordance with which lines are rimed in successive pairs: *aabbccdd*.

CRITICISM, NEW: See NEW CRITICISM.

CUBISM (*cubisme,* m.): A movement in painting in the years just preceding the First World War that was characterized by an emphasis on geometrical solids rather than on more directly representational forms; it exerted a considerable influence on certain poems of (primarily) Max Jacob and Guillaume Apollinaire.

DACTYL (*dactyle,* m.): adj. DACTYLIC: In English prosody, a foot (*q.v.*) consisting of a stressed syllable followed by two unstressed syllables (/◡◡), as in the word "*hes*itate."

DEAD METAPHOR: See METAPHOR.

DECASYLLABLE (*décasyllabe,* m.): The French line of ten syllables, usually containing a caesura (*q.v.*) after the fourth syllable.

DENOTATION (*désignation,* f.; *signification primaire,* f.): The literal, primary meaning of a word, phrase, or allusion. (See CONNOTATION.)

DICTION (diction, f.): The choice and arrangement of words in a poem. "Restrictive diction" is used in this book to refer to the kind of language from which the poet excludes certain words or concepts *a priori,* on the ground that they are not, for one reason or another, "poetic." One form of restrictive diction is "archaic diction" in which the poet imitates the language of an earlier age. "Permissive diction" is the term used here to describe the kind of poetic diction which accepts any term or concept as potentially proper poetic material. "Neologistic diction" is the type of language in which the poet creates new words, often by adapting one part of speech to another. "Hypocoristic diction" is the kind of language marked by the frequent use of endearing terms or nicknames.

DIDACTIC VERSE (*poésie didactique,* f.): The sort of verse which has as its primary purpose the communication of ideas, usually moral injunctions.

DIGRAPH (*digraphe,* m.): Two letters used together to represent a single sound, as in the French *ai, eu, ph,* etc.

DIMETER (*dimètre,* m.): A French line containing two *mesures* (*q.v.*), or an English line containing two feet. (See FOOT.)

DIMINUTION: The term invented by Kenneth Burke to describe the repetition of a consonant cluster with the consonants spaced out on their first appearance, thus: "*gory and grim.*" The term can also be applied to a similar treatment of vowels. (See AUGMENTATION.)

DISPLACEMENT: The Freudian term referring to the dream process whereby the significance attached to one object or situation is transferred to another logically unrelated object or situation. A similar effect sometimes occurs in poetic imagery. (See CONDENSATION.)

DISPOSITION: See ATTITUDE.

DISPOSITION DES RIMES: See RIME SCHEME.

DISSONANCE (*dissonance*, f.): (1) The use in close proximity to one another of not quite identical but closely related sounds; (2) cacophony (*q.v.*).

DI(S)SYLLABLE (*dissyllabe*, m.): A French line of verse containing only two syllables.

DISTANCE: See PSYCHIC DISTANCE.

DISTICH: See COUPLET.

DISTIQUE: See COUPLET.

DIZAIN (m.): A French stanza of ten lines.

DODECASYLLABLE (*dodécasyllabe*, m.): An alternate (but infrequently used) name for the alexandrine (*q.v.*).

DOUZAIN (m.): A French stanza of twelve lines.

DRAMATIC MONOLOGUE (*monologue dramatique*, m.): A poem expressing the words of a single person who reveals by what he says both his own character and the nature of the dramatic situation in which he finds himself.

DRAMATIC POETRY (*poésie dramatique*, f.): Poetry which requires (at least hypothetically) theater presentation.

DYNAMIC IMAGE: See IMAGE.

ECOLE DE L'ART POUR L'ART: See "ART FOR ART'S SAKE" SCHOOL.

ECOLE LYONNAISE: Sixteenth-century "school" of poets centered in Lyons, "led" by Maurice Scève.

ECOLE ROMANE: Late nineteenth century school of poets led by Jean Moréas.

ECOLE SYMBOLISTE: Late nineteenth-century school of minor poets, not to be confused with the Symbolist movement in general.

ELEGY (*élégie*, f.): A genre of lyric poetry usually devoted to mourning the death of an individual, a time of year, or the past in general. (See UBI SUNT ELEGY.)

ELLIPSIS (*ellipse*, f.): The omission of necessary words in a grammatical construction.

EMBRACED RIMES (*rimes embrassées*, f. pl.): The rime scheme (*q.v.*) in which a riming couplet is surrounded by another pair of riming lines: *abba*.

E MUET: See MUTE E.

ENJAMBEMENT (*enjambement*, m.): A construction in which one or more words belonging to a syntactical unit that has been begun in one line of verse are carried over uninterruptedly into the next line. (See CONTRE-REJET, RUN-ON LINE.)

ENNEASYLLABLE (*ennéasyllabe*, m.): A nine-syllable line of verse.

ENVOY (*envoi*, m.): A short final stanza at the end of a ballade (*q.v.*) or a chant royal (*q.v.*), usually addressed to an important personage. It normally begins with the word "Prince."

EPIC (*épopée*, f.): A poem relating heroic actions involving a nation and/or a legendary (usually national) hero.

EPIC POETRY (*poésie épique*, f.): Poetry having the characteristics of the epic (*q.v.*).

EPIQUE: The French adjective, "epic."

EPITHET, TRANSFERRED: See TRANSFERRED EPITHET.

EPOPÉE: See EPIC.

EQUIVOQUE: See AMPHIBOLE, AMBIGUITY.

ESTHETIC DISTANCE: See PSYCHIC DISTANCE.

ETYMOLOGY (*étymologie*, f.): The original meaning of a word, or the study of the historical development of the meanings of words.

EUPHEMISM (*euphémisme,* m.): A softening of the effect that would be created by the use of a word or phrase, usually achieved by substituting some other word or phrase.

EUPHONY (*euphonie,* f.): The "musical" effect produced by a series of easily pronounced or otherwise pleasing sounds.

EXCLAMATION (*exclamation,* f.): A sudden emotional outburst.

EXPLICATION DE TEXTE (f.): A formal presentation of the results of the textual analysis of a poem; often called an "explication" in English.

EXPRESSION IRONIQUE (f.): See IRONIC STATEMENT.

EXTENDED ONOMATOPOEIA (*onomatopée prolongée,* f.): The repetition of the key sounds of an onomatopoeic word in other neighboring words.

EXTRALITERARY TECHNIQUES (*techniques extra-littéraires,* f. pl.): Methods of elucidating literary texts involving techniques borrowed from such non-literary fields as psychology, history, or anthropology.

FABLIAU (m.), plural FABLIAUX: A short medieval story of a humorous or anecdotal type.

FALLACY: See AFFECTIVE FALLACY, INTENTIONAL FALLACY, NOSEGAY FALLACY.

FALLACY OF COMMUNICATION: Allen Tate's term for the attempt to use poetry as a vehicle for communicating ideas or feelings that should properly be expressed in prose.

FALLACY, PATHETIC: See PATHETIC FALLACY.

FARCE (*farce,* f.): A short play whose unique purpose is to cause laughter.

FEMININE RIME (*rime féminine,* f.): A rime involving words ending in a mute *e,* plural *-es,* or the verbal ending *-ent.*

FIGURATION (*représentation figurative,* f.): The method of indirect comparison by which A is partly compared to B in a way that directs attention to connotations of A that would not otherwise be obvious. Also called "tropology," the method includes metaphor (*q.v.*) and metonymy (*q.v.*).

FIGURE OF COMPARISON: See METAPHOR, SIMILE.

FIGURE OF CONTIGUITY: See METONYMY, SYNECDOCHE.

FIGURES DE RHÉTORIQUE: See RHETORICAL FIGURES.

FIGURES OF SPEECH: See RHETORICAL FIGURES.

FIXED FORM (*forme fixe,* f.): A pre-established conventional verse pattern involving a set number of lines to a stanza, a fixed number of stanzas, a predetermined rime scheme, or any combination of these.

FLOATING ACCENT (*accent mobile,* m.): One of the variable accents that may fall on any syllable in a French line of verse (as distinguished from the fixed accents preceding the caesura and at the end of the line).

FOND: See CONTENT.

FOOT (*pied,* m.): In English metrics, a group of syllables, usually including one stressed and one or two unstressed syllables, the accentual pattern of which recurs regularly in a poem.

FORM (*forme,* f.): The term often illogically used to refer to the manner in which the ideas "contained" by a poem are expressed. (See CONTENT.)

FORME: See FORM.

FORM, FIXED: See FIXED FORM.

FREE RIMES: See MIXED RIMES.

FREE VERSE (*vers libres,* m. pl.): Verse written without regard to standard rules of prosody. (See CADENCE, VERSET.)

GENRE (*genre,* m.): As used in this book, genre denotes a class of poems having in common a particular mode of "hypothetical presentation" (*q.v.*), an identifiable tone (*q.v.*), or a tendency to develop certain kinds of motifs (*q.v.*).

GUSTATIVE IMAGE: See IMAGE.

H MUET: See MUTE H.

HARMONY: See VERSE TEXTURE.

HEAD RIME: See ALLITERATION.

HEMISTICH (*hémistiche,* m.): The first or last half of a line of verse (usually an alexandrine).

HENDECASYLLABLE (*hendécasyllabe,* m.): The French line of eleven syllables.

HEPTAMETER (*heptamètre,* m.): A French line of seven *mesures* (*q.v.*), or an English line of seven feet (see FOOT).

HEPTASYLLABLE (*heptasyllabe,* m.): A seven-syllable line of verse.

HERESY OF COMMUNICATION: Cleanth Brooks' term for the mistaken notion that a poem is simply an ornament clothing an idea.

HERESY OF PARAPHRASE: Cleanth Brooks' term for the erroneous notion that a poem's meaning is fully expressed by a paraphrase of its ideas.

HÉROÏ-COMÉDIE: See MOCK EPIC.

HETEROMETRIC (*hétérométrique,* adj.): The term used to describe a stanza containing lines of various lengths. (See ISOMETRIC.)

HEXAMETER (*hexamètre,* m.): A French line of six *mesures* (*q.v.*), or an English line of six feet (see FOOT).

HEXASYLLABLE (*hexasyllabe,* m.): A six-syllable line of verse.

HIATUS (*hiatus,* m.): The immediate succession in the same breath group of two pronounced vowel sounds (without an intervening consonant sound).

HUITAIN (m.): A stanza of eight lines.

HYPERBOLE (*hyperbole,* f.): An exaggeration for rhetorical effect.

HYPOCORISM (*sobriquet,* m.): A nickname.

HYPOCORISTIC DICTION: See DICTION.

HYPOTHETICAL PRESENTATION, MODE OF: The manner in which a poem is ostensibly to be presented (as sung, or dramatized, etc.).

HYSTERON-PROTERON: A form of expression in which an item that should logically be named first is instead mentioned last.

Iᴀᴍʙ (*iambe*, m.), adj. Iᴀᴍʙɪᴄ: The English foot (*q.v.*) consisting of an unaccented syllable followed by an accented syllable (⌣⁄), as in "*alert.*"

Iᴍᴀɢᴇ (*image*, f.): A combination of words which evokes a sensory recollection. Critics differentiate between visual (sight), olfactory (smell), gustative (taste) tactile (touch), auditive (hearing), kinesthetic (motion or posture), thermal (heat), pressure, static, dynamic or kinetic (force or movement), and synesthetic (mixed sensory) images.

Iɴᴄᴏᴍᴘʟᴇᴛᴇ Mᴇᴛᴀᴘʜᴏʀ: See Mᴇᴛᴀᴘʜᴏʀ.

Iɴsᴛʀᴜᴍᴇɴᴛɪsᴛᴇs (m. pl.): Members of a minor school of poets at the end of the nineteenth century.

Iɴsᴜғғɪᴄɪᴇɴᴛ Rɪᴍᴇ: See Rɪᴍᴇ.

Iɴᴛᴇɴᴛɪᴏɴᴀʟ Fᴀʟʟᴀᴄʏ: The error, denounced by the New Critics, of judging the poem in terms of the author's intention. (See Nᴇᴡ Cʀɪᴛɪᴄɪsᴍ.)

Iɴᴛᴇʀɴᴀʟ Rɪᴍᴇ (*rime intérieure*, f.): A rime (*q.v.*) involving words in the interior of a line of verse.

Iɴᴠᴇʀsɪᴏɴ (*inversion*, f.): Also called "anastrophe," the reversal of the normal syntactical order of words.

Iʀᴏɴɪᴄ Sɪᴛᴜᴀᴛɪᴏɴ (*situation ironique*, f.): A situation in which there is a discrepancy between deserts and reward, expectancy and fulfillment; or one in which the character's total or partial ignorance is combined with the spectator's or reader's full knowledge.

Iʀᴏɴɪᴄ Sᴛᴀᴛᴇᴍᴇɴᴛ (*affirmation ironique*, f.): A statement intended to convey a meaning different from the one it professes to give.

Iʀᴏɴʏ (*ironie*, f.): A general term covering both ironic situation (*q.v.*) and ironic statement (*q.v.*).

Isᴏᴍᴇᴛʀɪᴄ (*isométrique*, adj.): The term used to describe a stanza all of whose lines are of uniform length. (See Hᴇᴛᴇʀᴏᴍᴇᴛʀɪᴄ.)

Iᴛᴀʟɪᴀɴ Sᴏɴɴᴇᴛ: See Sᴏɴɴᴇᴛ.

Jᴇᴜ-ᴘᴀʀᴛɪ (m.), (Provençal "*partimen*"): A medieval genre of lyric poetry in which two poets engage in a debate.

JONGLEURS (m. pl.): Medieval wandering minstrels who sang *chansons de geste* (*q.v.*).

KINESTHETIC IMAGE: See IMAGE.
KINETIC IMAGE: See IMAGE.

LAIS (m. pl.): Short, versified medieval love stories. Also Villon's spelling of *legs,* "legacy."
LAISSE (f.): The name given to the assonanced stanza of the medieval *chansons de geste* (*q.v.*).
LAPIDARY (*lapidaire,* m.): A medieval treatise on precious stones in the form of didactic verse (*q.v.*).
LIAISON (f).: Sometimes called "linking" in English; the pronunciation of a normally silent consonant at the end of a word because the following word begins with a vowel.
LITOTES (*litote,* f.): The form of understatement (*q.v.*) in which something is affirmed by the denial of its opposite.
LYRIC POETRY (*poésie lyrique,* f.): The form of poetry, usually brief, which is written as though it were to be sung.

MASCULINE RIME (*rime masculine,* f.): A rime involving words with endings other than mute *e,* plural *-es,* or the verbal ending *-ent.*
MATERIALS (*matière,* f.): Wellek and Warren's term for the "aesthetically indifferent" elements of a poem, i.e., the words themselves. (See STRUCTURE.)
MEIOSIS: See UNDERSTATEMENT.
MESSAGE HUNTING: The attempt to express the meaning of a poem by paraphrasing its raw ideas.
MESURE (f.): A group of syllables occurring between pauses in a French line of verse.
METAPHOR (*métaphore,* f.): A figure in which two objects are indirectly compared by substituting one for the other or by identifying them, it being understood that the objects are dissimilar except in one essential characteristic. A "dead metaphor" is an overworked metaphor that has become a cliché (*q.v.*). A "mixed metaphor" is the simul-

taneous indirect comparison of one object with two or more other unrelated objects. An "incomplete metaphor" is a metaphor in which the substitution of terms is not fully carried out. (See SIMILE.)

META-REALITY (sometimes *para-réalité*, f.): As used in this book, the term refers to the reconstruction or transposition of reality that is portrayed in poetry.

METONYMY (*métonymie*, f.): The indirect comparison (by identification or by substitution of one for the other) of two objects between which there exists a logically analyzable quantitative or causative relationship. (See SYNECDOCHE.)

MIMESIS (*harmonie imitative*, f.): As used in this book (in John Ciardi's sense), this term refers to the effect produced when the quality of sound of a word seems particularly appropriate to the word's denotation in cases where the denotation is not an onomatopoeia (*q.v.*). This effect is also called "pseudo-onomatopoeia."

MIRACLE PLAYS (*miracles*, m. pl.): Medieval dramas based on the lives of saints.

MIXED METAPHOR: See METAPHOR.

MIXED RIMES (*rimes libres* or *mêlées*, f. pl.): Also called "free rimes"; the use in verse of an unpredictably varying rime scheme.

MOCK EPIC (*héroï-comédie*, f.): A form of satire in which a trivial subject is treated with epic solemnity.

MONOLOGUE, DRAMATIC: See DRAMATIC MONOLOGUE.

MONOMETER (*monomètre*, m.): A French line containing one *mesure* (*q.v.*), or an English line of one foot (*q.v.*).

MONOSYLLABLE (*monosyllabe*, m.): A one-syllable line of verse.

MOOD (*disposition*, f.; *ambiance*, f.): A term often used (ambiguously) to refer to either attitude (*q.v.*) or atmosphere (*q.v.*).

MORALITY PLAY (*moralité*, f.): A medieval comedy that aimed (ostensibly) at both the edification and the amusement of its audience.

Motif (*motif*, m.): A type of character, verbal pattern, or situation that recurs regularly in literature, art, or folklore.

Muscular Enactment: John Ciardi's term for the sort of mimesis (*q.v.*) in which the muscles of the speaker's vocal organs seem to reënact the denotative meaning of a word.

Muted Alliteration (*allitération sourde*, f.): The use of closely related but not quite identical sounds at the beginning of words in close proximity to one another.

Mute E (*e muet*, m.): In French, *e*'s not carrying a written accent or followed by a consonant in the same syllable (other than final plural *-s* or verbal ending *-nt*).

Mute H (*H muet*, m.): French non-aspirate *h*.

Mystery Play (*mystère*, m.): A lengthy (usually fifteenth century) religious play representing in part the drama of the Redemption.

Myth (*mythe*, m.): A narrative intended to dramatize a fundamental speculation of mankind.

Mythos: The Greek word for "plot," "fable," "story," from which the word myth (*q.v.*) is derived.

Narrative Poetry (*poésie narrative*, f.): The kind of poetry which relates a story.

Neologistic Diction: See Diction.

Neuvain (m.): A French stanza of nine lines.

New Criticism: A movement in British and especially American criticism dating from the 1920's which favors close textual analysis over biographical or historical criticism.

Nonce Word (*mot de circonstance*, m.): A word created for use on a single occasion.

Non-Poetry: See Prose and Verse.

Nosegay Fallacy: The mistaken idea that the poem is a collection of attractive but separate "ingredients" which can be "extracted" from the text and evaluated.

Oblique Expression (*expression indirecte*, f.): Any method of expression in which what is literally said is something other than what is meant.

OCTOSYLLABLE (*octosyllabe,* m.): An eight-syllable line of verse.

ODE FUNAMBULESQUE (f.): A humorous genre of light verse invented by Théodore de Banville in 1857.

OLFACTORY IMAGE: See IMAGE.

OLORIME (f.): A pair of lines which, being completely identical in sound, rime with each other from beginning to end.

ONOMATOPOEIA (*onomatopée,* f.): The effect produced when the sound of a word imitates the denotation of a word which is also a sound.

ONZAIN (m.): A French stanza of eleven lines.

OVERSTATEMENT (*exagération,* f.): An exaggeration.

OXYMORON (*oxymoron,* m.): A verbal paradox reduced to the minimal number of words.

PACE (*allure,* f.): The rate of speed at which a line is read, or the quality of the line which causes it to be read at a certain rate relative to other lines.

PADDING: See CHEVILLE.

PANTOUM (*pantoum,* m.): A Malayan fixed form (*q.v.*) with an indefinite number of stanzas, each a quatrain (*q.v.*) rimed *abab.* The second and fourth lines of each stanza become the first and third lines of the next stanza, and the last line of the last is the first line of the first stanza, so that the poem ends with the same line with which it began.

PARADOX (*paradoxe,* m.): A seemingly self-contradictory statement which contains a basis of truth.

PARAGRAPH, VERSE: See VERSE PARAGRAPH.

PARAPHRASE, HERESY OF: See HERESY OF PARAPHRASE.

PARNASSIAN MOVEMENT (*mouvement parnassien,* m.): An anti-romantic poetic movement, led by Leconte de Lisle, centered upon *Le Parnasse contemporain* (1866), its goal being a synthesis of the "Art for art's sake" tradition with the spirit of positivism.

PARODY (*parodie,* f.): The satirical imitation of one work by another.

PARONOMASIA (*paronomase*, f.): The illogical association of one word with another because of similarities in their sounds.

PARTIMEN: See JEU-PARTI.

PASTICHE (*pastiche*, f.): The satirical imitation of one work by another, theoretically created by pasting together bits taken from different parts of the work which is being ridiculed.

PASTORAL (*pastorale*, f.): An "irregular" dramatic genre characterized by an Arcadian setting and a quasi-comic plot with a happy ending.

PASTOURELLE (f.): A medieval lyric poem portraying the wooing of a shepherdess by a knight or by the poet.

PATHETIC FALLACY: Ruskin's term for the ascription of human traits to nature, as in "a pitiless storm."

PENTAMETER (*pentamètre*, m.): A French line of five *mesures* (*q.v.*), or an English line of five feet (see FOOT).

PENTASYLLABLE (*pentasyllabe*, m.): A five-syllable line of verse.

PERIPHRASIS: See CIRCUMLOCUTION.

PERMISSIVE DICTION: See DICTION.

PERSONIFICATION (*personnification*, f., *prosopopée*, f.): Also called "prosopopoeia," the investing of abstract ideas or inanimate objects with human qualities or actions.

PETRARCHAN SONNET: See SONNET.

PIED: See FOOT.

PLÉIADE, LA: A group of seven sixteenth-century poets associated with Ronsard.

PLEONASM (*pléonasme*, m.): the unnecessary addition or repetition of a word in expressing an idea.

POETRY (*poésie*, f.): As distinguished in this book from "verse," the word "poetry" refers to those serious works of literature, whether or not they are in verse, which are capable of inspiring strong emotions in the reader with the greatest economy of literary means. (See also NARRATIVE, DIDACTIC, SATIRIC, DRAMATIC, LYRIC, and EPIC POETRY, and VERSE.

PRECIOSITY (*préciosité,* f.): The literary tradition, strong in seventeenth-century France, in which delicacy of feeling was expressed with a nicety of language involving elaborate circumlocutions that soon became coy, finical, and ridiculous.

PRESSURE IMAGE: See IMAGE.

PROSE (*prose,* f.): A term used ambiguously to refer on the one hand to writing which is not versified, and on the other hand to writing which is "prosaic," "pedestrian," i.e., not poetic.

PROSOPOPOEIA: See PERSONIFICATION.

PSEUDO-ONOMATOPOEIA: See MIMESIS.

PSYCHIC DISTANCE (*distance,* f.): Also called "esthetic distance" by the New Critics, "psychic distance" describes the reader's detachment from the work of art, which prevents him from confusing it with reality.

QUATRAIN (*quatrain,* m.): A four-line stanza.

QUINTAIN: See CINQUAIN.

QUINTIL: See CINQUAIN.

REDOUBLED RIME (*rime redoublée,* f.): A rime involving more than two words.

REJET (m.): The words run on to the second line in a case of enjambement (*q.v.*).

REJET A L'HÉMISTICHE (m.): A form of *contre-rejet* (*q.v.*) in which only the first half of the second line is given over to the completion of the statement.

REPETEND (usually *refrain,* m.): Any repeated element of a poem, with or without variations.

RESTRICTIVE DICTION: See DICTION.

RHETORICAL FIGURES (*figures de rhétorique,* f. pl.): Special syntactical organizations of words intended to produce a specific emotional effect.

RHÉTORIQUEURS, LES GRANDS: A group of poets who, at the end of the fifteenth and beginning of the sixteenth centuries, devoted themselves almost exclusively to experimenting with elaborate forms of versification.

RHYME: See RIME.

RHYTHM (*rythme*, m.): A regularity of recurrence of a sound phenomenon such as stress, pause, or change of pitch.

RICH RIME: See RIME.

RIME (*rime*, f.): In French, an identity of sound involving the last audible sound(s) of two or more words. If the last three sounds are involved the rime is "rich" (*riche*); if two sounds are involved the rime is "adequate" or "sufficient" (*suffisante*); if only one sound is involved, the rime is "insufficient" or "weak" (*faible*). (See ALTERNATE RIMES, ASSONANCE, COUPLET RIMES, EMBRACED RIMES, FEMININE RIME, INTERNAL RIME, and MASCULINE RIME.)

RIME COUÉE: See TAIL RIME STANZA.

RIME INTÉRIEURE: See INTERNAL RIME.

RIME SCHEME (*disposition des rimes*, f.): The pattern according to which rimes are distributed in the stanza.

RIMES ALTERNÉES: See ALTERNATE RIMES.

RIMES CROISÉES: See ALTERNATE RIMES.

RIMES EMBRASSÉES: See EMBRACED RIMES.

RIMES PLATES: See COUPLET RIMES.

RIMES REDOUBLÉES: See REDOUBLED RIMES.

RIMES TIERCÉES: See TERZA RIMA.

RITUAL (*rite*, m.): A communal activity which is the dramatic equivalent of a myth.

ROMAN BRETON (m.): One of a group of *romans courtois* (*q.v.*) of Celtic inspiration centered on the legends of King Arthur, Tristan, and the Quest of the Holy Grail.

ROMAN COURTOIS (m.): One of a number of courtly romances, aristocratic in inspiration, popular in the twelfth and thirteenth centuries.

ROMAN D'AVENTURE (m.): A freer and more realistic development of the *roman courtois* (*q.v.*).

"ROMANTIC" TRIMETER (*trimètre "romantique*," m.): An alexandrine (*q.v.*) inaccurately termed "romantic" because

Victor Hugo popularized it, though examples can be found in the seventeenth century. In the "romantic" trimeter, the central caesura is replaced by two caesuras, one after the fourth syllable and one after the eighth.

RULE OF ALTERNATION (*loi d'alternance*, f.): The rule in strict French versification that masculine and feminine rimes (*qq.v.*) must alternate with each other throughout a poem.

RUN-ON LINE (*vers enjambé*, m.): A line involved in enjambement (*q.v.*).

SATIRIC POETRY (*poésie satirique*, f.): The kind of poetry in which persons, types, or ideas are ridiculed.

SEPTAIN (m.): A French stanza of seven lines.

SERVENTOIS (m.), (Provençal *sirventes*): A medieval genre based on moral or political causes and characterized by many pointed allusions to current events.

SESTINA (*sextine*, f.): A complicated fixed form (*q.v.*) composed of six unrimed *sixains* (*q.v.*). The last word of each line of the first stanza recurs as the last word of a different line of each of the next five stanzas. The poem concludes with a tercet (*q.v.*) the three lines of which end in three of the six terminal words of the poem; the other three words may also appear elsewhere in the three respective lines. The scheme in accordance with which the final words appear is indicated in the following diagram, in which the letters are the last words of the six respective lines of each stanza: *abcdef, faebdc, cfdabe, ecbfad, deacfb, bfdeca, eca.*

SHAPE (*forme*, f.): The term used in this book to refer to the design of a poem that results from the combination of the lengths of the lines, the number of lines in a stanza, and the rime scheme.

SIMILE (*comparaison*, f.): A direct comparison of one object with another involving the words "like" or "as" (*comme, pareil à, ainsi que*, etc.). (See METAPHOR.)

SIRVENTES: See SIRVENTOIS.

SIXAIN (m.): A French stanza of six lines.

SOLECISM (*solécisme,* m.): A deviation from standard usage, particularly in matters of syntax.

SONNET (*sonnet,* m.): A fourteen-line fixed form (*q.v.*) which in French is always of the Italian (Petrarchan) type, *viz.,* two quatrains (*q.v.*) rimed *abba, abba,* followed by two tercets (*q.v.*) rimed variously; *ccd, ede* or *ccd, dee* are common types.

SOTIE (f.): A kind of satirical morality play (*q.v.*).

STATIC IMAGE: See IMAGE.

STANZA (*strophe,* f.): A group of lines in a poem serving roughly as the equivalent of a paragraph, often held together by a predetermined rime scheme (*q.v.*). (See VERSE PARAGRAPH.)

STOCK RESPONSE: An unthinking reaction to a text based on purely conventional grounds.

STRESS (*accent,* m.): The accent or emphasis placed on certain syllables of a spoken phrase. In French it is usually weak and accompanied by a distinct shift in vocal pitch.

STROPHE: See STANZA.

STRUCTURE (*structure,* f.; *facture,* f.): (1) Warren and Wellek's term for the manner in which poetic "materials" (*q.v.*) "acquire aesthetic efficacy." (2) As used in this book, the system of interrelationships engaged in simultaneously by all the elements of the poem. (See STRUCTURE OF CONNOTATIONS.)

STRUCTURE OF CONNOTATIONS: The phrase used in this book to refer to the process by which the implied meanings of a poem are expressed as a result of the interaction of all of the significant elements of the poem.

SUBJECT (*sujet,* m.): The literal, denotative meaning of a poem. (See THEME.)

SUFFICIENT RIME: See RIME.

SUJET: See SUBJECT.

SURREALISM (*Surréalisme,* m.): A twentieth-century poetic movement purporting to express the raw content of the poet's unconscious mind by means of a succession of freely associated images.

SYLLEPSIS (*attelage*, m.): A rhetorical device in which one word links two constructions, each of which implies a slightly different meaning of the yoking word.

SYMBOL (*symbole*, m.): A recurring image or other device standing for a broader, more pervasive area of meaning than a metaphor can represent.

SYMBOLIST MOVEMENT (*mouvement symboliste*, m.): A rather vague and ill-defined term characterizing the work of such poets as Baudelaire, Mallarmé, Verlaine, Rimbaud, and a number of lesser writers.

SYMBOLIST SCHOOL (*école symboliste*, f.): A minor school of poets at the end of the nineteenth century, not to be confused with the symbolist movement.

SYNECDOCHE (*synecdoque, synecdoche*, f.): A form of metonymy (*q.v.*) in which the relationship between compared items is one of part to whole.

SYNESTHESIA (*synesthésie*, f.): The faculty of responding with one sense to the stimulation of another, as in those persons who see colors when music is played or *vice versa*.

SYNESTHETIC IMAGE: See IMAGE.

TACTILE IMAGE: See IMAGE.

TAIL RIME STANZA (*rime couée*, f.): A fixed form (*q.v.*) stanza usually having the rime scheme *aabccb*, the *b* lines being shorter than the *a* and *c* lines.

TAUTOLOGY (*tautologie*, f.): The useless repetition of an idea or a word; a redundancy.

TENSON (m.), (Provençal *tenso*): A medieval poetic genre involving a debate between two poets.

TERCET (*tercet*, m.): A three-line stanza.

TERZA RIMA (*tierce rime* or *rime tiercée*, f.): A succession of tercets (*q.v.*) rimed *aba, bcb, cdc, ded*, etc., concluding with either a single line riming with the middle line of the previous tercet (*yzy z*), or with a tercet whose middle line rimes with the first and third lines of the first tercet of the poem (*zaz*).

TETRAMETER (*tétramètre*, m.): A French line of four *mesures* (*q.v.*), or an English line of four feet (see FOOT).

TETRASYLLABLE (*tétrasyllabe*, m.): A four-syllable line of verse.

TEXTURE, VERSE: See VERSE TEXTURE.

THEME (*thème*, m.): The implied meaning of the subject (*q.v.*) of a poem.

THERMAL IMAGE: See IMAGE.

TONAL CHIASMUS: Kenneth Burke's term for the effect caused by the repetition of two successive sounds in reverse order, as in "Et les *f*ruits *p*asseront la *p*romesse des *f*leurs."

TONE (*ton*, m.): The quality of the poem which suggests the way in which the poet wants the reader to react toward him or toward his subject.

TRAGI-COMEDY (*tragi-comedie*, f.): An "irregular" dramatic genre characterized by a complicated, romanesque plot with a happy ending.

TRANSFERRED EPITHET: An adjective applied to a noun to which it does not properly belong since it actually modifies another (usually unexpressed) noun.

TRAVESTY (*parodie*, f.; *travestissement*, m.): A broad or grotesque parody (*q.v.*).

TRIMÈTRE (*trimètre*, m.): A French line of three *mesures* (*q.v.*), or an English line of three feet (See FOOT).

TRIOLET (*triolet*, m.): A fixed form (*q.v.*) in eight lines, of which the first two are repeated as the last two and the fourth is the same as the first. Rime scheme: *abaaabab*.

TRISYLLABLE (*tri[s]syllabe*, m.): A three-syllable line of verse.

TROCHEE (*trochée*, m.), adj. TROCHAIC: The English foot (*q.v.*) composed of an accented syllable followed by an unaccented syllable (/⌣), as in the word "*temp*er."

TROPE (*trope*, m.): (1) A brief Latin paraphrase of a sacred text introduced into the Liturgy; (2) A figure of speech.

TROPOLOGY: See FIGURATION.

TROUBADOUR (m.) A medieval lyric poet of the South of France (Provence).

TROUVÈRE (m.): The Northern counterpart of the troubadour (*q.v.*).

UBI SUNT ELEGY: An elegy (*q.v.*) like Villon's "Ballade des dames du temps jadis" containing an expressed query beginning "Where are . . . , *e.g.*, "Where are the snows of yesteryear?"

UNDERSTATEMENT (*litote*, f.): Also called "meiosis"; the indirect method of expression which presents something as less significant than it really is.

VERBE (m.): as used by and in connection with certain symbolist poets, "le verbe" refers to the poetic "Word" in a sense analogous to that of the Divine Word, *Verbum*, or *Logos*, in which a mystical creative power is implied.

VERS (m.): In the singular, a line; in the plural, verse (*q.v.*).

VERS BLANCS: See BLANK VERSE.

VERSE (*vers*, m. pl.): a composition in metrical form with regular rhythm and usually (unless it is free verse) (*q.v.*) predetermined line lengths and rime scheme (*q.v.*).

VERSE, FREE: See FREE VERSE.

VERSE PARAGRAPH: A group of lines of verse not strictly a stanza, corresponding to a prose paragraph.

VERSET (m.): A free verse line invented by Paul Claudel intended to imitate the effect of Biblical verses.

VERSE TEXTURE (*harmonie*, f.): Sometimes called "harmony"; the over-all sound quality of a poem or passage of verse.

VERS LIBRES: See FREE VERSE.

VERSLIBRISTE (m.): A writer in free verse.

VILLANELLE (*villanelle*, f.): A fixed form (*q.v.*) consisting of five tercets (*q.v.*) followed by a quatrain (*q.v.*), all on two rimes. The opening line is repeated at the end of the second and fourth tercets; the final line of the first tercet

also comes at the end of the third and fifth. The two refrain
lines are repeated at the end of the quatrain. Rime scheme:

1 2   1   2   1   2   12
aba, aba, aba, aba, aba, abaa.

VISUAL IMAGE: See IMAGE.

WEAK RIME: See RIME.

ZEUGMA (*zeugma,* m.): A figure in which a yoking word links
two constructions with only one of which it is grammatically connected.

BIBLIOGRAPHY

Bibliography

The following list of books and records is, of course, merely suggestive rather than exhaustive, and the categories are not entirely rigid. It is hoped, however, that this catalogue will provide a jumping-off point for the reader who wishes to investigate further some of the aspects of French poetry (or poetry in general) touched upon in this book.

I. Dictionaries

a. *All French (modern):*
   Petit Larousse. Paris, Larousse, 1959.
b. *English-French, French-English (modern):*
   Bellows' French Dictionary, 4th ed. London, Longmans, Green & Company, 1951.
   The Concise Oxford French Dictionary, Abel and Marguerite Chevalley, comp. Oxford, Clarendon Press, 1940.
   Mansion, J. E., *Shorter French and English Dictionary.* New York, Henry Holt & Company, Inc., n.d.
   The New Cassell's French Dictionary, Denis Girard and others, ed. New York, Funk & Wagnalls Company, Inc., 1962.
c. *Old French-Modern French:*
   Grandsaignes d'Hauterive, Robert, *Dictionnaire d'ancien français, moyen âge et renaissance.* Paris, Larousse, 1947.

II. Grammars

a. *Modern French:*

French grammars (elementary and intermediate) appear so frequently and in such abundance that even a list of suggestions would be pointless. The following are good reference grammars, useful for checking on the finer details of French syntax.

Fraser, W. H., Squair, J., and Parker, Clifford S., *French Composition and Reference Grammar.* Boston, D. C. Heath and Company, 1942.

Mansion, J. E., *French Reference Grammar for Schools and Colleges,* rev. ed. Boston, D. C. Heath and Company, n.d.

b. *Old French:*

Foulet, Lucien, *Petite syntaxe de l'ancien français,* 3rd ed. Paris, H. Champion, 1930.

Anglade, Joseph, *Grammaire élémentaire de l'ancien français.* Paris, 1918.

III. Poetry Collections (Bilingual Translations)

Editions of the works (complete or partial) of individual poets range from the inexpensive *Classiques Larousse* series to the expensive and authoritative *Pléiade* editions published by Gallimard, with all the intermediate stages amply represented. The same is true of anthologies covering given periods or kinds of poetry. The following list is therefore limited to a selection of bilingual editions of French poems in which the original French texts and the English translations are both printed.

a. *Collections of poems by various poets:*

Abbott, Claude Colleer, ed. and trans., *Early Medieval French Lyrics.* London, Constable & Company, Ltd., 1932.

Eldridge, Richard Burdick, trans., *Flowers from a Foreign Field.* Trenton, N. J., Agency Press, 1959.

Fowlie, Wallace, ed. and trans., *Mid-Century French Poets: Selections, Translations, and Critical Notices.* New York, Twayne, 1955.

MacIntyre, Carlyle F., trans., *French Symbolist Poetry.* Berkeley, University of California Press, 1958.

————, and Carmody, F. J., ed. and trans., *Surrealist Poetry in France.* Berkeley, California Book Company, 1953.

Mackworth, Cecily, ed., *A Mirror for French Poetry, 1840–1940: French Poems with Translations by English Poets.* London, George Routledge & Sons, Ltd., 1947.

Martin, Charlotte Hunnewell, trans., *A Few Early French Verses Done into English.* Albany, Argus Press, 1949.

The Penguin Book of French Verse. V. 1. *To the Fifteenth Century,* ed. by Brian Woledge. V. 2. *Sixteenth to Eighteenth Centuries,* ed. by Geoffrey Brereton. V. 3. *Nineteenth Century,* ed. by Anthony Hartley. V. 4. *Twentieth Century,* ed. by Anthony Hartley. Baltimore, Penguin Books, 1957–61. 4 vols.

Thorley, Wilfred Charles, ed. and trans., *A Bouquet from France: One Hundred French Poems with English Translations in Verse and Brief Notes.* Boston, Houghton Mifflin Company, 1926.

b. *Collections of poems by single poets:*

Apollinaire, Guillaume, *Alcools; Poems 1898–1913,* trans. by William Meredith, Introduction and notes by Francis Steegmuller. Garden City, N. Y., Doubleday & Company, Inc., 1964.

————, *Selected Writings,* ed. and trans. by Roger Shattuck. New York, New Directions, 1950.

Baudelaire, Charles, *One Hundred Poems from Les Fleurs du mal,* trans. by Carlyle F. MacIntyre. Berkeley, University of California Press, 1947.

Corbière, Tristan, *Selections from Les Amours jaunes,* trans. by Carlyle F. MacIntyre. Berkeley, University of California Press, 1954.

Gautier, Théophile, *Gentle Enchanter: Thirty-four Poems,* trans. by Brian Hill. Chester Springs, Pa., Dufour Editions, 1961.

Laforgue, Jules, *Poems,* trans. by Patricia Terry. Berkeley, University of California Press, 1958.

Mallarmé, Stéphane, *Poems,* trans. by Roger Fry with commentaries by Charles Mauron. New York, Oxford University Press, 1937.

————, *Selected Poems,* trans. by Charles F. MacIntyre, Berkeley, University of California Press, 1957.

Perse, Saint-John (pseud. of Alexis Léger), *Seamarks,* trans. by Wallace Fowlie. New York, Pantheon Books, 1958.

Rimbaud, Arthur, *The Drunken Boat, Thirty-six Poems by Arthur Rimbaud,* ed. and trans. by Brian Hill. London, R. Hart-Davis, 1952.

————, *Rimbaud's Illuminations, a Study in Angelism,* ed. and trans. by Wallace Fowlie. New York, Grove Press, 1953.

————, *A Season in Hell,* trans. by Louise Varèse. Norfolk, Conn., New Directions, 1952.

Verlaine, Paul, *Selected Poems,* translated by Carlyle F. MacIntyre. Berkeley, University of California Press, 1948.

Villon, François, *Complete Works,* trans. by Anthony Bonner. New York, Bantam Books, 1960.

IV. RECORDINGS OF FRENCH POETRY

A considerable amount of French poetry has been recorded both in France and in the United States. Many libraries have facilities for listening to such poetry records. The following list includes some of the more noteworthy collections:

Disques Véga and Disques Adès (Editions Seghers): "Poètes d'Aujourd'hui." The following poets are recorded on 33⅓ rpm, 7-inch records: Apollinaire, Aragon, Baudelaire, Carco, Cendrars, Claudel, Desnos, Eluard, Hugo, Jacob, Jammes, Musset, Nerval, Péguy, Perse, Rimbaud, Verlaine.

L'Encyclopédie sonore (Librairie Hachette): "Trésor de la poésie lyrique française." Six 33⅓ rpm, 12-inch records (320 E 810 to 320 E 815), as follows: No. 1 Moyen âge. No. 2. Renaissance. No. 3. Dix-septième siècle. No. 4. Dix-huitième siècle et préromantiques. No. 5. Grands romantiques. No. 6. Romantisme et Parnasse. (Each record contains poems of a number of poets read by a variety of readers.)

Lumen: "Anthologie de la littérature de langue française." Each of the following poets is represented in this collection by one 45 rpm, 7-inch record unless otherwise indicated: Apollinaire, Baudelaire (2 records), Cendrars, Charles d'Orléans, Chénier, Eluard, Hugo (4 records), La Fontaine (3 records), Lamartine, Mallarmé, Péguy (4 records), Prévert, Rimbaud (2 records), Ronsard (2 records), Supervielle, Valéry, Verlaine (3 records), Villon (2 records). There is also a record devoted to the Parnassians, and one to the Pléiade.

Pléiade: "Les Classiques vous parlent." Each of the following poets is represented in this collection by one 45 rpm, 7-inch record unless otherwise indicated: Baudelaire, Boileau, Hugo, La Fontaine (2 records), Ronsard, Verlaine, Vigny.

V. BOOKS ON POETIC THEORY AND PRACTICE

In addition to books cited earlier in the text, this list includes works which raise and discuss theoretical questions of the kind treated in Part I of this book, and also a few books which take up matters of practical analysis. It is hoped that those readers interested in such questions will find the volumes listed here stimulating and provocative.

Barfield, Owen, *Poetic Diction, a Study in Meaning,* 2nd ed. London, Faber & Faber, Ltd., 1952.

Bloom, Edward A., Philbrick, Charles H., and Blistein, Elmer M., *The Order of Poetry, An Introduction.* New York, Odyssey Press, 1961.

Brooks, Cleanth, *Modern Poetry and the Tradition.* Chapel Hill, The University of North Carolina Press, 1939.

———, *The Well Wrought Urn, Studies in the Structure of Poetry.* New York, Harcourt Brace & Company, Inc., 1956.

———, and Warren, Robert Penn, *Understanding Poetry; An Anthology for College Students.* New York, Henry Holt & Company, Inc., 1946.

Burke, Kenneth, *The Philosophy of Literary Form: Studies in Symbolic Action,* rev. ed. New York, Vintage Books, 1957.

Ciardi, John, *How Does a Poem Mean?* Boston, Houghton Mifflin Company, 1960.

Crane, Ronald S., *The Languages of Criticism and the Structure of Poetry.* Toronto, University of Toronto Press, 1953.

Empson, William, *Seven Types of Ambiguity,* 3rd ed. Norfolk, Conn., New Directions, 1953.

Frye, Northrop, *Anatomy of Criticism.* Princeton, Princeton University Press, 1957.

Hyman, Stanley Edgar, *The Armed Vision: A Study in the Methods of Modern Literary Criticism,* rev. ed., abridged. New York, Vintage Books, 1955.

Pottle, Frederick A., *The Idiom of Poetry,* new ed. Ithaca, Cornell University Press, 1946.

Ransom, John Crowe, *The New Criticism.* Norfolk, Conn., New Directions, 1941.

———, *The World's Body.* New York, Charles Scribner's Sons, 1938.

Richards, I. A., *Practical Criticism: A Study of Literary Judgment.* New York, Harcourt, Brace & Company, 1954.

Rukeyser, Muriel, *The Life of Poetry.* New York, Current Books, Inc., 1949.

Sewell, Elizabeth, *The Structure of Poetry.* London, Routledge & K. Paul, 1951.

Spire, André, *Plaisir poétique et plaisir musculaire; essai sur l'évolution des techniques poétiques.* New York, S. F. Vanni, 1949.

Stauffer, Donald, *The Nature of Poetry.* New York, W. W. Norton & Company, Inc., 1946.

Wellek, René, and Warren, Austin, *Theory of Literature,* 2nd ed. New York, Harcourt, Brace & Company, Inc., 1956.

Wimsatt, W. K., and Beardsley, M. C., *The Verbal Icon, Studies in the Meaning of Poetry.* Lexington, University of Kentucky Press, 1954.

Wheelwright, Philip, and others, *The Language of Poetry,* ed. by Allen Tate. New York, Russell & Russell, 1960.

VI.   VERSIFICATION, DICTION, RHETORIC, AND SYMBOL

Bodkin, Maud, *Archetypal Patterns in Poetry; Psychological Studies of Imagination.* London, Oxford University Press, 1934.

Banville, Théodore de, *Petit traité de poésie française.* Paris, Bibliothèque Charpentier, 1891.

Boileau-Despréaux, Nicolas, *L'Art poétique.* (This classic work has been published and republished steadily since the seventeenth century and has been translated into English. It appears in an inexpensive edition in the "Classiques Larousse" series published by Larousse, together with *Le Lutrin* of Boileau.)

Charpier, Jacques, and Seghers, Pierre, ed., *L'Art poétique.* Paris, Seghers, 1956.

Du Bellay, Joachim, *La Deffense et illustration de la langue françoyse,* ed. by Henri Chamard. Paris, M. Didier, 1948.

Grammont, Maurice, *Petit traité de versification française,* 12th ed. Paris, Armand Colin, 1947.

————, *Le Vers français, ses moyens d'expression, son harmonie,* 4th ed. Paris, Delagrave, 1937.

Kastner, Leon Emile, *A History of French Versification.* Oxford, The Clarendon Press, 1903.

Konrad, Hedwig, *Etude sur la métaphore.* Paris, M. Lavergne, 1939.

Martinon, Ph., *Les Strophes.* Paris, Champion, 1911.

Morier, Henri, *Dictionnaire de poétique et de rhétorique.* Paris, Presses Universitaires de France, 1961.

Nowottny, Winifred, *The Language Poets Use.* London, The Athlone Press, 1962.

Patterson, W. F., *Three Centuries of French Poetic Theory.* Ann Arbor, University of Michigan Press, 1935. 2 vols.

Thieme, Hugo P., *Essai sur l'histoire du vers français.* Paris, Champion, 1916.

Tobler, Adolf, *Le Vers français, ancien et moderne,* traduit sur la 2e édition allemande par Karl Breul et Leópold Sudre. Paris, F. Vieweg, 1885.

Verrier, Paul, *Le Vers français.* . . . Paris, H. Didier, 1931–32. 3 vols.

VII.   Histories of French Literature

Adam, Antoine, *Histoire de la littérature française au XVIIe siècle*. Paris, Domat, 1948–56. 5 vols.

Bédier, Joseph, and Hazard, Paul, *Littérature française*, rev. ed. by Pierre Martino. Paris, Larousse, 1948–49. 2 vols.

Brereton, Geoffrey, *An Introduction to the French Poets, Villon to the Present Day*. London, Methuen, 1956.

Castex, Pierre, and Surer, Paul, *Manuel des études littéraires françaises*. Paris, Hachette, 1946–53. 6 vols.

Clouard, Henri, *Histoire de la littérature française du symbolisme à nos jours*. Paris, A. Michel, 1947–49. 2 vols.

Jasinski, René, *Histoire de la littérature française*. Paris, Boivin, 1947. 2 vols.

Lalou, René, *Histoire de la littérature française contemporaine (1870 à nos jours)*, rev. ed. Paris, Crès, 1924.

Lanson, Gustave, *Histoire de la littérature française*, remaniée et complétée pour la période 1850–1950 par Paul Tuffrau. Paris, Hachette, 1955.

Neuf siècles de littérature française, des origines à nos jours, ed. by Emile Henriot. Paris, Delagrave, 1958.

Nitze, William A. and Dargan, E. Preston, *A History of French Literature from the Earliest Times to the Present*, 3rd ed. New York, Henry Holt & Company, Inc., 1938.

Paris, Gaston, *La Littérature française au moyen âge*, 6th ed. Paris, Hachette, 1913.

Wright, Charles Henry Conrad, *A History of French Literature*, rev. ed. New York, Oxford University Press, 1925.

VIII.   Biographical and Critical Studies of Major Poets, Short Historical Periods, and Genres

An attempt has been made in this section to provide a starting point for the study of particular poets, periods, or genres. In the case of each poet, whenever possible, a biography and a critical study have been mentioned unless one existing volume deals satisfactorily with the poet's life and work. Since this section is intended to complement Part III of this book, the order of presentation of these entries is chronological by subject rather than alphabetical by author.

a. *Middle Ages*

    1. *Chansons de geste:*

        Faral, Edmond, *La Chanson de Roland, étude et analyse*. Paris, Mellottée, 1948.

Fawtier, Robert, *La Chanson de Roland, étude historique.* Paris, Boccard, 1933.

2. Chrétien de Troyes:
Cohen, Gustave, *Un Grand romancier d'amour et d'aventure au 12ᵉ siècle, Chrétien de Troyes et son œuvre.* Paris, Boivin, 1931.

3. Marie de France:
Hoepffner, Ernest, *Les Lais de Marie de France.* Paris, Boivin, 1935.

4. Early lyric poetry:
Cohen, Gustave, *La Poésie en France au moyen âge.* Paris, Richard-Masse, 1952.
Hoepffner, Ernest, *Les Troubadours dans leur vie et dans leurs œuvres.* Paris, Armand Colin, 1955.
Jeanroy, Alfred, *Les Origines de la poésie lyrique en France au moyen âge,* 3rd ed. Paris, Champion, 1925.

5. Rutebeuf:
Clédat, Léon, *Rutebeuf,* 2nd ed. Paris, Hachette, 1909.

6. *Le Roman de Renard:*
Foulet, Lucien, *Le Roman de Renart.* Paris, Champion, 1914.

7. *Les Fabliaux:*
Bédier, Joseph, *Les Fabliaux,* 4th ed. Paris, Champion, 1914.
Nykrog, Per, *Les Fabliaux; étude d'histoire littéraire et de stylistique médiévale.* Copenhagen, Ejnar Munksgaard, 1957.

8. *Le Roman de la rose:*
Thuasne, L., *Le Roman de la rose. Les Grands événements littéraires.* Paris, 1929.

9. Late lyric poetry:
Chamard, Henri, *Les Origines de la poésie française de la Renaissance.* Paris, Boccard, 1920.
Champion, Pierre, *Histoire poétique du XVᵉ siècle.* Paris, Champion, 1923. 2 vols.

10. François Villon:
Champion, Pierre, *François Villon, sa vie et son temps.* Paris, Champion, 1913. 2 vols.
Lewis, D. B. Wyndham, *François Villon.* New York, Coward-McCann, 1928.

11. Medieval drama:
Cohen, Gustave, *Le Théâtre en France au moyen âge.* Paris, Rieder, 1929–31. 2 vols.

b. *Sixteenth century*

    1. Clément Marot:

        Kinch, Charles E., *La Poésie satirique de Clément Marot*. Paris, Boivin, 1940.

        Plattard, Jean, *Marot, sa carrière poétique, son œuvre*. Paris, Boivin, 1938.

    2. *L'Ecole lyonnaise:*

        O'Conner, Dorothy, *Louise Labé; sa vie et son œuvre*. Paris, Les Presses françaises, 1926.

        Saulnier, V. L., *Maurice Scève*. Paris, Klincksieck, 1948–49. 2 vols.

    3. *La Pléiade:*

        Bishop, Morris, *Ronsard, Prince of Poets*. New York, Oxford University Press, 1940.

        Chamard, Henri, *Histoire de la Pléiade*. Paris, Didier, 1939–40. 4 vols.

        Champion, Pierre, *Ronsard et son temps*. Paris, Champion, 1925.

        Cohen, Gustave, *Ronsard, sa vie et son œuvre*. Paris, Boivin, 1924.

        Saulnier, V. L., *Du Bellay, l'homme et l'œuvre*. Paris, Boivin, 1951.

    4. Agrippa d'Aubigné:

        Buffum, Imbrie, *Agrippa d'Aubigné's Les Tragiques; a Study of the Baroque Style in Poetry*. New Haven, Yale University Press, 1951.

    5. Sixteenth-century drama:

        Lebègue, Raymond, *La Tragédie française de la renaissance*. Bruxelles, Office de publicité, 1944.

        Lintilhac, Eugène François, *Histoire générale du théâtre en France;* vol. II, *La Comédie: moyen âge et renaissance*. Paris, Flammarion, 1905.

c. *Seventeenth and eighteenth centuries*

    1. First half of the seventeenth century:

        Audibert, Raoul, and Bouvier, René, *Saint-Amant, capitaine du Parnasse*. Paris, La Nouvelle Edition, 1946.

        Celles, Jean de, *Malherbe: sa vie, son caractère, sa doctrine*. Paris, Perrin, 1937.

        Lebègue, Raymond, *La Poésie française de 1560 à 1630*. Paris, Société d'Edition d'Enseignement Supérieur, 1951. 2 vols.

        Vianey, Joseph, *Mathurin Régnier*. Paris, Hachette, 1896.

Weingarten, Renée, *French Lyric Poetry in the Age of Malherbe*. Manchester, Eng., Manchester University Press, 1954.

2. Nicolas Boileau:
   Bray, René, *Boileau, l'homme et l'œuvre*. Paris, Boivin, 1942.
   Hervier, Marcel, *L'Art poétique de Boileau, étude et analyse*. Paris, Mellottée, 1938.
   Mornet, Daniel, *Nicolas Boileau*. Paris, Calmann-Lévy, 1941.

3. Jean de La Fontaine:
   Clarac, Pierre, *La Fontaine, l'homme et l'œuvre*. Paris, Boivin, 1947.
   Sutherland, Monica, *La Fontaine*. London, Cape, 1953.

4. Seventeenth-century drama:
   Lancaster, Henry C., *A History of French dramatic literature in the seventeenth century*. Baltimore, Johns Hopkins Press, new ed., 1952. 9 vols.

5. Pierre Corneille:
   Brasillach, Robert, *Pierre Corneille*. Paris, Fayard, 1938.
   Dorchain, Auguste, *Pierre Corneille*. Paris, Garnier, 1918.
   Herland, Louis, ed., *Corneille par lui-même*. Paris, Editions du Seuil, 1954.

6. Jean Racine:
   Brereton, Geoffrey, *Jean Racine; A Critical Biography*. London, Cassell, 1951.
   Clark, Alexander F. B., *Jean Racine*. Cambridge, Harvard University Press, 1939.
   Moreau, Pierre, *Racine; l'homme et l'œuvre*. Paris, Boivin, 1943.

7. Molière:
   Audiberti, Jacques, *Molière dramaturge*. Paris, L'Arche, 1954.
   Bray, René, *Molière, homme de théâtre*. Paris, Mercure de France, 1954.
   Brisson, Pierre, *Molière, sa vie dans ses œuvres*. Paris, Gallimard, 1943.

8. André Chénier:
   Walter, Gérard, *André Chénier, son milieu et son temps*, 10th ed. Paris, Laffont, 1947.

d. *Nineteenth and twentieth centuries:*

   1. Romanticism:
      Martino, Pierre, *L'Epoque romantique en France, 1815–1830*. Paris, Boivin, 1944.

2. Alphonse de Lamartine:
   Guyard, M.-F., *Lamartine*. Paris, Editions Universitaires, 1956.

3. Victor Hugo:
   Barrère, Jean Bertrand, *Hugo, l'homme et l'œuvre*. Paris, Boivin, 1952.
   Hugo, Victor, *Victor Hugo par lui-même*, ed. by Henri Guillemin. Paris, Editions du Seuil, 1951.

4. Alfred de Musset:
   Van Tieghem, Phillippe, *Musset, l'homme et l'œuvre*. Paris, Boivin, 1944.

5. Alfred de Vigny:
   Castex, Pierre, *Vigny, l'homme et l'œuvre*. Paris, Boivin, 1952.

6. Gérard de Nerval:
   Cellier, L., *Gérard de Nerval, l'homme et l'œuvre*. Paris, Hatier, 1956.

7. Le Parnasse:
   Martino, Pierre, *Parnasse et symbolisme* (1850–1900). Paris, Armand Colin, 1925.

8. Leconte de Lisle:
   Flottes, Pierre, *Leconte de Lisle, l'homme et l'œuvre*. Paris, Hatier-Boivin, 1954.

9. José-Maria de Heredia:
   Ibrovac, Miodrag, *José-Maria de Heredia, sa vie—son œuvre*. Paris, Les Presses françaises, 1923.
   Moussat, Emile, *Expliquez-moi . . . les sonnets de José-Maria de Heredia*. Paris, Editions Foucher, n.d.

10. Charles Baudelaire:
    Austin, L. J., *L'Univers poétique de Baudelaire; symbolisme et symbolique*. Paris, Mercure de France, 1956.
    Jones, Percy M., *Baudelaire*. Cambridge, Eng., Bowes & Bowes, 1952.
    Ruff, Marcel A., *Baudelaire, l'homme et l'œuvre*. Paris, Hatier-Boivin, 1955.

11. Paul Verlaine:
    Adam, Antoine, *Verlaine, l'homme et l'œuvre*. Paris, Hatier-Boivin, 1953.

12. Arthur Rimbaud:
    D'Eaubonne, F., *La Vie passionnée de Rimbaud*. Paris, Intercontinentale du livre, 1956.

Cartier, M., *Rimbaud, sa vie, son œuvre*. Bienne, Boillat, 1957.

Hackett, C. A., *Rimbaud*. London, Bowes & Bowes, 1957.

Starkie, Enid, *Arthur Rimbaud*. New York, W. W. Norton & Company, Inc., n.d.

13. Stéphane Mallarmé:

Mondor, Henri, *Vie de Mallarmé*. Paris, Gallimard, 1941.

Schérer, Jacques, *L'Expression littéraire dans l'œuvre de Mallarmé*. Paris, Nizet, 1947.

14. Jules Laforgue:

Ramsey, Warren, *Jules Laforgue and the Ironic Inheritance*. New York, Oxford University Press, 1953.

15. Symbolism and Post-Symbolism:

Clancier, G. E., *De Rimbaud au Surréalisme: panorama critique*. Verviers, Marabout, 1959.

Cornell, Kenneth, *The Post-Symbolist Period: French Poetic Currents, 1900–1920*. New Haven, Yale University Press, 1958.

————, *The Symbolist Movement*. New Haven, Yale University Press, 1951.

Dinar, André, *La Croisade symboliste*. Paris, Mercure de France, 1943.

Raymond, Marcel, *De Baudelaire au surréalisme*, new ed. Paris, José Corti, 1940.

16. Paul Valéry:

Bémol, Maurice, *Paul Valéry*. Clermont-Ferrand, G. de Bussac, 1949.

Mackay, Agnes Ethel, *The Universal Self; a Study of Paul Valéry*. Toronto, University of Toronto Press, 1961.

17. Guillaume Apollinaire:

Adéma, Marcel, *Guillaume Apollinaire, le mal-aimé*. Paris, Plon, 1952.

18. Surrealism:

Balakian, Anna E., *Surrealism, the Road to the Absolute*. New York, Noonday Press, 1959.

Read, Herbert E., ed., *Surrealism*. London, Faber & Faber, Ltd., 1937.

19. Independents and contemporaries:

Gros, Léon Gabriel, *Poètes contemporains*. Paris, Cahiers du Sud, 1944–51. 2 vols.

Michel, Henri, *Henri Michaux*, ed. by René Bertelé. Paris, P. Seghers, 1949.

Roy, Claude, *Jules Supervielle*. Paris, P. Seghers, 1949.

INDEX

Index

256

This manuscript was edited by Francine Rosemberg. The book was designed by Eleonore Valencia. The text typeface is Mergenthaler Linotype Caledonia designed by W. A. Dwiggins in 1937. The display face is American Type Founder's Garamond based on a face cut by Jean Jannon in the 16th Century. Inspired by the designs of Aldus Manutius and Claude Garamond, this present version was designed in 1917 by M. F. Benton and T. M. Cleland.

The book is printed on Glatfelter's Antique paper and bound in Holliston Mills Kingston cloth. Manufactured in the United States.